PROFOUND AWARENESS

LIVING, LEARNING, LOVING, LAUGHING, AND LEADING IN HIS PRESENCE

DR. ERIC J. PALMU

WESTBOW
PRESS®
A DIVISION OF THOMAS NELSON
& ZONDERVAN

WestBow Press books may be ordered through booksellers or by contacting:

WestBow Press
A Division of Thomas Nelson & Zondervan
1663 Liberty Drive
Bloomington, IN 47403
www.westbowpress.com
844-714-3454

ISBN: 979-8-3850-4052-0 (sc)
ISBN: 979-8-3850-4053-7 (e)

Library of Congress Control Number: 2024927187

Print information available on the last page.

WestBow Press rev. date: 01/24/2025

To God be the glory!

To God be the glory.

CONTENTS

Preface.. ix
Introduction xi

PART I
Covenant Design to Teach Love

1 The Pre-Creation Planning: God Designs, Jesus Builds, the
   Spirit Hovers.. 1
2 Original Freedom: Life in Eden.. 9
3 Choice: A Critical Theme in a Covenant.. 27

PART II
Adamic Covenant: A Relationship of Love

4 Adam and Eve's Accepted Choice: Dominion, Marriage,
   and Work 33
5 A Choice for Angels: Emergence of Evil... 39
6 Created Discontent: A Broken Covenant 44
7 Separation: They Call on God 51

PART III
Noahic Covenant: Covenant Renewal

8 Pride and Covenant: Preparations for a Family 61

PART IV
Abrahamic Covenant: A Covenant of Family

9   Reconciliation and Dependence: Now and in the Future...................... 71
10 God Is with His People: The Everlasting Covenant of Family 78

PART V
Mosaic Covenant: The Law of Love and Worship

11 Covenant Protection: Reverence for God 89
12 Covenant Family Arrives Home: The Promised Land 103
13 God-Serving Leadership: Judges and Prophets.............................. 110
14 A Troubled Leadership: Kings and Prophets................................. 116

PART VI
Davidic Covenant: Seeking the
Heart and Vision of God

15 King David and King Solomon: Wisdom and Understanding 129
16 An OT Thematic Review: Lessons and Trials 148

PART VI
A New Covenant for Eternity

17 Jesus Restores Us to the Father: Wilderness and Sermon
    on the Mount 157
18 The New Covenant Ministry: The Crucial Themes 177
19 Bride of Christ: A Galilean Wedding and the Bridegroom 199
20 A New Wine: Spiritual Formation, Holy Spirit, the Great
    Commission.. 206
21 Spiritual Maturity: A Full Measure of Joy 220
22 Christian Leadership: God-Serving Men and Women 240
23 A Choice for Reality: Kingdom of Man or Kingdom of God 249
24 The Whole Truth: Nothing but the Truth..................................... 266
25 Eternity: A New Heaven, a New Earth, a New Jerusalem................. 281
26 Profound Awareness: In the Public Square 292

Appendix 1: Spiritual Formation.. 317
Appendix 2: Thematic Lessons to the Whole Counsel of God.............. 319
Appendix 3: God's Design... 323

PREFACE

I have spent much of my life studying God and how I fit into the big picture. Not because I had to (I lied—in some cases I had to), but because I was truly interested in the God/man relationship. (Let's be clear: when I use the terms *man* or *mankind*, I am using them to speak about humanity as a whole.) Despite the fact that I attended Sunday school, church, and theological training, and experienced encounters with the supernatural, I have held deep reservations about the existence of God. I have behaved in ways that would demonstrate nonbelief in anything beyond living my own life. However, time has moved on, and I am now in my late sixties. I've learned that submission to the King of the Universe is a reality that cannot be ignored.

Curiously, this realization about Yahweh, or the God of Christianity, was more about my authentic response to Him than it was about scripture memorization or church attendance. I did all the things that "practicing" Christians do. What I missed was understanding the essence of a relationship with Him. In short, I had to first believe the Story of God in order to know Him. That's the point of the sinner's prayer. In this simple prayer, you state that you believe in the work of Jesus on the cross, you release control of your life over to Him, and you submit to His leading in your life. That's it. You're in! But, other than having your sins forgiven, you're not sure what it means. And you're not sure you *are* in.

Yes, the sinner's prayer is also known as the believer's prayer or the prayer of salvation. The best part: you experience a supernatural "something" (peace) at that moment of earnestly seeking Him. This elation is the Holy Spirit taking up residence in your soul. After that, your pastor, church leader, or friend tells you to start reading the Bible—oh, begin your reading in John. You are excited because the Holy Spirit, now in you, is prompting your heart to read as well. Unfortunately, it doesn't take long before the distractions of the world draw you away from your supernatural encounter with God. Discontent sets in again.

Well, the truth is you are not alone. Disappointingly, this scenario happens more often than it should because we haven't understood spiritual formation. Why not? That's another story. I can't tell you how many times I have prayed for my salvation, run to the altar, or raised my hand at the pastor's request—mostly after every fall from grace or long periods of selfism. Consequently, my age-old question was "Why does this keep happening? Why isn't my walk more Christlike?" So I started my search with theological training in Christian education.

Understanding the supernatural work of the Holy Spirit in my spiritual formation was slow in coming. It shouldn't have been, but I guess I was a slow learner about this sanctification process. I've come to learn that my teachers lacked a more profound understanding of spiritual growth. Eventually, the Story of God revealed some mysterious and crucial issues that led me to a deeper relationship with God. I discovered that the most important details were in the themes I found in His Story. That's the focus of this book: the themes that bridge each of us to a deeper relationship in which we experience the everlasting love and daily intervention of God.

Let's start here, at the root of our Judeo-Christian family story. Jesus was asked by an expert in the Law, "What is the greatest commandment?"

Jesus answered, "Love the Lord your God with all your heart and with all your soul and with all your mind and with all your strength."[1]

The cornerstone of this greatest commandment is a relationship with God and loving Him like no other. Yes! *It means possessing an authentic relationship with your unseen God.* As His people, with a relationship grounded in faith, believers must aspire to live and behave by the example Christ taught as He walked the earth.

As mentioned, I *know* the highs and lows, the joys and pains, as well as the many prayers for salvation found in the journey with God. The Story of God teaches us about the incredible love you can experience. He will reveal Himself as you *run* after Him with all your heart, soul, mind, and strength! But know this: He will *not* force you into a relationship with Him. The choice is yours to be in relationship with Him or not.

Dr. Eric J Palmu
December 22, 2021

---

[1] Luke 10:27.

INTRODUCTION

Let's look at the last words Jesus spoke prior to leaving the disciples and others. Those final words are referred to as the Great Commission. This is what He called His followers to do. It is crucial that we honor the final instructions of our Lord.

> Then Jesus came to them and said, "All authority in heaven and on earth has been given to me. Therefore go and make disciples of all nations, baptizing them in the name of the Father and of the Son and of the Holy Spirit, and teaching them to obey everything I have commanded you. And surely I am with you always, to the very end of the age."[2]

The challenge is how to accomplish His commission. The mission is clear. What is also clear is that Jesus has all the power and authority to lead His people into the mission. And He is in this with us. We must be ready in our hearts to lead. The church is fully aware of what we are called to do.

The focus of this book is deepening our relationship with God in order that we can teach and lead. Said another way, *the purpose of our existence is to be in a relationship with Him* so as to follow His leadership, teach His Story, and lead others to restoration with Him in order to establish the kingdom of God on earth. Whether you believe it or not, your lived reality is found in Him and only Him. The true reality will be discussed throughout this book. God began planning Creation before the foundations of the world. He walked in the garden with us. We failed to learn *a choice to love Him*. He is still working with us in order to bring us home.

THE ORCHARD EXPERIENCE

Due to an allergic reaction to fiberglass material used in his trade, my dad, a Finnish immigrant, needed to transition to another vocation. He chose commercial construction. We had to move out to the country because it

---

[2] Matthew 28:18–20.

was much more affordable than living in the city. With the family income dramatically reduced, cutting costs became Mom and Dad's priority. Their eventual dream was for Dad to find stable employment and for the two of them to build their own home. A rural area of the county provided a low-rent, two-story, and very old farmhouse. Despite the lower standard of living, the hills, fields, farms, and openness turned out to be a paradise for me.

It was on this farm that I first encountered a moment with God. It was a warm spring morning. The apple orchard behind the house was a postcard scene. The orchard, about the size of a football field, was on a gentle hill, sloping away from the back of the house toward a field. I was admiring the scenery when I remembered an old doghouse on the edge of the hill, a few feet away. I climbed on its roof and made myself comfortable.

As I sat there motionless, I was mesmerized by the orchard's beauty and quiet. The trees were full of apple blossoms. The air was so still, I could hear the buzz of the bees doing their thing as they searched the flowers for nectar.

I found myself curiously introspective. Why was I, a ten-year-old boy, sitting there admiring an apple orchard in the spring? I was amazed by what was obviously God's handiwork. For several minutes, one thought led to another. Then these words came from my mouth: "God, this is just beautiful. You have given your people an incredible planet. You have taken care of us. I want to do something great for you someday."

At that moment, I saw a significant movement of branches in the tops of the trees at the far end of the orchard. It was not like the tranquility surrounding me. The branches showed that the movement was coming through the orchard in my direction. A very obvious breeze was moving the trees—but there was not a cloud in the sky.

I was surprised by how quickly the stillness around me was interrupted by the firm but gentle wind now moving past me. I was a bit anxious but not scared as the wind moved through the orchard. I said what seemed obvious to me: "God, you heard me?" I was not sure why I asked that question, other than the overwhelming sense of majestic presence that filled the senses within me.

Then I heard, "You will."

Tears filled my eyes. I realized I was in the presence of God.

The breeze lessened, and the orchard returned to its state of peaceful calm. Less than a minute later, I could hear the bees flitting about. His words had not been audible, but I knew they belonged to Him (that still, small voice, a wispher I had read about in Bible class). I had no idea how that experience would be a lighthouse in my life.

I remember this supernatural occurrence as if it happened yesterday. Interestingly, I never shared this story with another human being until I was an adult. Yet I spoke to God about it often. The memory of that experience usually surfaced when I was considering a life change or an unexpected job opportunity. The same question would arise in my prayers: "Is this what you want me to do?"

PROFOUND AWARENESS

This book will highlight the two significant aspects of *go* (lead) and *teach* (make). The first is learning to teach others about our relationship (spiritual connection) with God. We'll study the challenges found in spiritual formation for those responding to God's call. We'll also study biblical characters stymied by this relationship with God because they didn't fully understand how God wants this relationship to work. First, you must learn the Story of God.

God absolutely loves you and is continuing the work He began in us in Creation. Unfortunately, there also seems to be a lack of understanding on the part of our church leadership to teach what it means to live in the presence of God. Being a good Christian isn't a membership; it is an authentic connection to our Creator!

This takes us to the second area: learning to lead (*go*) in the presence of God. Godly leadership must begin with a deep-seated intimacy, a conversational closeness with God to hear "the still small voice."[3] What does that mean? When Elijah found himself in a desperate situation, God approached him, not in an angry or overbearing fashion, but softly:

> Then a great and powerful wind tore the mountains apart
> and shattered the rocks before the Lord, but the Lord was
> not in the wind. After the wind there was an earthquake, but
> the Lord was not in the earthquake. After the earthquake

---

[3] 1 Kings 19:12.

came a fire, but the Lord was not in the fire. And after the
fire, came a gentle whisper.[4]

This is a reminder that God is not in the natural calamities we often attribute to Him. God is the peace amid calamity.

Also in the second part, we'll take a look at the linking nature of covenants and the imperfect church leadership that set the stage for the Messiah, as well as for the Messiah's return. The church is often referred to as the bride, and Jesus is the Bridegroom. The intimacy between the bride and the Bridegroom is soul-deep, gentle, kind, patient, and good. It is filled with soft conversation about future and an eternity with Him.

These connective themes are interwoven throughout the Story of God. They provide guideposts of incredible insight, a profound awareness found in the firm foundation of the relationship between God and man.

I want to say this: this book will not take a chapter-and-verse approach to Bible study, nor will it follow a theological doctrine or approach, but will review significant passages to support a *theme-based hermeneutic found in the whole counsel of God*.[5] The process begins with teaching the big-picture themes found in the Story of God. These themes, when connected, are foundational (building your house on rock) to a genuine spiritual growth that will provide a greater understanding of God and your relationship with Him. The themes are the footings of the supernatural reality we all live within. He has revealed to all of us who He is. He can be known. Equally, we must present ourselves to be known. This is His communication plan for humanity and, more importantly, our intimacy with Him. Unfortunately, like Adam in the garden, we hide. We must come out of hiding and approach Him in the naked and vulnerable attitude in which we left Him.

The Story of God is filled with divine conversation about the future. Believe it or not, this is the way it is for the believer in submission to God. In the same way, the church must surrender, in part and as a whole, to God. Becoming a sweetly surrendered church depends on whether the Christ-followers have deepened and embraced their relationship with God.

---

[4] 1 Kings 19:11–12.

[5] Acts 20:27 NKJV. The *whole counsel* is interpreted also as *purpose of God* (ESV) or *will of God* (NIV).

I refer to this soul-deep, supernatural relationship with God as a *profound awareness* directed by God through His Holy Spirit that is a display of the fruit of the Spirit. Here's the rub: most believers, and certainly nonbelievers, have no understanding of what the profound awareness looks like. However, when they observe the fruit of the Spirit in Christ-followers, they recognize something in that believer they don't possess, and they want it.

The seeker wants to know and be known by God, but too often struggles to understand this divine connection between God our Creator and humanity. Embracing your spiritual formation will lead to a profound awareness. This journey begins at the Sermon on the Mount.

EMBRACING OUR DIVINE RELATIONSHIP

Usually, the connection the church wishes to develop is distorted by bad theology, poor sermon prep, autocratic leadership, or a poorly developed leadership curriculum. Too often church leaders select for leadership good people who have earthly success and work ethic, without first determining whether these people possess an intimate relationship with God. God-serving leadership requires an intimate and dependent fellowship with Him.

Intimacy with God is about dependence: leaning on Him, waiting on Him, and embracing an ongoing conversation with Him, all day long and every day. It is difficult to be a God-serving leader without a God-serving relationship. God-serving leaders display actions from the oneness of heart and mind that exists supernaturally.

The challenge for the church is growing each follower to own and cultivate their spiritual formation. We'll examine *owning*, built off the Story of God and what He has done through and for humanity. We'll also focus on *cultivating*, the biblical events and other substories as well as the critical motifs regarding that cut to the heart of each person.

I believe God wants us *all* to serve Him as His leaders in the kingdom. But God-serving leadership is inextricably tied to an authentic and intimate dependence on Him. A relationship is not about scripture memorization. It is not about church membership. It is not about a work ethic. These characteristics are all part of earthly stewardship, but they are not what a relationship is about. A relationship is about the Author of those words.

I've heard it said, "We can't know God." That's not true! We can know God because He desires a relationship with us.[6] The believer's struggle in this relationship is separation from the *in the world* distractions.

Together, the two parts, owning and cultivating, will direct your path to becoming a soul-deep believer, that possesses a profound awareness of God and His plan for humanity. Your role is as a *God-serving leader,* because that's the Great Commission.[7] It's simple. You will be directed by God *to go* and *to make,* leaders in your story with God.

GOD'S LOVE IS IN THE CHOICE

It begins with one single and personal act in your life that possesses eternal consequences through responsibility. Yes, we all face decisions and must take responsibility for our actions! Every individual living on this planet must decide how he or she is going to exist and interact with others. Some will say they do not have a choice; life is already determined. Others will say that the circumstances of their lives forced their situations, or their parents didn't correct their bad behavior. On and on the excuses go. There are a plethora of ways humans will seek to defend or justify what has taken place in their lives. Ultimately, each of us must decide responsibility for our behaviors, independent of worldly expectations.

BEING RESPONSIBLE FOR YOUR BEHAVIOR

We will begin with a universal precept found in a conversation between God and Cain, the firstborn son of Adam and Eve. Here's the context: Cain behaved poorly in his relationship with the Creator. Specifically, he didn't demonstrate gratitude (giving thanks to God) for God's blessing. God called him out for his actions. Cain became angry, and God addressed his anger:

---

[6] James 4:8: "Come near to God and he will come near to you. Wash your hands, you sinners, and purify your hearts, you double-minded."

[7] Matthew 28:19–20: "[G]o and make disciples of all nations, baptizing them in the name of the Father and of the Son and of the Holy Spirit, and teaching them to obey everything I have commanded you."

Then the Lord said to Cain, "Why are you angry? Why is your face downcast? If you do what is right, will you not be accepted? But if you do not do what is right, sin is crouching at your door; it desires to have you, but you must rule over it."[8]

The universal truth here is that *a person is responsible for their own behavior.* Clearly, Adam and Eve, considering their lived experience, would have brought up both of their sons with an understanding of God's expectation for appropriate behavior. The secondborn, Abel, learned about gratitude. Obviously Cain chose not to accept this parental teaching.

The universal truth is to do what is right. This brings us to the purpose of part one: embracing a right relationship with our Creator. Clearly, God instructed Cain to take command of his own behavior.

FAILING TO FOLLOW GOD IS SIN

Of greater importance, God calls out Cain with a warning: "Sin is crouching at your door."[9] It is the first time we see the word *sin* used in the Bible.

Understanding the word *sin* is critical to your spiritual development. It isn't a bad action or habit. Most theologians define *sin* as "missing the mark or the way." You can't read the word *sin* without asking, "What is the mark or the way?" That is a very good question, and I am glad you asked. It has to do with the usage in this passage. In short, Cain is missing the mark because he is failing to observe holy living, not attending to God's expectations.[10] Both Cain and Abel were raised by parents who were fully aware of what holy living meant and looked like. Abel was grateful for God's blessings; Cain was not. In other words, sin is not following God's instruction. It isn't the action, it's ignoring God's leading.

Sin for all humanity is the same. It is obvious that humanity is missing the mark of holy living or bringing the kingdom of God to earth. Recognizing the distinction of holy living is fundamental for all believers.

---

[8] Genesis 4:6–7.

[9] Genesis 4:7

[10] Chata. TWOT 638a, Vol. I, p.277; Strongs H2398, means *missing the mark* https://biblehub.net/searchhebrew.php?q=2398.

VALUING WHAT IS REAL

Most of us begin with an ideal about how life should be. We build a mental world of right and wrong, love and peace. It is our utopia—a place where we love and are loved.

My utopia has always included God because I grew up in the church. Even as a person of God, I pondered my personal responsibility for creating a meaningful relationship with God. I vacillated between a human understanding of value and a divine design from God. Was there an inherent value that gave me significance? The journey and my lack of confidence were intense. The highlights and lowlights were always testing the limits of my relationship with others. I looked heavenward for answers because that is what I had learned to do in Sunday school. Still, I didn't find a consistent path to perfected living. My life was all about me and what I valued.

I was challenging righteous (morally sound) living in ways that only a sinful, self-righteous narcissist would behave. My selfish actions hurt family and friends. I let people down. I was all of that until I realized I was out of control. I continually looked for ways to make life better—not just for that day, but in the days to come. Too often my selfish emotions ruled over me, and bad things followed. My prideful decisions took advantage of others. My rebellious attitude left me with a real sense of separation from what I knew was right. Surprisingly, I always seemed to look up for answers. I will be eternally grateful for His everlasting love.

A righteous life should be about learning and teaching others about the critical themes and events that lead to a genuine connection with Him. It is an authentic and supernatural relationship requiring *personal responsibility*. We must value what is good in the sight of God. I had many lessons to learn.

LIBERATING YOUR SOUL FROM THE INFLUENCE OF YOUR PRIDE AND THE WORLD

This is not a hermeneutic for liberation theology. It is not about Calvinist doctrine, Catholicism, or Arminian theology. The journey is a faith-walk, or more specifically, *a soul liberation*! The theological perspective is a liberation from the enslavement of forces controlled by a world that hates God, seeks to possess self-indulgent minds, and furthers the enslaved heart's narcissistic choices for happiness. The minds and hearts of humans are locked in this cycle of independent decision-making without God, while not knowing that the real and eternal dependence on God reigns in our lives.

Seeking spiritual freedom from this cyclical and deafening process through a covenant relationship with God will allow the *transformed soul* to participate in a deeply engaging relationship with God, if earnestly sought. Turning away from the old lifestyle *will* give back the wholesome and thriving life God desired to grow in Eden. This journey is only possible through a deepening submission to God. Through this mysterious tour, He will nurture your heart and mind to become one with Christ—a Christlike unity. This supernatural, connective relationship leads to the *vision*. It is a sort of theological zeitgeist or a biblical vision, *haza* (ka-za), that leads to a supernatural unity or oneness.

THE CRITICAL UNDERSTANDING IN THE FAITH-JOURNEY

This is huge! A real relationship with Him is not about what you think the Bible says. It is not about feeling good because you went to church. It is not about your introspection and comparisons with other Christians and non-Christians. In God's realm, we are either believers or we live in unbelief. There is no middle ground; there are no denominations. When you give an accounting for your life, He will never ask you what church you attended, if you prayed in tongues, or how many Sundays you attended church, or about your eschatological views. It matters not what group you identify with. *God sees his believing sons and daughters as they are.*

Which leads to the paramount issue: How do you see yourself? Can you really see into the why of your actions? Because God does. A faith-journey is about choosing to be true to yourself and God as the Lord of your life.

Unfortunately, the Jews, God's chosen people, live in denial of the Lord God's one and only Son because He didn't fit their theological vision. This is where the followers of the Story of God begin: the truth is we all live under the King of the universe. Let's be clear. Your choice of what to believe will have eternal consequences. Choose wisely.

Love Him or leave Him, God has given you the gift of this choice. Even contemplative religious ideas of spiritual awareness, like Buddhism and Hinduism, do not seek restoration with the One true God. Islam, from

Mohammed's Koran, leads millions astray through a horrific rewrite of God's Word. Mohammed led his followers to a counterfeit eternity.

FACING THE DECISION OF WHICH REALITY IS TRUE

When you are alone—sitting in your living room, lying in your bedroom, walking through an open field, or perhaps strolling on a beach—familiar, recurring thoughts enter your mind. You think about your relationships with others and with the truth. Maybe your thoughts are introspective and focus on you: wondering who you are or how lonely you are. Maybe you think that life doesn't make sense. Maybe you remember a funny experience from weeks or months earlier. Maybe you relive a challenging moment at work or in a significant relationship. Maybe you take a serious look at where you are in your life.

You want to be happy about your finances, job, relationships, community, and future. Curiously, these reflections are both enlightening and, mostly, alarming. When you think about past memories of happiness or about painfully poor decisions, you wonder why happiness is fleeting. Is there long-term happiness? Frequently, these thoughts have connections to friends as well as bad characters in your life. You may recall the depth of emotional pain resulting from not being included or from being the butt of someone's joke.

You seem to find more questions than answers stemming from the trauma of parental divorce, the death of a loved one, or horrific sexual abuse. Each recollection takes you deeper into your connectedness with pain and loneliness. But you keep looking for happiness, a real joy that is lasting. Each thought presses you to deeply consider your lived experiences. The compilation of the past leaves you with one nagging question: What really matters?

This troubling introspection pushes you further into questions about your value, your identity, and that illusive sense of loving and being loved. Just when you think you are "in love," something happens that jolts you from that place. The probability of whether things are going to get better, coupled with the inner truth that you just don't know what or who to trust, adds anxiety. The reality of self-determination reveals the truth about your aloneness.

Friends, family, job, educational pursuits, social upheaval, and political turmoil can divert your attention from these moments of self-discovery. It is then that you realize your thoughts have spiraled out of control and you are questioning what is authentic and moral about life and living. Adding to these ever-pressing issues, you look for ways to soften or remove the tension, driving you to question your own behavior and morality. Examining the world around you, you discover that your reality is much different than others. You wonder, "How should I act?"

Eventually, what you discover is that we *all* have these introspective moments as we search for that utopia of life! The challenge is discerning what is real and what is an illusion, because it affects the utopian picture you created. It is the difference between subjective and objective, and how our emotions affect the two views. If you look long enough, you will grapple with the truth of significance and what makes you joyful.

Until that point, your significance was likely anchored in a talent, status, dream, position, good deed, cause, or money. What I have learned is that we seldom talk about these anchors with friends, even our closest friends. When we do, we discover that our friends can be in a very different place. More frightening, your confidence in a reality—the way you understand the world—is shaken. You may ask, "Is there something other than me at work here? Is there a reality that I am missing? Can I be whole and find true happiness?"

WHERE MY FAITH-JOURNEY HAS LED ME

My journey led me to question whether my pursuits were meaningful. I also asked a bigger question: "Is God real, and does He play a role in my life?" I had to ask myself, in all honesty, whether there was a part of the *self* that I was ignoring.

In college I had been taught that humans are considered mind and body. I laughed when I realized that's why I talked to myself. Yet in church I discovered something different that made more sense: humans are mind, body, and soul. That soul is real. In my quiet conversations with my soul, or inner being, I was alone but not lonely. Someone else was there. I had spent a lifetime avoiding those secret conversations with the inner me; now I embrace the curious heart-to-heart chats.

I was driven to figure it out. I wanted to know what was true and authentic about human life and my place in it. If life is simply a free-for-all with no real meaning, then what's the sense? Should I cultivate a life of using the perspectives of these "wise" people to pursue my happiness?

I decided to focus on courses in the human sciences: sociology, psychology, political science, and philosophy, which is humankind's view of itself. I used my academic pursuits to become a certified teacher. After my undergraduate work, I followed up with graduate work in theology, the study of God. My quest for understanding was on fire. I had to answer these critical observations and questions. I had to find true happiness—joy.

This journey led me to write and compile the good, bad, and the ugly of my life experiences. The book you now hold results from research for my first book, *Reversing Eden: Owning Your Transformation* (2015); my dissertation, *Developing Spiritual Maturity in Ministry Leaders through Whole-Bible Thematic Instruction* (2019); and other graduate work in theology and prayer life. This book reveals my understanding of how people come to truth about wholeness, which I define as significance and meaningfulness grounded in something bigger than the self, leading to a thriving and flourishing life is available *only* through an authentic relationship with God.

BOOK OVERVIEW

This book will focus on the truth of the God Story, in particular its application for our lives as individuals, as a church community, and, most importantly, as the bride of Christ. A biblical theology will be used as the roadmap. A hermeneutic, or way of deciphering God's Word, is to discover the overarching themes and motifs interwoven throughout the God Story upon which we can build our lives. We'll examine the relational themes of each covenant and its application to our lives. The relational themes construct a *vision* in the God Story that will sink deep within your inner being, your *soul*.

To assist you in understanding, we'll follow a covenantal structure in the God Story. The covenants reveal God's love and the truth about our separation from Him. Moreover, the covenants reveal the truth about what *restoration* really means. In the New Testament are the steps to living in an authentic, grace-filled, profound awareness of God. If the church can wrap its heart around this truth, it will bring the kingdom to earth.

Each chapter exists in a covenant, its primary story, and its substories. Christlike relationships require a kingdom vision that is an accurate understanding of one's position and responsibility in the God Story.

In most chapters there will be a consideration of the pre-creation planning session. In all likelihood, you've never heard of pre-creation planning. It is about a dialogue that might have taken place among God, Jesus, and the Holy Spirit. Despite the fact that you may never have heard a sermon about these alleged conversations, we do find reference to these discussions in the phrase "before the foundations of the world." Specific pre-creation planning conversations will be offered and footnoted where applicable.

Finally, most chapters will cover a biblical period, with a focus on the biblical theme(s) connected to profound awareness. I'll include a specific perspective supporting the spiritual development of profound awareness.

Each part is essential to understanding the dynamic connection of themes and motifs necessary for an authentic relationship with God. Be sure to read carefully each highlighted verse or passage included in a chapter. These verses reveal the mysteries of God.

This book is not about you or me. It is about the Story of God. Your significance is grounded in Him. The God Story is what you should believe first; then your life will possess the significance you pursue.

PART I
Covenant Design to Teach Love

1

THE PRE-CREATION PLANNING: GOD DESIGNS, JESUS BUILDS, THE SPIRIT HOVERS

IN THE BEGINNING OF ANY STORY, THERE IS A MAIN CHARACTER TO BE known. And with any great book, it is of great interest to understand the author and the point of the story. So in the God Story, we read to identify the issues and themes interwoven within the biblical account for our understanding. The themes crisscross throughout, but the Story of God remains the same.

"In the beginning, God created the heavens and the earth."[11] As a matter of fact, most readers don't realize that the story begins before Creation.

THE REAL BEGINNING

Curiously, "in the beginning" has met with a large theological discussion. However, there is something to be said about a time before Creation. A deeper look reveals that the apostle John had a vision for what I refer to as the *time before time*: "In the beginning was the Word, and the Word was with God, and the Word was God."[12] Time before time is a different kind of time.

There is connection in the two phrases, specifically a *continuity* in time, but they are different. *The Eerdmans' Bible Commentary* states, "The Word that is now was the Word before creation began."[13] The Hebrew word *arche* reveals an *existence* before time and the Creation. Said another way, before time as we know it, Jesus came in the flesh as the Word and was with His

---

[11] Genesis 1:2.

[12] John 1:1.

[13] *The Eerdman's Bible Commentary* (Eerdmans 1970), using the term "apxn," 930.

Father before Creation. The word *arche* is different than *resit*.[14] The phrase "in the beginning" more likely refers to the first step or the starting point.

I have only met one pastor in fifty years of chasing after God who would speculate about and discuss what might have been in the pre-creation conversations before the God Story begins.

"Now the earth was formless and empty, darkness was over the surface of the deep, and the Spirit of God was hovering over the waters."[15] Here we find another view of the story going back to a time before Genesis. It is believed by King David:

> Before the mountains were born or you brought forth the
> whole world, from everlasting to everlasting, you are God.[16]

That is the real starting point: to understand that God was before Genesis and that He has a plan to bring forth the whole world. The time before our creation may have been very different from the time of post-Eden Adam and Eve. What we do know is this: "But do not forget this one thing, dear friends: With the Lord a day is like a thousand years, and a thousand years are like a day."[17]

The apostles Paul and John (John to a greater extent) recognize that in God's creative planning and process, He was *not* alone. God is invisible, and Jesus is in His image! Jesus is before *all things*. Before anything else, He was part of Creation, and everything in existence is contingent on His work!

> The Son is the image of the invisible God, the firstborn over
> all creation. For in him all things were created: things in
> heaven and on earth, visible and invisible, whether thrones
> or powers or rulers or authorities; all things have been
> created through him and for him. He is before all things,
> and in him all things hold together.[18]

---

[14] *resit*. The first thing. TWOT. Vol. 2, pg. 826, 2097e. (Read John 1:1), https://www.blueletterbible.org/lexicon/h7225/niv/wlc/0-1/.

[15] Genesis 1:2.

[16] Psalm 90:2.

[17] 2 Peter 3:8.

[18] Colossians 1:16.

> Through him all things were made; without him nothing
> was made that has been made.[19]

In his letter to Timothy, Paul speaks about Jesus being before time (as we understand time): "This grace was given us in Christ Jesus before the beginning of time, but it has now been revealed through the appearing of our Savior."[20]

Clearly, to John, Jesus is a vital connection in Creation. With God's Son, Jesus, all things were made. It is Jesus who connects God and humankind.

> But in these last days he has spoken to us by his Son, whom
> he appointed heir of all things, and through whom also he
> made the universe.[21]

The Son's role is designed by the Father. The Son is in unity with the Father. The letter to the Hebrews establishes the Savior as the builder and His Father as the designer.

> The Son is the radiance of God's glory and the exact
> representation of his being, sustaining all things by his
> powerful word. After he had provided purification for sins,
> he sat down at the right hand of the Majesty in heaven. So
> he became as much superior to the angels as the name he
> has inherited is superior to theirs.[22]

God announces his Son, Jesus, to the angels and the heavens. The believing Hebrews and Gentiles understood this story in the depths of their hearts. They knew their God and recognized their long-promised Savior!

According to Paul, God has announced that Jesus is the pinnacle of their faith:

> For to which of the angels did God ever say, "You are my
> Son; today I have become your Father"? Or again, "I will be

---

[19] John 1:3.
[20] 2 Timothy 1:9
[21] Hebrews 1:2.
[22] Hebrews 1:3–4.

his Father, and he will be my Son"? And again, when God brings his firstborn into the world, he says, "Let all God's angels worship him." In speaking of the angels, he says, "He makes his angels spirits, and his servants' flames of fire."[23]

To make the reality of this Creation planning more poignant, I can imagine a discussion taking place between Father and Son, as revealed in Jesus's request (in John's account) for the believers, as his Father promised *before* Creation:

And now, Father, glorify me in your presence with the glory I had with you before the world began.[24]

Father, I want those you have given me to be with me where I am, and to see my glory, the glory you have given me because you loved me before the creation of the world.[25]

Jesus reminded His Father that the believers who would follow would be His. This is a powerful and intimate love between Father and Son! It is an everlasting love the Father and Son desire to share with you. John notes in Jesus's words that He is clearly referencing a conversation with the Father prior to Creation.

In the next passage, Paul implies that this planning session occurred to predestine or set into motion believers to participate in the inheritance.[26] The plan was to unfold for those who would believe and conform to His will. God's plan is in motion. Are you honoring His plan for you?

For he chose us in him before the creation of the world to be holy and blameless in his sight.[27]

---

[23] Hebrews 1:5–8.
[24] John 17:5.
[25] John 17:24.
[26] *Proorizo:* the predetermined plan of salvation was set into motion for all Israelites and Gentiles who would believe in their inheritance with Christ. Focus is on the preset plan, not chosen individuals. BLB Strong's G4309; Theological Dictionary of the NT Vol. 5, p. 456; Moody Bible Dictionary, p. 1847 (Eph. 1:11–12).
[27] Ephesians 1:4.

> In him we were also chosen, having been predestined
> according to the plan of him who works out everything in
> conformity with the purpose of his will.[28]

To the Ephesians, Paul proclaims that God's design is to complete His work in us. That was the plan from before the *in the beginning*: "For we are His workmanship, created in Christ Jesus for good works, which God prepared beforehand so that we would walk in them" (Eph. 2:10). We must all build our faith on the truth of God's everlasting love for His people. We are members of His divine design that will lead His people into eternity.

THE MAJESTIC CONCLAVE

It is significant that we consider the nature of this loving trinitarian conclave as it prepares our eternity with the Creator even *before* Creation. In this planning session are two very powerful thought processes: His plan for and knowledge of the future. The success of the plan rests on His prior knowledge regarding the actions of humanity, as well as evil grown by the evil one. We know from Isaiah that God is imminently filled with wisdom and understanding. His creative strategy for the created is unfolding as planned from the beginning, before the foundations of the world.

> "For my thoughts are not your thoughts, neither are your
> ways my ways," declares the Lord.
>
> "As the heavens are higher than the earth, so are my
> ways higher than your ways and my thoughts than your
> thoughts."[29]

Paul makes reference to this trinitarian assembly as well. He recognizes that the work of God and Jesus started before time as we know it.

> The Son is the image of the invisible God, the firstborn over
> all creation. For in him all things were created: things in

---

[28] Ephesians 1:11.
[29] Isaiah 55:8–9.

heaven and on earth, visible and invisible, whether thrones
or powers or rulers or authorities; all things have been
created through him and for him. He is before all things,
and in him all things hold together.[30]

You can see that, before Creation, God had a plan. This plan would
counter the challenges found in a world separated from God. Moreover, this
plan had an end in mind but not a finality, an eternity. John reveals a new
heaven and new earth but also the final disposition for all.

In the following passage from Revelation, John identifies four themes
critical to understanding the beginning and the end of the God Story: (1)
the new heaven and earth, containing Jerusalem; (2) God's kingship over
those who choose to be in relationship with Him; (3) the veracity of His
Word; and (4) the eternal consequences for those who choose not to be in
relationship with God.

> Then I saw "a new heaven and a new earth," for the first
> heaven and the first earth had passed away, and there was
> no longer any sea. I saw the Holy City, the new Jerusalem,
> coming down out of heaven from God, prepared as a bride
> beautifully dressed for her husband.
>
> And I heard a loud voice from the throne saying,
> "Look! God's dwelling place is now among the people, and
> he will dwell with them. They will be his people, and God
> himself will be with them and be their God. 'He will wipe
> every tear from their eyes. There will be no more death' or
> mourning or crying or pain, for the old order of things has
> passed away." He who was seated on the throne said, "I am
> making everything new!"
>
> Then he said, "Write this down, for these words are
> trustworthy and true." He said to me: "It is done. I am the
> Alpha and the Omega, the Beginning and the End. To the
> thirsty I will give water without cost from the spring of the
> water of life. Those who are victorious will inherit all this,
> and I will be their God and they will be my children.

---

[30] Colossians 1:15–17.

> But the cowardly, the unbelieving, the vile, the
> murderers, the sexually immoral, those who practice magic
> arts, the idolaters and all liars—they will be consigned to
> the fiery lake of burning sulfur. This is the second death."[31]

Let's be very clear: believing the God Story and trusting His sovereign intervention in our lives is *faith* and the *hope* we believe in for eternity with Him. Consequently, we are called to pursue God's will for our lives. Through faith, we believe His Word, trust His sovereignty over our lives, and pursue His purposes. That is our choice. "By faith we understand that the universe was formed at God's command, so that what is seen was not made out of what was visible."[32]

Another passage tells what will happen at the judgment that has been planned since the pre-creation planning session:

> When the Son of Man comes in his glory, and all the angels
> with him, he will sit on his glorious throne. All the nations
> will be gathered before him, and he will separate the people
> one from another as a shepherd separates the sheep from
> the goats. He will put the sheep on his right and the goats on
> his left. Then the King will say to those on his right, "Come,
> you who are blessed by my Father; take your inheritance, the
> kingdom prepared for you since the creation of the world."[33]

Wow! What an incredible day that will be. All who have pressed into their faith and remained steadfast in serving the Lord will take their inheritance as promised.

This is the foundation of the Christian faith: the invisible God designed the universe, and He worked through His Son, the Builder. We *must* earnestly seek Him. "And without faith it is impossible to please God, because anyone who comes to him must believe that he exists and that he rewards those who earnestly seek him."[34]

---

[31] Revelation 21:1–8.

[32] Hebrews 11:3.

[33] Matthew 25:31–34.

[34] Hebrews 11:6.

It is clear that belief and earnest seeking are required of believers. Believing and seeking are the most difficult tasks for us to learn. Believing in the Story of God is a tough decision, because we must abandon everything we've been taught about *knowing*.[35] In short, humans must know in order to believe. On the other hand, in God's realm, His people must first believe in order to know. The distinction is critical if God's people are to be willing to walk into the unknown. Unfortunately, too many approach God from the wrong perspective.

DEVELOPING A PROFOUND AWARENESS

There is a compelling reason for believers to understand the Story of God from the very beginning as we know it. The first and most significant aspect of the vision is that God is the King of the universe. This truth must be emblazoned on the hearts, minds, and souls of all believers.[36] The God Story must permeate our hearts and minds to cause us to reach back to Him. Pray with all your heart for God's vision to fill your soul.

Secondly, the Hebrews were taught this vision about their God as truth from an early age. They lived their lives believing that God could and would intervene in their lives. God was part of their daily thought processes and actions. They did nothing without considering God's Word!

To participate in an authentic relationship with God requires, first, that one possess an indisputable belief in the existence of a Creator God, and second, that one earnestly seek a relationship with Him daily.

Meditate on this: we'll see in the New Testament that the writer of Hebrews was speaking directly to the people of the synagogue, the people of the Book. Steeped in their Jewish covenantal history and traditions, they did not consider budging from the vision of the priests, because that vision was grounded in the Law. The author implored them about what is necessary to be in a personal relationship with God. No longer were they required to seek the priests. They could do the unthinkable: enter the Holy of Holies through an intimate relationship with God. The covenants of old are still important to teach and learn, but the new covenant seeks to *resurrect the heart that God created in His people.*

---

[35] *Regarding Jesus* (A&F Publications, 2020), 7.

[36] Deuteronomy 6:4–9.

2

ORIGINAL FREEDOM: LIFE IN EDEN

MY ORCHARD EXPERIENCE HAS REMAINED WITH ME THROUGHOUT MY life. I never doubted its reality. However, it didn't protect me from asking questions or keep me from living a disobedient life. Sound familiar? While I believed God was there, I had no way of understanding how He would intervene in my life. I was brooding over questions: Does God really intervene in our lives? Is the Bible true? What is real about a supernatural God?

Even though much of the Bible has proven historically factual, its miracles and supernatural events have long been questioned. Ironically, most committed Christians will confess moments of deep reservation regarding God, the Bible, and the Bible's application to their lives. I will admit the same. However, those questions were answered for me in deeply moving moments in my search for truth.

One of those issues was understanding the Trinity. Again, the nuggets of biblical truth act as markers for our understanding. John reveals the truth about Jesus being with humanity:

> No one has seen the Father except the one who is from God; only he has seen the Father.[37]

> No one has ever seen God, but the one and only Son, who is himself God and is in closest relationship with the Father, has made him known.[38]

This theme is momentous! Only Jesus has seen God, the Father. If no one has seen God, who was walking in Eden with Adam and Eve? If no one

---

[37] John 6:46.
[38] John 1:18.

9

has seen God, who wrestled with Jacob? If no one has seen God, who walked with God in Abraham's covenant-cutting dream? Jesus is the Son of God whom the world sees. The theophany is our in-the-world visitor and reveals two pieces of the trinitarian collective. Jesus comes to earth as an image of the Father. The only one who came close to seeing God was Moses, and he had to hide because God was so bright.[39]

WALKING IN AN EDENLIKE RELATIONSHIP WITH JESUS

Watching for God's actions is one thing; living as a person of God is another. My personal lack of self-control or poor obedience provided me with continual obstacles, but my belief in Jesus was unshakable. I lived in a world in which my moral choices were a significant challenge. My own selfish desires marred my ability to determine what good Christian behavior was. I am sure the God who met me in the orchard was disappointed, but I know His *grace*. I know a *mercy* I don't deserve. But I also know a freedom in grace to make my mistakes. Grace is given to us by the Father because He knows we will struggle in *missing the mark* (sin). We all have the responsibility to learn from His grace. The Holy Spirit is our Comforter in His forgiveness, and also our Guide for the next day.

Much like a rock thrown in a pond, the choices we make as to how we will exist in this world—our thoughts, actions, interactions, intentions, attitudes, and motives—have a ripple effect on our worldview that leaves no facet of our lives untouched. Every person on the planet is faced with this question of being: How then should I live? Not a single person can escape it.

You were born because God willed your existence and restoration before Creation. Therefore it is your *responsibility* to respond to God and determine how you will live. Tragically, our greatest challenge in life is understanding and contending with our pride. Victory over your pride will lead to an Edenlike relationship with God.

---

[39] Exodus 33:15–22.

SOUL

After Genesis 2, we find the next usage of the word *soul* in Deuteronomy, from the Hebrew word *nepes* (pronounced neh-fesh). Strongs and the *Theological Wordbook of the Old Testament* (TWOT) reveal that providing an understanding of its usage is challenging. In this context, the word *soul* encompasses a wholeness of self—a unity of flesh, will, and vitality.[40] Understanding the soul is also connected with longing or yearning. I am fond of Willard's description of soul:

> The soul is that aspect of your whole being that correlates, integrates, and enlivens everything going on in the various dimensions of self. It is the life-center of the human being. It regulates whatever is occurring in each of those dimensions and how they interact with each other and respond to surrounding events in the overall governance of your life.[41]

Wholeness is a fully functioning soul that is able to thrive and flourish in any situation. God's kingdom on earth requires each person's heart, mind, and strength to be whole and nourishing. Willard states that a person of such wholeness "is prepared for and capable of responding to the situations in life in ways that are good and right. For such a person, the human spirit will be in correct relationship to God. With His assisting grace, it will bring the soul into subjection to God and the mind (thoughts, feelings) into subjection to the soul."[42] This is where we find joy as our character and vision line up with God.

Joy is broken when self-destructive choices are being made, causing bitterness and torment that result in a conflict arising within. Dallas Willard states, "The individual soul's specific formation—the character it has taken on through its life course—is seen in the details of how thoughts, feelings, social relations, bodily behaviors, and choices unfold, and especially how

---

[40] Soul. TWOT 1395a, Vol. II, p.587; Strongs H5315, https://biblehub.com/hebrew/5315.htm.
[41] Dallas Willard, *Renovation of the Heart* (NavPress, 2002), 199.
[42] Willard, *Renovation of the Heart*, 199.

they interact with each other. In most actual cases, the individuals are not at harmony with themselves, much less with truth and with God."[43]

As I perused the *soul* selections in my concordance, I discovered that in eighteen of twenty listings, the phrase "with all your heart and soul" is used. The other two usages are in Hannah's prayer, "pouring out my soul to the Lord,"[44] and Job's lament about his predicament causing a "bitterness in my soul."[45] The distinction is that the first group are about the uplift of heart and soul, while the latter group show how life struggles arrest the soul. In both cases the Hebrew word for *soul* is the same. In the psalms of King David, *soul* is used in both contexts, one rejoicing and the other weary.

Together, these usages reflect good and bad influences on one's growth. Of special note, one's belief or nonbelief in God has a powerful impact on a vision and on the soul. The soul's discernment culminates in a vision. Ultimately, as the vision grows and matures, its effects become a more observable character. And because of one's growth, personality development and spiritual formation will unfold.

As we'll see, the maturing process is ever-present in the lives of self-aware humans. Human aspects, such as vision and character, experientially unfold with each day. Ultimately, this reveals a dynamic interworking of the soul. It will work through a process that amends, modifies, adapts, revises, or reshapes attributes, both negatively and positively. Consequently, please recognize that very little in life remains static. One thing is for sure: change is inevitable. God is in pursuit of you.

Biblically speaking, there are four parts to the soul in the greatest commandment: mind, heart, will, and emotions. Humanistic psychology prefers the term *self* because the self can be demonstrated by objective evidence. The soul is not seen. In Creation, the living soul was breathed into humankind by God.[46] Man's soul required the breath of God, its life force (*nismat hayyim*), which includes mind, desire, emotion, and passion.[47]

---

[43] Willard, *Renovation of the Heart*, 201.

[44] 1 Samuel 1:15.

[45] Job 7:11.

[46] Genesis 2:7, "[T]he man became a living being." The Hebrew word *nepes* means soul, self, life, creature, mind, living being, desire, emotion, passion," https://www.blueletterbible.org/lexicon/h5315/niv/wlc/0-1/.

[47] Blue Letter Bible, @2022BlueLetterBible, "soul," https://www.blueletterbible.org/lexicon/h5315/niv/wlc/0-1/.

I maintain that humanity (both natural man or woman and spiritual man or woman) interprets the world from the soul through the collective heart, mind, will, and emotions. Inherent in each person is a mind that collects the sense data and, together with the heart, interprets and discerns respective perceptions, which become their experiences. The will acts on the products of the soul, the critical piece in vision development. Discernment, a facet of the heart, is the evaluation of the perceptions and interpretations. Discernment is the faculty that determines whether to accept, reject, or modify the experience.

THE SOUL'S INNER CONFLICT

In my search for truth, meaningfulness, and joy, I found it fascinating to study history, humanities, writing, learning, philosophy, sociology, and psychology. During college, my passion to understand the plight of humankind intensified. Yet I struggled to understand my own choppy, disconnected, and incoherent reflections.

Surprisingly, in some class discussions I did discover a commonality in the observations of my classmates. For the first time in my life, I heard others pondering the bigger questions of our realities. This proved to be an important piece in my pursuit of self-discovery. I was pleased to learn there were others considering man's predicament. Some thoughts were much more developed than mine; others were not.

What I found so surprising was the clash of my to-that-point hidden beliefs with the views of most of my professors. The contrast was stark. I recognized that I possessed a perspective that was in opposition to their existential thinking. The academics' views were distinctly humanistic and secular. They excluded the spiritual element and the transcendence of God as religious fantasy.

More concerning, I discovered that I was ill-prepared to argue the points from my Sunday-school understanding of the Bible. However, the works of the late Dr. Francis Schaffer brought me great satisfaction. He addressed the detrimental changes in the thought processes of scientific man.[48] I was deeply engaged in listening to the wisdom of humankind. The more

---

[48] Francis A. Schaeffer, *Escape From Reason* (Crossway Books, 1990), 207.

I understood, the more I was troubled by the lack of continuity in thought that ended in existentialism and without any parameters.

> The purposes of a person's heart are deep waters, but one
> who has insight draws them out.[49]

I could see where this was going. It was very disconcerting. No matter what the final analysis of man's wisdom, arriving at Kant's moral imperative was a pipe dream. Ultimately, the results of humanism would still have to be accepted by all. The possibility of that happening in me was nil.

THE GARAGE EXPERIENCE

What I call "the garage experience" was another profound experience in my life. I had a day off, and it was time to change the oil in my car. I was sitting on a crate in the garage, listening for the soft sound of the final drip. It was an introspective moment. I pondered the greatest questions of existence. I started a one-sided conversation with and about God, sincere and thoughtful. I was literally telling Him of my dilemma with the humanistic teaching of college and its challenges to my faith, whatever that was. My concern was that if He was not real, then the humanists were right. We're alone in this universe.

The secular world had a finely tuned, deterministic machine.[50] Existential philosophy clearly described the place of humankind in time and space. If existential man was right, then faith in God was useless. Life simply means that we are born, we live, and then we die. In all of space, we are a tiny species on a small, inconsequential planet among billions of celestial bodies, alone in this gigantic universe. In all of time, no one knew I was going to be here one hundred years ago, and no one is going to care one hundred years from now except for my progeny. In all of time and space, we exist for less than a blink of an eye. There is a name for that moment when a person recognizes the truth of one's existential reality. Human existence in and of itself, in all of time and space, has no "real" meaning, value, or purpose, other

---

[49] Proverbs 20:5.
[50] Schaeffer, *Escape From Reason*, 229–230.

than that which each individual decides for himself or herself. Existentialism calls this *existential dread*.

My mundane conversation with God continued. I realized that each person must ascribe value to their choices. Ascribing value to our pursuits and materialism can be equally challenging. What is valuable to one person is not valuable to another. Many of my classmates and I recognized that there is nothing in secular life that possesses an inherent value. That's why so many students leave college before graduation. They decide that a college education is not their path to a self-sufficient and meaningful life. Humans must choose to ascribe value to their own endeavors. No job, profession, or element of material well-being has ultimate value in and of itself. Our hope is that what we give value to will return a level of significance and meaning. It would be such a waste of time to live, work, and die in unhappiness. So, in the quiet of my garage, my question to God was "Can you make sense of all this for me? Is that all there is for humankind? That we are born, live, and die? Are the existentialists right, God?"

It was then that I heard it: a clear and distinct and audible voice that said, "Abide in Me." The voice was followed by several lesser voices. None were audible; they were just in my head.

"Study His Word."

"No shortcuts."

"Don't doubt His Word."

"Trust Him in everything."

"Seek His will."

The voice that had spoken aloud was so real, I stood up and looked around the garage to see if anyone else was in there. I was alone. Whatever part of me had been sullen and disturbed by my disparaging thoughts, I was startled and alert now, goose bumps everywhere. What had just happened? Curiously, my physical reactions were similar to those I had experienced in the orchard, but the audible voice was new.

I immediately went down to the basement, built a desk, and began a daily study and prayer schedule. I got up early every morning before my duty, read the Bible, and spent fifteen minutes talking to God (praying). I journaled about the biblical passages I read and my thoughts for the day. The biblical principles I was discovering, I applied to my life. Overnight, life took on another meaning. I was being moved by God's Holy Spirit.

15

My personal journey is not the same as yours. He wants a relationship with you. The Story of God isn't just for me; it is for all humankind. I will share how this relational journey has gone awry for so many.

As humans, we live from our personal histories. Personal histories are created from our collective experiences and, as mentioned, are influencing the way in which we perceive the world around us. Just as important, the experiences affect our responses. Personal histories include family interactions, social influences, the culture of the community, education, faith or nonfaith, work ethic, trauma, political upbringing, stress, and so on. Both positive and negative experiences will habitually influence a person's outlook and behaviors.

If you are a humanist, you must value and seek your own significance. Philosophers and psychologists have identified the paths of life choices. You can commit to a work ethic, attend college or not, own a business, enlist in the military, or choose a life of nefarious criminal activity. Parental influence and compulsory education oversee the training of the youth in our society and, one hopes, provide a nurturing home that teaches ethical values. Socialization, or how to interact and behave within a culture, can also prepare each of us for a lifetime of work and raising a family. The choice is to allow which experiences will or will not influence our actions.

In short, family and education are necessary to guide you to an existence of working and living. The educational process is designed to enhance employable skills so that students can sell their labor to the highest bidder. We all hope work will give our lives meaning, not only subsistence for living.

CRITICAL DEFINITIONS AND THEMES

Before moving forward, I need to address some critical concepts that will assist you in your reading. A *presupposition* is what you choose to believe in your heart and mind, with or without evidence. A presupposition is like the given information for solving a geometric proof. You remember—in order to solve the proof, you were given specific information to depend on. In the same way, each presupposition is the given information you use to understand phenomena in life and living. It is something you are taught or have learned to believe. We all have presuppositions about existence, whether we recognize them or not.[51] We call these differing perspectives about the universe and humankind *worldviews*.

WHOSE WORLDVIEW?

My initial study, following the garage experience, produced an uncanny truth about presuppositions and the humanistic worldview. The first discovery had to do with the *existential crisis* that I had recognized in my academic discussions with others. The existentialist's view of the universe and existence comes from a naturalist worldview. Naturalists rely exclusively on scientific study to determine the laws and forces of nature they will accept as truth. Clearly, naturalism has no place for God, because it anchors itself in natural properties and causes that can be verified.

Naturalists believe that humankind evolved naturally to its current state. Consequently, the human species on this planet must determine how to assign meaning to life and living, giving human existence values that most of civilized humankind can agree upon.

Philosophy is a mindful process, according to Dictionary.com—the use of reason to conduct a rational investigation of the truths and principles of being, knowledge, or conduct. Philosophy is humankind's wisdom pertaining to a described reality and humankind's place in it. Existentialism is philosophy's reigning worldview. The naturalist maintains that life has a natural end, death. There is nothing to follow. Some hold a fantasy of reincarnation.

On the other side of the worldview discussion is the supernaturalist perspective. Greg Koukl refers to the two sides of the conversation as a competition: "The Christian view is not the only way of viewing the world, of course. It is a competition. Every religion and every secular philosophy will claim to represent reality in a true and accurate way."[52] The supernaturalist worldview is set on God's vision of creation and an eternity, a reality that He designed. God assigns value and meaning to life, according to which all human beings can thrive through a community. For the supernaturalist, there is an eternity for some—an eternity with God.

---

[51] Francis A. Schaeffer, *The God Who Is There* (Crossway Books, 1990), 6.
[52] Greg Koukl, *The Story of Reality* (Zondervan, 2017), 23.

In light of the fact that I hold God to be the Originator of the supernatural worldview, I looked to Scriptures for understanding. The word *vision* can refer to a purely spiritual understanding of existence. A *vision* of the supernatural occurs when one recognizes a truth that transcends natural reality in an intense aha moment, and the truth of reality and its existence is in the One who created reality. The biblical characters we'll soon discuss all experienced an *epiphany*, that life-changing moment when reality took on a new face.

Therefore, the critical presupposition to vision is that God exists. God's vision gives the lives of His image bearers—humankind—meaning, value, and purpose. I'll never forget what a favorite high school teacher and coach once said: "Eric, nothing is as it seems. Look harder." It signaled for me an alternative universe.

SEEKING AN AUTHENTIC RELATIONSHIP

Incredibly, I realized that God was changing my heart from the inside out. I didn't recognize it right away in my life journey with Him, but about two months later I noticed my heart was softening toward others and the world around me. A level of mercy for the lost was building within me as I recalled how much God forgives me. It was an emotionally intense moment when I looked up and said, "You are really changing my heart." Tears rolled from my eyes as I remembered that day in the orchard. I now understood what the apostle Paul meant by the mysteries of God: a profound understanding of the supernatural mystery of the God-vision.

My mind, trained for objective reasoning, recognized that my heart change was inexplicable and not discernible by science. Dr. Craig Keener agrees that reliance on human wisdom is humanity's error: "Those who, based on worldly philosophies, think themselves divine should instead cultivate a true embrace of the divine perspective."[53] It dawned on me that I was now open to the spiritual intervention of God in my life. I was connected to centuries of the biblical history of God's people. Even the way I perceived life was changing.

Within a few weeks, I was pursuing more deeply God's direction for my life. It was a vision for a new reality. Initially, I was seeking out men of God to pray with. Unexpected blessings also came my way. In my military job,

---

[53] Craig Keener, *The Mind of the Spirit* (BakerAcademics, 2016), 173.

I was promoted and assigned to a new position that allowed me to attend college full-time. God was intervening in my life.

The changes were noticed by others. When on leave, I would return to my hometown and visit with the pastor of my home church. He told my parents that in twenty-five years of ministry, he had never observed such a phenomenal change in a human being. I can only attribute this change to God. Supernaturally—not overnight, but in the days and weeks following the garage experience—I studied, prayed, and practiced righteous living. I was not perfect. I struggled with my own wants and needs and my own desire to live this new life on my own terms. I was learning just how much of a hold that self-fulfilling human nature had on nonbelievers, believers, and me.

I learned that my personal desires, wants, and ambitions never stop, but power over the natural self (biblical flesh) does grow. I observed that drawing near to God is directly proportional to a desire to have God draw near to you.[54] I continued my studies, prayer, and daily conversations with God.

As I studied, I was gaining more understanding, and I was observing and experiencing the regular intervention of God in my life. I could see it. Yes, I knew that, in many of my life events and circumstances, God was intervening. Circumstances were changing without explanation. His intercession was real. I was changing from the inside out. I could tell there was a transformation happening in my heart. I was experiencing love, joy, and peace.

Today, I believe God to be authentic and intimate. His Word is truth. His intervention in my life is trustworthy. It was wise to pursue His goals for my life. Throughout this book, I begin with this premise: God exists. I will unequivocally demonstrate God's presence in the life of His believers.

Let's clarify a few distinctions when walking through spiritual transformation.

SEARCHING FOR A TRUE REALITY

The *reality presupposition* is the distinction between secular humanity's view and spiritual humanity's view of truth. My garage experience drew a line in the sand between the secular man and the Christ-man welling up within

---

[54] James 4:8.

me. My vision was forever altered. I learned that, for the natural man, the existential goal is first to know his reality and then to believe the reality he creates. For the spiritual man, the goal is to first believe God's reality for life and living and then to know the truth.

These are very distinct approaches to discerning and responding to the world. Both the natural person and the spiritual person possess minds that perceive and learn through the gathering and organizing of experience. This is how they both know. However, the way each interprets those perceptions is markedly different.

In this work, we will presume the Scriptures are true. God's Word aligns with this discernment process; this is a truth that startled me at times. It was my understanding of the differing interpretations of others that led me to acknowledge that there are other ways to respond to the circumstances in reality.

A biblical passage led me to subordinate my perceptions to a heart under the control of this godly influence within.[55] Without a doubt, there is a distinct demarcation between the perceptions and understanding of the secular self, and those of "trust in the Lord with all your heart" anchored in biblical truth.[56] My theological studies affirmed the powerful transcendence of an authentic truth that exists in reality. That profound awareness was guiding my heart to new understandings that affected my interpretations. The discernment grew sharper as I studied and learned of God's vision for humanity.

As a major bonus, this profound awareness was accompanied by a peace that I could not explain.[57] Our hearts and minds need to be in Christ.[58] I didn't understand it, but people saw it in me. Even a childhood friend, greatly unchurched, whom I ran into a year after my garage experience, said, "I can tell you are at peace."

He was right. I was filled with a mercy for humankind and its ways. I understood what the biblical account means by the word *lost*. Those who do

---

[55] Proverbs 3:5–6: "Trust in the Lord and lean not on your own understanding."
[56] Ibid.
[57] Philippians 4:7: "And the peace of God, which transcends all understanding, will guard your hearts and your minds in Christ Jesus."
[58] 1 Corinthians 2:16.

not possess God's vision are lost in the wilderness, searching for significance and meaningfulness.

Interpreting reality is a part of the presupposition developmental process. We organize and store that knowledge differently. Natural man understands the interpretative process as a part of the mind. Theologically, spiritual man also organizes and stores. More importantly, he interprets or discerns through the heart, mind, and will. The science of natural man holds that humans possess a duality of mind and body. The heart is not identified in human philosophy. Consequently, the natural mind holds the interpretive process.

UNDERSTANDING DISCERNMENT VERSUS JUDGMENT

Discernment can be defined as the interpretation of what the mind and heart perceive. According to Scriptures, discernment by the heart is critical and must be guarded.[59] The verse implies that from this central point of a person, an interpretation of one's perceptions is advanced. On the one hand, these interpretations are highly influenced by one's personal history, harbored within the dynamic *soul*. On the other hand, the decisions and behavior of the *self* are directed by the heart's influence. In short, the soul is autonomous and responsible for the effect discernment has on behaviors.

Another way of saying it is that your personal history is your frame of reference. A self-aware frame of reference discerns and guides future perceptions, actions, and observations of others, now and in the future.[60]

---

[59] Proverbs 4:23: "Above all else, guard your heart, for everything you do flows from it."
[60] Magazine Pro Theme on Genesis Framework, https://psychology.iresearchnet. com/social-psychology/self/. People experience their selves in two senses. The first is as an active agent who acts on the world as well as being influenced by that world. This type of self is usually referred to as the I, and focuses on how people experience themselves as doers. The second is as an object of reflection and evaluation. In this type of self, people turn their attention to their physical and psychological attributes to contemplate the constellation of skills, traits, attitudes, opinions, and feelings that they may have. This type of self is referred to as the me and focuses on how people observe themselves from the outside looking in, much like people monitor and contemplate the competence and character of other people.

LIVING IN A REVERENT RELATIONSHIP

Living in a reverent relationship means grasping a reverence for the authenticity of your relationship with God. A reverent fear is a relational response that recognizes His everlasting love for us is unmerited, but He still loves us. We pursue in our lives a continued effort to walk in right living or righteousness. A reverent fear implies an intimate and personal relationship with Him that is cherished because He is God.

Paul warns that this grace isn't a pass to go on in unrighteous behavior.[61] The nature of a covenant relationship is an intimate companionship. Such a relationship will be an understanding of your response to that relationship. Inherent in that understanding is a reverence for a precious intimacy with Him, such that you fear its brokenness.

My garage experience led me to prayer, study, and a life of *confession*. My contrite and broken heart forced me to face every selfish action or evil thought and ask God time and time again for forgiveness. Thank goodness, I did not face everything all at once. It has been an agonizing and painful process throughout my life.

At times, this exercise of approaching God seemed like a life of purposeful desertion and humbling reunion. But, in a very internal and spiritual way, it was freeing. With each act of contrition, I felt lighter and freer of my debilitating self-condemnation. The mystery is the peace, love, and joy He returned that filled my heart. Crucially, my confession and His forgiveness gave me freedom. Now I am able to approach the Holy One in surrender and humility. It is a soul liberation like nothing else!

DEVELOPING A PROFOUND AWARENESS

Profound awareness does not mean perfection. The battle will continue because of our human nature. It is a battle "against the authorities, against the powers of this dark world and against the spiritual forces of evil in the heavenly realms."[62] We will continue to engage in confusing behaviors because seeking right living with God reveals a nature of selfishness.

---

[61] Romans 6:1–2: "What shall we say, then? Shall we go on sinning so that grace may increase? By no means! We are those who have died to sin; how can we live in it any longer?"
[62] Ephesians 6:12.

However, the good news is, if you continue to pursue God with all diligence, victories will follow.

I experienced the joy as I learned to believe, trust, and pursue the God Story. There is always another side to a story. My new relationship with God did not give me a perfect life. I could spend the next ten pages sharing the poor decisions I made on my on-again, off-again spiritual journey. There were highs and lows. My only regrets stem from the fact that the selfish actions I took and the poor decisions I made often left a wake of disappointment and pain for me, my family, and my friends.

Our lives in Christ can result in living righteous lives, but like the apostle Paul, "I don't know why I do the things I don't want to do."[63] That is not an excuse, but a clear warning that our hearts and minds require a godly relationship.

Let's be very clear: this journey is not a life of self-righteous hubris. The journey is one of radical change resulting in a deep humility and reverence for our Creator God. The pride in human nature is a powerful and ego-protecting force. Modern psychology shows that we are products of our upbringing. I could say that upbringing played a role in my misguided behavior, but to what end? Yes, the mind and heart harbor the effects of the good and bad elements of childhood and youth. It is God's mystery of grace that overcomes it all.[64]

God provides an avenue to wholesome health and moves our selfish actions to a place where they are not to be repeated. We were not designed to hold the pain of our sin. Mercy means He moves sin as far as the east is from the west.[65] He doesn't see it, and we're not supposed to hold on to it. Grace is given to those who fear Him.[66]

As I learned, I found myself more forgiving and merciful to others and less likely to be offended, all of which made me freer! I began to live in an

---

[63] Romans 7:14–25.

[64] Psalms 103:8–18.

[65] Psalms 103:12: "For as high as the heavens are above the earth, so great is his love for those who fear him; as far as the east is from the west, so far has he removed our transgressions from us."

[66] Psalm 103:11. TWOT Vol. I, 907a, pg. 399 *yare – reverence or awe, righteous behavior or piety.* Strongs H3373.

unimaginable joy, knowing that God has placed my selfish actions (and they are many) out of His sight.

But that was not to be the end of living an ungodly life of self-determination. The most distasteful actions are those we commit after deepening our relationship with God. Some behaviors result in a gut-wrenching despair reminiscent of King David.[67] I know the pain King David described in his prayer seeking forgiveness. In the same way, I was selfish and only thought of my own fleshly desires. I experienced that very painful place of fully understanding my grievous behavior. At times this caused despondency and a sense of spiritual detachment from my joy-filled relationship with God.

I was soon to learn about the unfailing love of God. God does not want us to wallow in the weight of our pain to the point that it destroys us from within. However, sin is bitter. The pain ensures we will never forget the sin, but His forgiveness has removed it. It makes no sense to relive the unrighteousness in our lives. Living in that accusative state of mind will not lead us to wholeness. What is worthy to note is the unfailing love of God. With each confession comes His healing touch.

I have experienced the anguish of my sin against God, I have also known the sweet forgiveness in His love. I disappointed my God, but He loved me back. I have experienced healing release through the pain of confession. Why? Because He loves a broken and contrite heart.[68] God knows a broken and contrite heart. It is the deepest love I have to offer Him, and He accepts it. I know this because He still provides for my needs as I commune with Him. He hears my prayers. I have experienced many God-guided moments that have resulted in His will being accomplished through my life. I pray each day for those righteous victories and the avoidance of my potential for unrighteousness.

The garage experience was about my faith-walk. The journey has resulted in a lifelong soul-yearning for a relationship with God. God has intervened in my life on innumerable occasions, leading me to the truth of His presence. Unfortunately, that proof is not enough for scientific man, but it is nonetheless real in my lived experience.

---

[67] Psalm 51:1–17.
[68] Ibid. The broken and contrite heart is essential to experiencing a profound relationship with God.

Again, *vision* refers to a realm of spiritual understanding, beyond the natural epiphany or aha moment. God has given me an understanding of His realm that is a great source of joy. Let me be clear: God has answered prayers and guided me in many powerful and real-life circumstances. All of it has led me to an indisputable faith in Him. Your faith-walk will be different. No two journeys with God are the same, because each of us is as unique as our fingerprints. However, the mystery of the growth process will possess a joyous similarity.

All the powerful circumstances we experience are very different, but because of our profound vision, we understand the supernatural mysteries of God. Through the fruit of the Spirit, the profound joins in mercy, purity of heart, and peacemaking for God.[69] Vision glows, understands, and pursues with the joy of God's intervention. I rely on Him alone. I have no fear of the future. A divine plan is in place and is victorious at the end.

Understanding the God Story requires an undaunted belief that He is God and you are not. Nothing about the mysteries of God make sense without this unequivocal faith. Your vision must emanate from serving God! If you remain steadfast in your unbelief, you will wander and end up in eternal torment. The apostle Paul presents it best:

> This, then, is how you ought to regard us: as servants of Christ and as those entrusted with the mysteries God has revealed. Now it is required that those who have been given a trust must prove faithful. I care very little if I am judged by you or by any human court; indeed, I do not even judge myself. My conscience is clear, but that does not make me innocent. It is the Lord who judges me. Therefore judge nothing before the appointed time; wait until the Lord comes. He will bring to light what is hidden in darkness and will expose the motives of the heart. At that time each will receive their praise from God.[70]

Meditate on this: your inner being, to bring it into unison with God, will be transformed. The deeper you go in reconstructing your vision, the deeper

---

[69] See Galatians 5:22–23; Matthew 5:7–9.
[70] 1 Corinthians 4:1–5.

will be the resulting closeness with God. It will be a closeness that you *never* imagined possible. It is referred to as being "one with God," like Jesus. It can be a treacherous journey, but one that *will* result in unspeakable joy.

God made you. He knows you better than you do. As King David learned, God sought to return to the relationship God had created David for: to be a man to be after God's own heart.[71]

> For you created my inmost being; you knit me together in my mother's womb. I praise you because I am fearfully and wonderfully made; your works are wonderful, I know that full well. My frame was not hidden from you when I was made in the secret place, when I was woven together in the depths of the earth. Your eyes saw my unformed body; all the days ordained for me were written in your book before one of them came to be.[72]

You *must* ask God to cultivate the soil of your heart to possess His vision. God began a good work in you; let Him have all of you.[73] Do not delay in this conversation with Him. You will hear from Him.

---

[71] 1 Samuel 13:14.

[72] Psalm 139:13–16.

[73] Philippians 1:6.

3

CHOICE: A CRITICAL THEME IN A COVENANT

IN THE PRIOR CHAPTERS, THE FOCUS WAS ON UNDERSTANDING THE essence of your soul and your relationship with God—a relationship that is *soul-deep* or, in other words, *set deep within your soul*. You want the God Story embedded in your soul, the place you live from every day.

Our vision is set on a foundation that God's plan is one of freedom and choice. The vision rests in an indisputable relationship with God, seeing the kingdom on earth on a daily basis. Understand the precarious nature of this relationship and its eternal consequences. Eternity is a long time. I suggest that you ponder carefully the truth the Bible offers you. Submission and a surrendered relationship with the Father are required to believe; anything less is unbelief.

As I have learned through those brothers and sisters who have walked beside me, this joy-filled mystery is *only* available to those who believe. So please set aside your questions and focus on believing instead of knowing. If you don't understand, ask God to make it clear. I mean it: ask God.

The truth discussion is not done. We'll revisit this several times. For now, we'll go a little deeper into the pre-creation planning session that took place "before the creation of the world" to learn what the God Story really looks like.[74] Crucial to this chapter and many of the following chapters is an *imagined conversation within the Trinity*. These imagined conversations are often found in scriptural themes and verses. We will focus on the Father as Designer and Jesus as Builder. *Pre-creation planning* is the preparation for a universe, a special planet, and its people.

Eden is an incredible place. It has the smells of jasmine and roses, the songs of mockingbirds and macaws, a foliage canopy more beautiful than the

---

[74] Ephesians 1:4; 1 Peter 1:20; John 17:24.

Amazon River region, varieties of fruits for the taking, perfect temperatures from the warming sun and cool evenings, rivers running through it, a night sky filled with stars and planets, docile animals, and no death. Eden is a garden of unimaginable peace and tranquility! And the *choice* to live in this solitude will be an incredible gift given to its inhabitants!

PRE-CREATION PLANNING

Pre-creation planning must have been extensive. As I consider what might have been discussed, I am most thoughtful about the themes of love, choice, and covenant. I can only imagine that the planning between Father and Son centered on the significant topic of love. Love must be the foundation of this creation: a love that is learned and then taught; a love that offers trust, respect, and honor without reservation, as demonstrated through Creation. A covenant would provide the relational boundaries, with critical anchors in love and trust for one another. All humanity would be taught love from one generation to next.

Most important here is the choice. The created, Adam and Eve, must have the choice to participate in a divine relationship. Anything else is not love. In their freedom, the created can choose to love or leave. Their lives will be wonderful in Eden. In the wholeness of being who they are, they will thrive and flourish. Wholeness is freedom, innocence, and holiness. They will commune with the Trinity. The earth will rest in the universe, surrounded by stars and galaxies.

THE GIFT

This is the beginning of eternity, the Alpha and Omega of human history. God has given a precious gift, *choice*. What He begins in the Garden of Eden will be completed in a new garden.[75]

With the end in mind, God designs a plan for his created. He begins by placing them in the garden, knowing they will disobey and rebel. God will send His Son to draw them away from their rebellion and into relationship for an eternity, if they accept the truth of His Story.

---

[75] Revelation 22:1–5.

The God Story is for those who will believe. It has a beautiful beginning. Human beings are created in His image and placed in a beautiful garden. But because He gives them a *choice*, they rebel. The rest of the story is about God drawing us back to Him. This is how the God Story begins, with the victorious end in mind.

The planning session continued with critical themes. The design includes a heavenly host.

DEVELOPING A PROFOUND AWARENESS

The objective of God's plan design could never be overstated. God desires a relationship with the created, His people. He designed an incredible environmental context, Eden, in which to be with His children. He wanted to meet them in a glorious place, a garden, to nurture and guide Adam and Eve. His love was immeasurable because He was willing to give them a *choice*. Love is a choice. They were free to be all they could be.

God knows what He is facing, and His love will lead Him to win His people back. It is a reckless kind of love, knowing that He was going to lose them. He knew how the story would start and how it would end.

It is absolutely necessary, in an authentic relationship with God, for the believer to experience a profound love of God. Only those believers possessing a profound awareness of the truth of God's love for them will engage in a personal and intimate relationship with Him. This is truly the mystery of knowing God.

Everyone else is just playing religion. That may sound harsh, but it is backed up by recent Barna research that reveals that only 17 percent of churchgoers possess a biblical worldview.[76] This means that only 17 percent of worshippers—people who attend church weekly, read their Bible daily, and pray—live their lives knowing full well that God is intimately intervening in their lives. This is exactly the same percentage of leaders ready to enter the Promised Land.[77]

Unfortunately, too many pastors and priests don't experience the profound awareness of a genuine relationship in knowing God. Only a

---

[76] "Competing Worldviews Influence Today's Christians," Barna, published May 9, 2017, www.barna.com/research/competing-worldviews-influence-todays-christians/.
[77] Numbers 14:6–9.

profound believer will comprehend a profound experience. God's desire is to draw His people into a profound relationship with Him.

Meditate on this: an essential detail of God's plan is to create an environment of love, both a material world and a spiritual world. His plan is for a place in the universe designed for Him and His created. It is a perfect place, amid the stars and planets, to be in an intimate relationship with Him.

PART II

Adamic Covenant:
A Relationship of Love

4

ADAM AND EVE'S ACCEPTED CHOICE: DOMINION, MARRIAGE, AND WORK

EDEN IS THE GARDEN OF GOD, WHERE HE DESIRES TO BE IN RELATIONSHIP with the created. You can only imagine the glory and splendor! There He instructs them about His precepts and teaches them about wholeness and the pursuit of a joyful life. In the critical God work between the beginning and the end, God seeks to build on a covenantal structure. However, between those two ends—the Alpha and the Omega—is the Story of God drawing us back unto Himself through Jesus.

In short, God's planning began with Creation and the created living with Him in Eden. There is an agreement, a covenant of sorts. The created participate in a relationship with the Creator and possess dominion over the earth—*if* they stay away from the fruit of a specific tree.[78] In Eden, God walks in the cool of the day with Adam and Eve.[79] He is in a *covenant relationship* with them. In the end, God will lead those who choose to commit themselves to a personal and intimate relationship with Him.

---

[78] Genesis 2:17.

[79] Genesis 3:8: "Then the man and his wife heard the sound of the LORD God as he was walking in the garden in the cool of the day, and they hid from the LORD God among the trees of the garden. In all likelihood, they walked with Jesus since no man has seen God (John 1:18).

PRE-CREATION PLANNING SESSION

I can only imagine that the Father and the Son built a plan with the end in mind: to create and harvest a relationship of love.[80] The planning included a beginning point, a foundation on which all eternity would stand. The covenantal structure would begin in Eden. The conversation may have included what the covenant would look like and how its purpose would be to teach love. The created would be given the breath of life. An agreement would be a binding covenant between humanity and their Creator. This set the stage for a robust and intimate relationship.

In this covenant of everlasting love, the created were given dominion over all the earth—if they remained true to their love and innocence through avoidance of a deadly fruit. They would be taught the facets of love, trust, and honor. Their pure hearts would be the basis of a thriving and flourishing relationship, as well as a culture of loving-kindness.

We find the Creation plan unfolding in the early verses of Genesis 1, as God designs it and Jesus builds it. We also see an introductory revelation regarding the created on the sixth day. They are created in God's image (*demuth*) and likeness (*selem*), male and female. They are given dominion over the earth, air, and sea, and instructed to be fruitful and multiply.

CREATION

Unlike the previous five days, God ends His review of the sixth day with excitement.

> Then God said, "Let us make mankind in our image, in our likeness, so that they may rule over the fish in the sea and the birds in the sky, over the livestock and all the wild animals, and over all the creatures that move along the ground." So God created mankind in his own image, in the image of God he created them; male and female he created them.

---

[80] John 1:2–3: He was with God in the beginning. Through him all things were made; without him nothing was made that has been made.

God blessed them and said to them, "Be fruitful and increase in number; fill the earth and subdue it. Rule over the fish in the sea and the birds in the sky and over every living creature that moves on the ground."

Then God said, "I give you every seed-bearing plant on the face of the whole earth and every tree that has fruit with seed in it. They will be yours for food. And to all the beasts of the earth and all the birds in the sky and all the creatures that move along the ground, everything that has the breath of life in it, I give every green plant for food." And it was so.

God saw all that he had made, and it was very good. And there was evening, and there was morning—the sixth day.[81]

We see, in an additional perspective in Genesis, the creation of man and God's agreement with Adam that defines their connection. God begins with the creation of Adam set in a *covenant relationship*.[82] In the first passage, we see God shaping His plan. He gives Adam life. Adam is placed in the garden and given work. Adam is given permission to eat from the tree of life but prohibited from eating from the tree of the knowledge of good and evil.

This is the account of the heavens and the earth when they were created, when the Lord God made the earth and the heavens.[83]

Here, God breathes or places His Spirit into the man through his nostrils, giving him life. The supernatural connection explains the human penchant to reach out or understand the Creator.

Now no shrub had yet appeared on the earth and no plant had yet sprung up, for the Lord God had not sent rain on the

---

[81] Genesis 1:26–31.

[82] The agreement between God and Adam possesses all the markings of a covenant (*beriyth*). A covenant is an alliance or pledge that holds both parties accountable to the other. TWOT ref. 282a Harris, Archer, Waltke.

[83] This quotation and the quotations immediately following are drawn from Genesis 2:4–17.

> earth and there was no one to work the ground, but streams came up from the earth and watered the whole surface of the ground. Then the Lord God formed a man from the dust of the ground and breathed into his nostrils the breath of life, and the man became a living being.

The biblical account reveals there are two trees in the garden. One is the tree of life, suggesting that the created can live forever, and the other is the tree of the knowledge of good and evil.

> Now the Lord God had planted a garden in the east, in Eden; and there he put the man he had formed. The Lord God made all kinds of trees grow out of the ground—trees that were pleasing to the eye and good for food. In the middle of the garden were the tree of life and the tree of the knowledge of good and evil.
>
> The Lord God took the man and put him in the Garden of Eden to work it and take care of it. And the Lord God commanded the man, "You are free to eat from any tree in the garden; but you must not eat from the tree of the knowledge of good and evil, for when you eat from it you will certainly die."

In the next passage, God states that Adam should not be alone. God also adds to Adam's work the responsibility of naming the animals. God is aware of the power of relationships among His created. So God creates a female partner. He provides an expectation of unity for the relationship. Adam is given work to do. Humankind will have a propensity to work.[84] However, work isn't enough for this relational creation of God.

> The Lord God said, "It is not good for the man to be alone. I will make a helper suitable for him."
>
> Now the Lord God had formed out of the ground all the wild animals and all the birds in the sky. He brought them to the man to see what he would name them; and

---

[84] Genesis 2:18–25.

whatever the man called each living creature, that was its name. So the man gave names to all the livestock, the birds in the sky and all the wild animals.

But for Adam no suitable helper was found. So the Lord God caused the man to fall into a deep sleep; and while he was sleeping, he took one of the man's ribs and then closed up the place with flesh. Then the Lord God made a woman from the rib he had taken out of the man, and he brought her to the man.

The man said, "This is now bone of my bones and flesh of my flesh; she shall be called 'woman,' for she was taken out of man." That is why a man leaves his father and mother and is united to his wife, and they become one flesh. Adam and his wife were both naked, and they felt no shame.

The work of the planning session was incredible. Jesus built as His Father designed. The created were in His image, male and female. Let's be clear: that answers the gender question for humankind. They are assigned work, given dominion over the earth, and married in physical as well as relational unity. They agree not to eat of the tree of the knowledge of good and evil. They commune with their Creator God. He teaches them.

DEVELOPING A PROFOUND AWARENESS

The God Story possesses a perfect design. The design is driven by relationship: the relational love of a parent raising children. The created are given chores and responsibilities. The God-Parent teaches important principles of living a life of wholeness—those things that are necessary to thrive.

The created were made in God's image; they are His image bearers. He gave them the capacity to think, sense the beauty of the world around them, and judge that beauty. He gave them the ability to gentle wild beasts. God's profound love and respect for His image bearers was demonstrated in giving them *dominion over it all.*

The God-man relationship was of a sovereign-vassal nature.[85] It was vital that the created's position required a behavioral compliance that confirmed their faithfulness to Him in this agreement, which we'll see is more like a covenant. They embraced their divine position relative to their Creator God.

A profound life as God's son or daughter, or as man and wife, means living an everlasting life filled with the *joy* of being in relationship with Him. In His compassion, He gave the created a *choice* in this agreement. All of humankind gets that choice as well. Biblical joy is *not* earthly happiness. Earthly happiness is a momentary and fleeting emotion. The choice is whether to be in relationship with Him and experience the deep-seated joy of being dependent upon Him.

Meditate on this: man is brought to life through his nostrils by the breath of God. Our life force is spirit. That undoubtedly places great value, a sanctity, on human life. We were given life by Him. God put them to work. This can only be considered a sacred responsibility in life. The work entailed caring for the earth.

God designed Adam and Eve to be one. He referred to them as husband and wife, a marriage. This is a fundamental belief or law for both Jews and Christians. Marriage is necessary for a thriving family and society.[86] The Christian faith embraces these fundamental truths regarding their vision relationship with God as paramount to life with God. Their choice is dependence upon the Creator for everything. They want for nothing! And they are safe and secure.

As you read, keep this in mind: in the planning session, the Trinity knew humanity would fail, but their love for humanity prevailed. The Son of God would be called upon to restore the rebellious and disobedient to right relationship with the Creator.

---

[85] Roy B. Zuck, ed., *A Biblical Theology of the Old Testament* (Moody Press, 1991), 18. God has created man for the express purpose of conveying to him the status and function of image—that is, that man was to represent God.
[86] Genesis 2:21–24.

5

A CHOICE FOR ANGELS: EMERGENCE OF EVIL

WE HAVE NO IDEA HOW LONG ADAM AND EVE SPENT IN THE GARDEN, being nurtured and taught by God. And we have no idea how long after Creation it was when Satan and his demons rebelled against God. Was the rebellion a great battle? Or was the great battle in the heavens because of their rebellion? God knew that the Lucifer's offer was going to be too much for Adam and Eve to resist. Lucifer was the guardian cherub. God knew that the offer would cause discontent in the hearts of the created. The created used their choice to choose their own destiny. God planned accordingly in the pre-creation planning session.

PRE-CREATION PLANNING SESSION

I can only imagine the challenges the intervention of evil would present to the trinitarian plan. The Trinity knew the plan would go awry, but they persisted. The only reason for their patience is His everlasting love and desire to be in relationship with the created. I imagine the planning conversation included a discussion about choice and rebelling against the covenant the created made with Him. Choice would be used for *selfish* reasons. The created would break covenant.

Lucifer had been appointed guardian over the garden.[87] Lucifer was the most beautiful and adorned angel! He was overcome with pride.[88] He envied and was jealous of all he saw. This guardian cherub rebelled. The deceiver persuaded one-third of the angels to follow him into a great battle.

---

[87] Ezekiel 28:14.
[88] Ezekiel 28:14–15.

In his selfish pride, he lured the created into believing they could be their own gods. They became discontented with all they had. They made their own decisions, believing they were right in their own eyes.[89]

God's gifts of love, choice, and freedom are all closely tied together. The created didn't have to choose another option. They only had to believe that being in covenant with their Creator was best for them, a blessing. In the cool of the evenings, they had conversations with their Creator about love and maintaining right behavior.

Emotions are good, but they can serve the *desires of the flesh*. The created made *self-satisfying* choices that made them feel good, but nothing filled their hearts' desires, nor would they find peace and contentment in their autonomy. They ceased to live in a holy innocence; they were filled with the knowledge of good and evil, which led them to horrific decisions.[90] They were banished from the garden. They were cut off from relationship with the Trinity. They were filled with disobedience and rebellion, making decisions on their own and violating the life-giving principles. They were alone and separated.

A HEAVENLY BATTLE

It isn't clear at what point after Creation that Lucifer led one-third of the angels into battle against God, Gabriel, Michael, and the angelic army. In all likelihood, Lucifer's angelic rebellion occurred after he saw all that God had done for the residents of the garden. Some of the story is in the book of Ezekiel, where the writer speaks for God as a prophet:

> You were the seal of perfection, full of wisdom and perfect in beauty. You were in Eden, the garden of God; every precious stone adorned you: carnelian, chrysolite and emerald, topaz, onyx and jasper, lapis lazuli, turquoise and beryl. Your settings and mountings were made of gold; on the day you were created they were prepared. You were anointed as a guardian cherub, for so I ordained you. You were on the holy mount of God; you walked among the fiery

---

[89] Isaiah 5:21: "Woe to those who are wise in their own eyes, and clever in their own sight."
[90] Proverbs 14:12: "There is a way that appears to be right, but in the end, it leads to death."

stones. You were blameless in your ways from the day you were created till wickedness was found in you. Through your widespread trade you were filled with violence, and you sinned. So I drove you in disgrace from the mount of God, and I expelled you, guardian cherub, from among the fiery stones. Your heart became proud on account of your beauty, and you corrupted your wisdom because of your splendor.[91]

Other biblical authors wrote of this angel of pride, Lucifer. "Widespread trade" is translated as *negotiations*. He offered the colluding angels key positions of authority.

Isaiah recorded what he heard from Lucifer. Lucifer's *pride* was the essence of his character. He was given responsibility to watch over Eden, but he wanted more. He was discontented with God's way of doing business. So Lucifer gathered together those angels he thought would listen and presented a plan to take over Eden and the created. He won them over by offering positions of power. God tells Isaiah what Lucifer said and what his goal was:

You said in your heart, "I will ascend to the heavens; I will raise my throne above the stars of God; I will sit enthroned on the mount of assembly, on the utmost heights of Mount Zaphon. I will ascend above the tops of the clouds; I will make myself like the Most High."[92]

In the book of Jude, it is revealed what will happen to those angels who followed Lucifer:

And the angels who did not keep their positions of authority but abandoned their proper dwelling—these he has kept in darkness, bound with everlasting chains for judgment on the great Day.[93]

---

[91] Ezekiel 28:13–18.

[92] Isaiah 14:13–14.

[93] Jude 1:6.

The apostle Paul establishes this for the followers of Christ:

> For our struggle is not against flesh and blood, but against the rulers, against the authorities, against the powers of this dark world and against the spiritual forces of evil in the heavenly realms.[94]

Satan's army was good, but not great enough to defeat the King of the universe:

> Its tail swept a third of the stars out of the sky and flung them to the earth. The dragon stood in front of the woman who was about to give birth, so that it might devour her child the moment he was born.[95]

Revelation reveals the eventual end of Lucifer and his demon angels:

> Then war broke out in heaven. Michael and his angels fought against the dragon, and the dragon and his angels fought back. But he was not strong enough, and they lost their place in heaven. The great dragon was hurled down— that ancient serpent called the devil, or Satan, who leads the whole world astray. He was hurled to the earth, and his angels with him.[96]

Satan's plan was a good one.[97] He presented to the created the same thing he presented to the rebelling angels: a choice of autonomy, power, and determination of their own destiny. They witnessed the power of their Creator God. On Judgment Day, Satan and his followers will be thrown into eternal torment.

---

[94] Ephesians 6:12.

[95] Revelation 12:4.

[96] Revelation 12:7–9.

[97] T. J. Allen, "Civil War in Heaven and Creation of Man," The Salty Eclectic (blog), April 22, 2018, https://thesaltyeclectic.com/2018/04/22/civil-war-in-heaven-and-creation-of-man/.

But the beast was captured, and with it the false prophet who had performed the signs on its behalf. With these signs he had deluded those who had received the mark of the beast and worshiped its image. The two of them were thrown alive into the fiery lake of burning sulfur.[98]

DEVELOPING A PROFOUND AWARENESS

Despite the wonderful life in Eden for the created, learning the precepts of holy living in Him was not enough. Lucifer's plan was devious. He worked the weaknesses of Adam and Eve.[99] All humans are familiar with the weakness of *discontentedness*, the loss of contentment with what the Creator God has given them. Generally economists say it best: human beings have insatiable desire for material well-being, as well as power and control.[100] Add to that the desire to choose one's own destiny, and you have a people with no vision other than self-gratification.

In our humanistic society, we teach values like independence, personal autonomy, and self-determination. You hear it throughout our media: be and do what you want. In God's economy, it doesn't work that way, as you'll see. The struggle humans experience with choice is *managing the self.* The daily work of assessing the many options we have and controlling our decisions is monumental. The magnitude of stress in the decision-making process is compounded by the need to determine consequences the decision may or may not have. In other words, will the perceived robust result of a decision be waylaid by an unanticipated black swan event?

Meditate on this: one who is in dependence on God is not anxious about a decision, because that person lives in a faith that brings assurance that God is leading them. Those who have the God Story anchored in their hearts have left the outcome to Him. They are focused on being in His will and not on personal gain or ambition. The believer is singularly in relationship with God.

Separation from the Creator is a lived experience. Adam and Eve know both sides of the chasm of disobedience and rebellion: one of love and intimacy, the other of sterility and aloneness.

---

98 https://www.gotquestions.org/sheol-hades-hell.html.
99 https://thesaltyeclectic.com/2018/04/22/civil-war-in-heaven-and-creation-of-man/.
100 https://www.intechopen.com/chapters/84741.

6

CREATED DISCONTENT: A BROKEN COVENANT

WHAT HAPPENED THROUGH THE PRE-CREATION PLANNING SESSION WAS unimaginable! Jesus built an entire universe, without flaw, using the Father's design. Adam and Eve were created in His image and likeness: joyful, intelligent, thriving, considerate, capable, loving, and gentle. They were offered dominion and given a choice to accept. Adam and Eve were placed in the garden to work it. They were given dominion over it. They united in marriage, named the animals, and, best of all, were in relationship with the Creator God and each other. They had the breath of God (*nesama*) within them. *Nesama* can be translated as "breath," but further research reveals that it is a breath of divine inspiration, spirit, or force that gives life.

With the end in mind, God will be victorious. Jesus has built an incredible universe. He is in an everlasting love relationship with the created!

Essential themes for understanding our relationship with God dictate the depth of our interaction with Him. In this case, embracing the specific details of the Eden tragedy are paramount in an engaging vision with the King of the universe at the center. Unpacking these passages should position you for understanding your deepening relationship with God, a soul-vision.

PRE-CREATION PLANNING

The significance of the broken relationship between Creator and created is interwoven in all that follows throughout human history. The damage is devastating. I can only imagine how difficult this would have been in the pre-creation planning meeting. The evil fallen angel was a great disappointment. The only goal of the deceiver was to lure these souls away from their Creator. The covenant was designed to protect the created by giving them the opportunity to choose thriving and flourishing lives that honored His precepts. Eden was intended to be a place of peace and intimacy.

However, God and Jesus would not be defeated. The lost would be given an opportunity to be restored to this divine relationship with the Father. Covenants and forgiveness would follow. The Holy Spirit would be sent to anoint those who believed.

BIBLICAL ACCOUNT (CA. 4000–2100 BCE)

The moment arrived. Lucifer was disguised as a serpent. This is important—had the deceiver revealed his true identity, the deception would have been over. The created would have recognized him. The deceiver approached Adam and Eve in the garden:

> Now the serpent was more crafty than any of the wild animals the Lord God had made. He said to the woman, "Did God really say, 'You must not eat from any tree in the garden'?" The woman said to the serpent, "We may eat fruit from the trees in the garden, but God did say, 'You must not eat fruit from the tree that is in the middle of the garden, and you must not touch it, or you will die.'" "You will not certainly die," the serpent said to the woman. "For God knows that when you eat from it your eyes will be opened, and you will be like God, knowing good and evil."
>
> When the woman saw that the fruit of the tree was good for food and pleasing to the eye, and also desirable for gaining wisdom, she took some and ate it. She also gave some to her husband, who was with her, and he ate it. Then the eyes of both of them were opened, and they realized they were naked; so they sewed fig leaves together and made coverings for themselves.[101]

---

[101] Genesis 3:1–7.

In the beginning of the conversation, Lucifer asked a seemingly harmless question, and Eve had the correct response. Unfortunately, the question itself caused Eve to question what she had been told. Then Lucifer countered with a very thought-provoking statement. He told Eve that she would not die. Eve's hesitation was tragic and set the stage for the next remark: "Your eyes will be opened, and you will be like God, knowing good and evil."

These alternative lifestyles were suggestive and seductive to Eve. Her next actions were crucial. Eve recognized that this fruit would be a tasty food, was appealing to the eye, and would give her wisdom.

Using feelings and senses to decide is catastrophic. Eve's three errors in judgment were pivotal. As we'll see, such errors are found throughout Scripture. Faith is clearly built on these.

- The created didn't believe God's Word.
- The created didn't believe in God's sovereignty over life and death.
- The created didn't favor God's plan for their lives.

This is a seminal moment for all humankind. This is the foundation to faith, with life-and-death influence over believers. This is the beginning of understanding the fundamentals of the faith theme.

Unfortunately, this disobedience was driven by *discontent*. Adam and Eve became discontented with what God had provided for them in the garden, as a consequence of learning that something else was better. They made decisions with their senses and trusted their feelings to seek what looked and tasted good. In this horrific moment, their discontent grew as they considered that what God had told them about the fruit may *not* have been true. What if God hadn't told them the truth? They realized they could be like God if they possessed knowledge and wisdom. With those thoughts building in their hearts and minds, they considered making alternative choices.

Their discontent became their nemesis. They considered having *independence* and *autonomy* from God. They might no longer be in *dependence* on Him. They could choose *self-determination* and no longer be concerned about the *sovereignty* of God. They would have *self-gratification* by enjoying what they wanted. They realized they would have control over their destiny.

46

IMPORTANT THEMATIC CONSIDERATIONS

God initially made His agreement with Adam. Eve told Satan that they couldn't touch the fruit. That isn't what God told Adam. Adam added to God's instruction when he told Eve what God had told him prior to Eve's arrival. The created were in the image of God and in His likeness. Adam and Eve were capable of their own reasoning and of making their own choices, but they were misled by their emotions.

Second, God never told Adam and Eve their eyes would be opened. He said they would die. For Satan, having their eyes opened through knowledge and wisdom was more important than their death or separation from God. When Eve ate the fruit, her eyes were not opened. However, when Adam ate the fruit, *their* eyes were opened. This was one of the terms of the agreement God had made with Adam, not Eve.

Finally, it is critical to note that, when their eyes were opened, *fear* coursed through their veins. *Fear* and *discontent* are damaging qualities for rebellious humanity. In proof of their fear, they hid from God. He asked what happened. That led to the blame game for Adam and Eve.

CRITICAL ISSUES

There are two significant issues here that clearly reflect God's everlasting love for Adam and Eve. A relational motif continues.

- Following God's inquiry and judgment is critical! The bloodshed sets the stage for our understanding of the blood theme throughout Scriptures. God shed blood in the garden. This was the first time that blood was shed on earth.[102] The skins of animals were prepared by God to cover Adam and Eve. It was an incredibly loving act by

---

[102] Genesis 3:21: "The Lord God made garments of skin for Adam and his wife and clothed them." According to TWOT (1589a), the usage here is very specifically about the hides of animals after skinning. No blood had been shed until that point.

47

God to cover their guilt and shame. Blood was shed to cover the choice to rebel and disobey. This is where the blood theme begins.

- God banishes Adam and Eve from the garden and shields them from reentry.[103] If they had returned to the garden, they could have eaten from the *tree of life* and thereby remained in a state of rebellious separation from God. God loved them too much to allow that to happen. Satan was correct: Adam and Eve henceforward possessed the knowledge of good and evil. God's pre-creation plan would restore His people back to Himself.

Understanding this is critical to your vision! The planning session demonstrates to us that God provided a way for us to return to relationship with Him. His heart's desire is an everlasting and intimate relationship with the created.

There is another significant issue here. Adam and Eve lost possession of the earth. God had given them dominion over it. Now this earth belonged to Satan. As God had likely informed Jesus in the pre-creation planning, "Their rejection will require restoration through You to heal the *broken relationship!*"

Let's review two details in this Eden tragedy that are critical to our vision and faith. After their eyes were opened, Adam and Eve recognized their nakedness. Their innocence was gone. God came walking through the garden.

> Then the man and his wife heard the sound of the Lord God as he was walking in the garden in the cool of the day, and they hid from the Lord God among the trees of the garden. But the Lord God called to the man, "Where are you?" He answered, "I heard you in the garden, and I was afraid because I was naked; so I hid."
>
> And he said, "Who told you that you were naked? Have you eaten from the tree that I commanded you not to eat

---

[103] Genesis 3:22–23 "And the Lord God said, 'The man has now become like one of us, knowing good and evil. He must not be allowed to reach out his hand and take also from the tree of life and eat, and live forever.' So the LORD God banished him from the Garden of Eden to work the ground from which he had been taken."

from?" The man said, "The woman you put here with me—
she gave me some fruit from the tree, and I ate it."

Then the Lord God said to the woman, "What is this
you have done?" The woman said, "The serpent deceived
me, and I ate."[104]

First, God called out to Adam even though He knew what had happened.
He knew Adam was hiding because of fear. God is calling out to humankind
despite the fact that we are selfish, rebellious people hiding in our own
choices.

Second, in the shadow of God's gracious love, Adam and Eve engaged
in a blame game, a horrific comparison of the two responses! Adam not
only blamed his wife, but God as well, referencing "the woman you put here
with me." To this very day, humankind existentially remains in a rebellious,
selfish, and greedy state of mind.

Finally, the curse upon the man was that he would toil for his existence.
Man would have to strive in his work to sustain his life and secure peace.
The curse upon the woman was childbearing and desire for her husband.
Her yearning is translated as master (*masal*), to control him.[105]

DEVELOPING A PROFOUND AWARENESS

The pursuit of knowledge to become like God led Adam and Eve and all of
humanity to a dark place. *Pride* and *discontent*, filled with *selfishness* and *evil*,
are born from *fear*. These crucial points are indispensable in developing a
faith-based relationship with God.

Jesus would come to repair the broken relationship. He would bring
heaven to earth. *We are still in our heaven on earth mode*, or the building of
the kingdom of heaven. Jesus has taught us how to be in relationship with
the Father. It is the desire of His heart that I yearn for, not my desires.[106]

---

[104] Genesis 3:8–13.

[105] Roy B. Zuck, ed., *A Biblical Theology of the Old Testament* (Moody Press, 1991),
21. As a part of God's judgment to choose rebellion, with its alienating results, *masal*
suggests that the wife will seek her husband's dominion.

[106] Psalm 37:4: "Take delight in the LORD, and he will give you the desires of your heart."

The essential qualities of faith require submission and surrender in order to (1) believe His Word, (2) trust His sovereignty, and (3) pursue God's purpose for your life. In a deepening relationship with Him, the profundity extends further into a peace that recognizes all that God is doing and will do for those who love Him.

Pride isn't arrogance, although the two can go hand in hand. Pride is an internal drive that is all about your wants and needs as a person. It is singularly about what you want. *Discontent* is not about what is or about being content with what is. Discontent is about what you don't have. This quality is a significant part of humanity's pride. The grass all too often appears greener on the other side of the fence.

SEPARATION: THEY CALL ON GOD

Adam and Eve began living their lives in separation from God and their garden relationship. They lived in despair, brokenhearted. Daily living must have been gut-wrenching, knowing what they had done. However, they used this new opportunity to teach the children of their children what they had done. They taught the grandchildren their personal responsibility as the people of God. The God Story is powerful, and Adam's influence over his progeny was formidable.

PRE-CREATION PLANNING

I can only imagine the trinitarian conversation as to what would follow the Eden tragedy. After Adam and Eve were banished, their situation became worse. They needed God's guidance more than ever. Their work was difficult. They lived in anguish, never forgetting what they had done. The memories of the garden were painful reminders of their discontent and what they had given up to become independent of their relationship with God.

However, God continued to watch over them. Adam's grandchildren received a powerful testimony about what happened. This great progenitor taught his grandchildren and those who came after them what happened. With their testimony, the created led their grandchildren *to call on the name of the Lord.*[107]

In their planning, God and Jesus must have discussed what would happen when Adam was gone. Lucifer would make things worse. Some of the created would hold tightly to their selfish choices, and some would learn that dependence on God is freedom. And when the great men left the earth, evil would abound.

---

[107] Genesis 4:26.

The covenants provided a vision for the restoration of God's people. There would be great pain as well as disappointment. The circumstances and trials Jesus would walk through presented opportunity for Creator and created to develop a deeper relationship. Some would become great leaders. Others would be distracted by their own visions, fears, needs, and mistakes.

Father and Son surely discussed sending Jesus to His people as a messenger.[108] No doubt teaching righteousness and wholesomeness was not a simple objective. Being His people required leaders who would cherish His vision in order to restore a lost people.

Adam taught his grandchildren, and they listened and obeyed the God Story. The grandchildren and their grandchildren witnessed the anguish of Adam and Eve. Next, the covenant-bearing leaders also taught God's precepts. They took responsibility for teaching a right way to live and what it means to be a joyful and wholesome people.

A BIBLICAL ACCOUNT

Adam and Eve were alone and working the soil to grow their own food. They also had to raise children. Their time must have been one of gut-wrenching discouragement, knowing what they had done. Adam and Eve taught their progeny about their rebellion and what happened in the garden. Here we find a serious sibling rivalry:

> Adam made love to his wife Eve, and she became pregnant and gave birth to Cain. She said, "With the help of the Lord I have brought forth a man." Later she gave birth to his brother Abel.
>
> Now Abel kept flocks, and Cain worked the soil. In the course of time Cain brought some of the fruits of the soil as an offering to the Lord. And Abel also brought an offering—fat portions from some of the firstborn of his flock. The Lord looked with favor on Abel and his offering,

[108] Ron Rhodes, *Angels Among Us: Separating Fact from Fiction* (2008), 117. See Genesis 16:7, 22:11; Exodus 3:2; Numbers 22:22, etc. A theophany is a visible manifestation or representative of God. God sent Jesus on several occasions to provide teaching or leadership, or to act as a warrior.

but on Cain and his offering he did not look with favor. So, Cain was very angry, and his face was downcast.

Then the Lord said to Cain, "Why are you angry? Why is your face downcast? If you do what is right, will you not be accepted? But if you do not do what is right, sin is crouching at your door; it desires to have you, but you must rule over it."

Now Cain said to his brother Abel, "Let's go out to the field." While they were in the field, Cain attacked his brother Abel and killed him.

Then the Lord said to Cain, "Where is your brother Abel?"

"I don't know," he replied. "Am I my brother's keeper?"

The Lord said, "What have you done? Listen! Your brother's blood cries out to me from the ground. Now you are under a curse and driven from the ground, which opened its mouth to receive your brother's blood from your hand. When you work the ground, it will no longer yield its crops for you. You will be a restless wanderer on the earth."[109]

God was looking after them. It is obvious that He blessed the work of Cain and Abel. We can't be sure whether Adam had a farm of his own. However, Adam and Eve had taught the boys about giving back the first fruits or best offering to God as a relational sign of gratitude in response to His blessing of the work. Adam and Eve taught their sons that giving back to God was a powerful sign of gratitude and worship.

Unfortunately, Cain did not honor what his parents taught. He did not bring his best first fruits. God showed disfavor. Abel brought the best of his flock to honor God. God's favor made clear the importance of this offering.

Cain was not happy with God's disfavor. A selfish person reveals how they feel when they are wronged. God saw in Cain's face a reflection of an attitude or feeling (*panim*) of the *self*, and He inquires why this is the case.[110]

---

[109] Genesis 4:1–12.
[110] *Downcast* or *countenance* refers to facial expressions that reveal the emotions or attitude of self. TWOT, 1782a, p. 727, Vol. 2, Harris, Archer, Waltke.

Curiously, God doesn't allow Cain to answer; He immediately asks about Cain's lack of responsible behavior: "If you do what is right, will you not be accepted?"

Two interesting points stand out here. First, an offering is a right and responsible action in Cain's relationship with God. It is sacrificial. Second, Cain is *responsible for his actions*. Cain does not get to blame his behavior on Mom and Dad rebelling in the garden, or on sibling rivalry. Cain and Cain alone is responsible for doing the right thing!

We learn another crucial lesson here. God not only taught Cain about honoring Him through offering and being responsible for his individual actions. God also informed Cain that Cain is vulnerable to sin because he is not listening to his Creator. This is the first time we see the word *sin* (*hattaat*) appear in Scripture. The root meaning is to miss the mark or the way.[111] *Missing the mark* is an abstract concept having to do with a path of right behavior. If you're not doing what is right, then your only choice is to do what is wrong. Furthermore, God provides a very specific imperative for Cain: "It [sin] desires to have you, but you must rule over it." This is a very clear message. Follow God's ways; otherwise rebellion leads to sin.

We know that Cain did not listen to God. Cain killed his brother, Abel, out of jealousy. We know the rest of this story. God withdrew his favor from Cain and sent him out to be a wanderer. Undoubtedly, Adam and Eve's discouragement over their past sin turned into grief and depression at the death and banishment of their boys. In all likelihood, Adam and Eve led in teaching about their experiences and their God. Their teaching would have been passed along through oral tradition following the tragedy in Eden. However, as great as their grief was, they continued to teach their offspring the ways of God.

A little history will help in understanding the lineage of God's family on earth. The oral tradition of storytelling provided to each generation the significance of the God Story. Adam taught his sons about their Creator God. Adam would have taught Seth what happened in the garden and how important it is to walk with God. The Story of God became a valuable and rich history by which to guide the spiritual and moral decisions of future generations.

---

[111] *Sin* means to miss the mark or, more specifically, to miss the way that God has purposed your life. TWOT, 638a, p. 277, Vol. 1, Harris, Archer, Waltke.

As grandfather, Adam taught his grandson, Enos, in great detail about what happened in the garden. Adam also taught Kenan the ways of God. Then, as a great-great-great-grandfather, Adam taught the son of Cainan, Mahalalel, the ways of God. Adam and these patriarchs taught Jared, Enoch (not Cain's son), and Methuselah. Enoch was especially gifted in his relationship with God.[112]

We can only imagine the incredible conversations as Adam shared with his progeny the deep pain of sinning against God. I expect that Adam, during family gatherings, told mighty stories about the beauty in the garden, as well as the punishment of using their choice for selfish decisions. Family gatherings would have been large, with several generations of grandchildren in attendance. What a party this must have been! The progeny of Adam learned these lessons well and together worshipped God.

Adam raised his great-great-grandchildren with a reverent fear of the Lord. He knew every reason why they should honor God. The oral tradition was filled with true stories that Adam passed along. His grandsons honored Adam. They believed him and lived righteous lives. God honored Adam's sons. None experienced the Flood, as seen in the Adam-to-Abraham chart.[113] The genealogical graphic provides an excellent perspective on Adam's lineage.

Noah's father, Lamech, was in all likelihood the last of the line to talk to Adam. Lamech passed the Story of God down to the next generations. Noah brought the Story through a flood and taught his grandchildren.

Noah's response to God's instruction to build an ark was truly the response of a faithful man. Noah built an ark in an arid climate that

---

[112] Genesis 5:24: "Enoch walked faithfully with God; then he was no more, because God took him away."

[113] https://davidscroll.com/new/graphics/. Dawid Bothma did some outstanding work on tracking the biblical genealogy from Adam to Joseph. Here is a graphic: https://i.pinimg.com/originals/48/86/ed/4886ed2a5f3d886cbafaf5ece48b2ab8.jpg. Dawid Bothma's research indicates that 1) Jewish tradition states that Adam and Eve had a total of twenty-three daughters and thirty-three sons; 2) they had their third son when Adam was 130 years old, and Adam died 800 years later, when he was 930 years old; 3) siblings did marry—Abraham married Sarah, his sister from the same father but a different mother; 4) marriage between siblings was only forbidden by Moses; 5) Lamech, descendant of Cain, was the first bigamist, and bigamy was never approved by God; and 6) at the end of his life, Adam lived with eight generations.

saw very little rain, on the basis of a voice! However, the credit goes to his father and great-grandfathers, including Methuselah. This is reason enough for grandparents to play an intimate role in the life of grandchildren.

Noah would likely have listened to and memorized the God Story from his father, Lamech; his grandfather, Methuselah; and his great-grandfathers, Jared, Mahalaleel, and Cainan, who all had sat under Adam's guidance. Noah was selected by God because he believed God, trusted God's sovereignty, and walked faithfully, pursuing God. God extended His covenant to Noah with the provision that Noah would not eat anything with lifeblood in it. And they were not to kill one another, because all humanity was in the image of God.[114]

There is no doubt that the motivation for Noah and his family to remain steadfast in building the ark came from those dynamic stories of the patriarchs living under the teachings of Adam and Eve.

Theologians and nonbelievers alike are divided as to the facts regarding the patriarchs and Noah.[115] In all likelihood, there were two groups of people, the righteous and the unrighteous. One group followed the patriarchs and the Story of God, remaining obedient to the ways of Adam. The progeny of Adam and Eve are said to have followed the stories told to them. They were moved by the God Story. Moses wrote, "At the time people began to call on the name of the Lord."[116] The other group, the Nephilim, "the heroes of old, the men of renown," possessed a very sinful nature.[117]

Curiously, Adam and Eve, along with their committed progeny, died before Noah completed the ark and it started raining. I believe that God did not want Seth's line to experience the Flood. In the absence of Adam and these great patriarchs, the people of the earth no longer believed the stories, and the evil in the hearts of humankind grew more wicked. Without the believing storytellers, the God Story turned from truth to fable. The void of men telling the Story of God resulted in wicked hearts. This is evidence that humanity needs God.[118]

---

[114] Genesis 9:5–6.

[115] "Genesis," *Moody Bible Commentary* (Moody Publishers, 2014), 55–56.

[116] Genesis 4:27.

[117] Genesis 6:4.

[118] Genesis 6:5.

The following passage speaks to the absence of godly men following the death of Adam. The moral decline of humankind was so horrific that the Spirit of God warned that His future presence was in question:

> When human beings began to increase in number on the earth and daughters were born to them, the sons of God saw that the daughters of humans were beautiful, and they married any of them they chose. Then the Lord said, "My Spirit will not contend with humans forever, for they are mortal; their days will be a hundred and twenty years."
>
> The Nephilim were on the earth in those days—and also afterward—when the sons of God went to the daughters of humans and had children by them. They were the heroes of old, men of renown.
>
> The Lord saw how great the wickedness of the human race had become on the earth, and that every inclination of the thoughts of the human heart was only evil all the time. The Lord regretted that he had made human beings on the earth, and his heart was deeply troubled. So the Lord said, "I will wipe from the face of the earth the human race I have created—and with them the animals, the birds and the creatures that move along the ground—for I regret that I have made them." But Noah found favor in the eyes of the Lord.[119]

Human behavior was so sinful that God "regretted" He had made man. *Regretted* here should be understood "in the sense of *was pained* or *sorrowful, grieved, sad*."[120] The absence of godly precepts makes room for the inclinations of natural man.

DEVELOPING A PROFOUND AWARENESS

God from the very beginning knew that life in the garden would not be enough to teach His children. However, despite their rebellion, Adam and

---

[119] Genesis 6:1–8.

[120] "Genesis," *Moody Bible Commentary*, 56.

Eve taught their progeny and set their vision on God. Until his death, Adam used his failure in order to teach his grandchildren. He was successful in his instruction; Enoch was taken up by God because he had an incredible relationship with Him.[121]

Adam's effort to teach each of his grandchildren, Enos to Lamech, was critical to living a good and righteous life. Very few understand the powerful role Adam took on in making sure the following generations loved and honored God despite Adam's rebellion. Adam learned and moved forward by training up his children in the way that they should go.[122]

In all likelihood, Adam and his grandsons were the "men of renown." Without the leadership of these men of God, evil grew rampantly, setting the stage for God to instruct Noah. Noah had heard the God Story from his father, Lamech, and from his grandfather, Methuselah, who had heard the testimony of his progenitor, Adam.

Surely Noah, having hear the oral tradition of the God Story, was motivated by it to complete the ark project. His vision and passion for this work were unwavering. He did everything as God required, even as the taunting, mocking, and provocative jeers grew during the 120-year build.[123]

The biblical account appears to indicate that it was following the death of Adam that evil grew rapidly. The patriarchs could not hold back the tide of evil. It is clear that the Spirit was deeply troubled. Wickedness was so bad that God was saddened by humankind.

In the garden, human beings learned and lived the precepts. What God taught Adam and Eve in the garden would have been the basis of what Adam and Eve taught their grandchildren. Despite the horrific and eternal nature of their rebellion, they went on to honor God through teaching His words. Adam taught principles of relationship with God that were the basis of a godly worldview. And the power of godly living should never be lost from our hearts and minds.

---

[121] Genesis 5:24.

[122] Proverbs 22:6: "Start children off on the way they should go, and even when they are old they will not turn from it."

[123] Genesis 6:3, 5–6.

PART III

Noahic Covenant: Covenant Renewal

8

PRIDE AND COVENANT: PREPARATIONS FOR A FAMILY

THE FLOOD CHANGED EVERYTHING, BUT THE COVENANTS CONTINUED with Noah and then with Abraham. The Deluge rid the earth of evil. It was a fresh start for a righteous man and his family, but their lifespan was reduced to 120 years.[124]

Noah and his family, armed with the God Story, built a new community to honor God. God set apart a people for Himself.[125] It is conceivable that Abraham met his very-great grandfather Noah. Noah would have shared the Story of God with Abraham and given a firm warning to do what God says.

PRE-CREATION PLANNING

I can only imagine God's disappointment in what would take place among humanity. The pain must have been gut-wrenching. He had done everything necessary for humankind to understand their relationship with Him and live flourishing and thriving lives. The downside of choice was that too many of humankind opted to go their own way according to their own reason.

The plan included a deluge. The Flood cleansed the earth of evil in order to begin again. Soon after the waters receded, the earth filled with people. This one-language people built a worship center to be like God. To counter this, God decided to divide them through language. The Trinity predetermined the use of relational covenants to identify believers who would be restored to the Eden relationship.

---

[124] Genesis 6:3.
[125] Deuteronomy 7:6–8.

The plan extended the covenant to Noah and eventually established a chosen people to announce that a messiah was coming to restore all believers back to relationship with God. There would be no more floods. God's people would be chosen for eternity by their belief in God's Word, trust in His sovereignty, and pursuit of His will for their lives. This covenant would be for all mankind. They would be filled with grace, and He would forgive their choice to rebel. The covenant would be with a people who would announce the coming of His Son to overcome evil and restore them. Abraham would establish his people.

The chosen people would be a stiff-necked people who did not understand the Messiah's presence.[126] Many did not receive the Savior. In time, through the covenants, a nation would be built that would believe, trust, and pursue God. Certainly the Trinity discussed that the Hebrews would not understand their mission. They would believe the Savior was coming to slay their enemy. The Hebrews ruled over them. They would be called the People of the Book.

BIBLICAL ACCOUNT

God renewed His covenant with Noah after the floodwater receded. As He had in the agreement with Adam, God told Noah and his family to be fruitful and multiply—which meant to thrive, to flourish, and to take dominion over all the animals from the ark. There would be no more floods.

> Then God said to Noah and to his sons with him: "I now establish my covenant with you and with your descendants after you and with every living creature that was with you— the birds, the livestock and all the wild animals, all those that came out of the ark with you—every living creature on earth. I establish my covenant with you: Never again will all life be destroyed by the waters of a flood; never again will there be a flood to destroy the earth."
> And God said, "This is the sign of the covenant I am making between me and you and every living creature with

---

[126] Exodus 32:9: "'I have seen these people,' the LORD said to Moses, 'and they are a stiff-necked people.'"

you, a covenant for all generations to come: I have set my rainbow in the clouds, and it will be the sign of the covenant between me and the earth."[127]

It was as He said. Unfortunately, as their numbers grew, the people of the earth wanted to experience authority and power—to be like God. This is the mark of human pride. God scattered the people by giving them different languages. They moved according to their languages.

According to the historical charts of language development, all languages grew out of a single location. Warrenfells has proposed that all human languages originated from a sub-Saharan region.[128] This is consistent with the biblical account of the region known as Shinar (Babel).

> Now the whole world had one language and a common speech. As people moved eastward, they found a plain in Shinar and settled there.
>
> They said to each other, "Come, let's make bricks and bake them thoroughly." They used brick instead of stone, and tar for mortar. Then they said, "Come, let us build ourselves a city, with a tower that reaches to the heavens, so that we may make a name for ourselves; otherwise we will be scattered over the face of the whole earth."
>
> But the Lord came down to see the city and the tower the people were building. The Lord said, "If as one people speaking the same language they have begun to do this, then nothing they plan to do will be impossible for them. Come, let us go down and confuse their language so they will not understand each other." So the Lord scattered them

---

[127] Genesis 9:8–13.

[128] Jay Warrenfells, *A Brief History of Language.* Warrenfalls's research maintains that all languages are born in this region as well as their migration to other places in the world. It can be found in the Odyssey Online, a learning browser: https://www. theodysseyonline.com/brief-history-language. Considered important in three of the world's major religions, Semitic languages are believed to have developed from a single tribal group in Arabia around 3000 BCE. These languages then spread throughout the Middle East and North Africa.

from there over all the earth, and they stopped building the city.[129]

The people of God were called by Him to be His chosen people.[130] God selected the Hebrews from all the people on the planet to be His people. And Abraham would be the leader of the family of God. Moreover, they became known as the covenant people.

> The Lord had said to Abram, "Go from your country, your people and your father's household to the land I will show you. I will make you into a great nation, and I will bless you; I will make your name great, and you will be a blessing. I will bless those who bless you, and whoever curses you I will curse; and all peoples on earth will be blessed through you."
>
> So Abram went, as the LORD had told him; and Lot went with him. Abram was seventy-five years old when he set out from Harran. He took his wife Sarai, his nephew Lot, all the possessions they had accumulated and the people they had acquired in Harran, and they set out for the land of Canaan, and they arrived there.
>
> Abram traveled through the land as far as the site of the great tree of Moreh at Shechem. At that time the Canaanites were in the land. The Lord appeared to Abram and said, "To your offspring will give this land." So he built an altar there to the Lord, who had appeared to him.[131]

By these words, it is clear that God is all-in regarding this covenant relationship. This was the second of two cascading covenants that were designed to keep the relationship between God and His people genuine and pure.

---

[129] Genesis 11:1–8.

[130] Deuteronomy 7:6: "For you are a people holy to the LORD your God. The LORD your God has chosen you out of all the peoples on the face of the earth to be his people, his treasured possession."

[131] Genesis 12:1–7.

Abram, a man of right thinking, was named the father of nations and followed God's instructions. He followed the instructions of the voice that he had heard about through the stories. It is likely that Abram had a significant relationship with Shem, son of Noah. Shem told Abram the stories he heard from Noah. It is conceivable that Abram shared his meeting with Shem. Abram was a righteous man, and because he was, God made him promises: "After this, the word of the Lord came to Abram in a vision: Do not be afraid, Abram. I am your shield your very great reward."[132]

Abram was not afraid. He picked up his family, livestock, women, and children to follow God's instruction. No doubt Shem encouraged Abram to follow God's instruction. Abram launched into the unknown based on God's instruction. He believed that God would be his shield for protection and his reward with blessings. "Abram believed the Lord, and he credited it to him as righteousness."[133]

God outlined specifically what the covenant meant:

> But Abram said, "Sovereign Lord, how can I know that I will gain possession of it?"
>
> So the Lord said to him, "Bring me a heifer, a goat and a ram, each three years old, along with a dove and a young pigeon." Abram brought all these to him, cut them in two and arranged the halves opposite each other; the birds, however, he did not cut in half. Then birds of prey came down on the carcasses, but Abram drove them away. As the sun was setting, Abram fell into a deep sleep, and a thick and dreadful darkness came over him.
>
> Then the Lord said to him, "Know for certain that for four hundred years your descendants will be strangers in a country not their own and that they will be enslaved and mistreated there. But I will punish the nation they serve as slaves, and afterward they will come out with great possessions. You, however, will go to your ancestors in peace and be buried at a good old age. In the fourth generation your descendants will come back here, for the

---

[132] Genesis 15:1.
[133] Genesis 15:6.

sin of the Amorites has not yet reached its full measure."
When the sun had set and darkness had fallen, a smoking
firepot with a blazing torch appeared and passed between
the pieces. On that day the Lord made a covenant with
Abram and said, "To your descendants I give this land."[134]

To *cut* a covenant literally means to cut pieces of meat and place them on each side of a path. The parties then pass between them. This signifies that if either of them violates the terms of the agreement, the other partner can cut the transgressor to pieces. The covenant is permanent. Abram, in his vision, saw two representatives walking the path between the pieces of meat, cutting the covenant.

According to Scriptures, the two representatives were the smoking firepot and the blazing torch. I submit that the smoking firepot represents God, and the flaming torch represents Jesus. This is crucial to understand the Story of God. God is walking this out with His Son, who will keep this covenant for all humankind. No man can keep the covenant. God's design is perfect, and Jesus understands His role as covenant-keeper.[135] In his book, Dr. Mark Rutland holds that both the firepot and the torch represent God.[136] In a sense, that's not wrong. However, covenants are always cut between two different individuals. Consequently, I see the flaming torch as the Son of God who will represent humanity.

The covenant with Adam had been that Adam had dominion over the earth, and he was to stay away from the forbidden fruit. Noah's dominion covenant was sealed by the rainbow as God's promise never to destroy humankind. The Abrahamic relational covenant also included a seal or sign: circumcision. All male participants in the covenant would be circumcised. As in the covenant made between God and Adam, the covenant between

---

[134] Genesis 15:8–18.
[135] Victor P. Hamilton, *Evangelical Commentary on the Bible* (Baker Book House, 1989), 21. Some commentaries do not specifically address the covenant-cutting walk in Abraham's dream. Many theologians only identify God as the covenant-cutter/walker. Historically, cutting a covenant requires two parties, both agreeing to the penalty of being cut to pieces if they did not abide by the provisions of the covenant. I maintain the fiery torch represents Jesus, standing for humankind as the only possible covenant keeper.
[136] Mark Rutland, *Of Kings and Prophets* (Charisma House, 2021), 44–45.

God and Abraham contained an action-sign to ensure compliance with the agreement.

Abraham experienced trials that shaped his faith in God. Of particular importance was the request by God that Abraham sacrifice his son, Isaac. Obviously, Abraham's relationship with God turned a corner as he prepared to travel to the region of Moriah to sacrifice Isaac. Abraham was not being asked to lead the people. Abraham was being asked to serve God in a very personal way—to prove his commitment to a jealous God. Abraham behaved as a *God-serving leader* despite the potential personal tragedy.

Dr. Hunter Sherman said this about Abraham's faith-journey:

> No man pursues a life of faith without his days of doubt, and there came a time when Abraham became obsessed with an awful thought. The voice of God which had so assuredly governed his conscience took on strange tones. Unbelievably, it told him to sacrifice his son, even as he had seen children die in the pagan cities from which he had drawn repugnance. With uncertain steps and many questions, he obeyed God's voice. Abraham, was convinced this terrible pressure on the mind must have a meaning, and set out to obey.[137]

DEVELOPING A PROFOUND AWARENESS

A theme of critical importance in the God design is the relational covenant. God established a relational boundary for believers in antiquity, with each covenant building on the previous. The covenant relationship exhibits the opposite position of the aloneness of independence in existentialism. Dependence is in the God design. Character is bound to relationship with God.

Abraham experienced a deep darkness at the beginning of his God-induced dream. That is what life is without a relationship with God: deep darkness and loneliness. Abraham was central to the development of humanity's covenant with God. God spoke to Abraham, and Abraham

---

[137] Hunter Sherman, *The Good, Bad, and Ugly* (LWG Publications, 2019), 22.

believed God.[138] Abraham left his secure surroundings and the protection of his extended family and went where God told him to go. When God calls you, He expects the same response.

Abraham emerged as a *God-serving leader.* God-serving leadership is not servant leadership. Nor is it a humanistic leadership paradigm. Servant leadership has a focus on serving those whom you lead. The clear distinction is that Abraham served God's vision—not his own, not that of the local rulers or authorities, but God's vision only!

I submit that a God-serving leader lives in a God-reality that responds to Him obediently. The focus is on listening to and waiting on God, even if, for Abraham, it meant sacrificing his only son. A God-serving leader possesses a profound awareness of who they are and how they are to live before God.

God's design was unfolding as anticipated. The central stage had emerged. The fiery torch stood for man as God cut a covenant with His people. Unfortunately, the vast majority of Hebrews did not see the Savior being cut to pieces as He was flogged by Roman soldiers prior to crucifixion. The Hebrews expected the coming Messiah to defeat their enemies.

The vision grows as people engage in the deep learning of the God Story.[139] The covenants are our guardrails for the vision. An authentic relationship with God is the most profound and precious relationship in the universe. It transcends any human connection known to humankind. The evidence of this God/man alliance is anchored in these eternal facts.

God introduced covenants for purposeful and meaningful relationships. The starting point is that God created humankind for a relationship of dependence. Mankind is given a choice of whether to be in a relationship with Him—in dependence on a trusting relationship. God teaches us through trials the covenant boundaries of relationships. He taught the created, Adam and Eve, how to live, love, marry, study, and work. God teaches the precepts to train the soul. Possessing a godly vision places us on a firm foundation until we are heaven-bound.

---

[138] Genesis 15:6: "Abram believed the Lord, and he credited it to him as righteousness."
[139] Proverbs 29:18: "Where there is no vision, the people perish: but he that kept the law, happy is he." Some have used this verse to emphasize the importance of vision in leadership. Without a vision, people are doomed to wander aimlessly. https://www.gotquestions.org/without-vision-people-perish.html.

PART IV

Abrahamic Covenant: A Covenant of Family

9

RECONCILIATION AND DEPENDENCE: NOW AND IN THE FUTURE

GOD'S DESIGN IS OUTSTANDING, BUT THE HUMAN RESPONSE TO HIS blueprint is dismal, to say the least. Abraham was the central figure of the renewed covenant family. As God's people, their prideful vision was one of fear. In each covenant, God's men and women led His people through one ordeal after another. Each covenantal experience taught the Hebrews about the vision of God and revealed their weaknesses in their relationship with Him.

PRE-CREATION PLANNING

I can only imagine the discussions about how the Trinity would teach love and the relationships they desired with humanity. Covenants bind believers to God. Covenants are deeply engaging commitments that have detrimental consequences if not honored. The Jews to this day recognize the covenantal relationship between Yahweh and Abraham, Isaac, Jacob, and Joseph.

Covenants were very different for the covenant patriarchs than for the children of Adam. Adam led well to teach godly precepts. However, the covenant with Abraham taught that God was Abraham's shield, a very great reward.[140] Abraham courageously left the protection of his people and trusted the God who spoke to him in this journey. God later extended the covenant to Isaac. Isaac learned from the trials of his father. Isaac became a quiet leader who focused on his family and submitted to God's will.[141]

---

[140] Genesis 15:1.
[141] Larry Richards, *Everyman in the Bible* (Thomas Nelson Publishers, 1979), 68.

Isaac's son, Jacob, deceived his brother for a birthright. Isaac gave Jacob the blessing that should have gone to Esau. Despite the deception, God's plan would not be thwarted. God called Jacob to lead His people through difficult times. Esau was blessed as well.

God planned a large family for Jacob. Unfortunately, it was a house of disharmony. Jacob deceived, and he would be deceived. From Jacob's family would come Joseph. He became a prominent leader in Egypt. The trials Joseph endured quelled his arrogance. He brought harmony to his father's divided house.

There will be turmoil in the families that don't teach the Story of God precepts. When His leaders don't wait on God's leadership, discontentedness will bring strife. God blessed Jacob's work and leadership. God sent His Son to wrestle with Jacob because Jacob wasn't sure about who he was. Ultimately, God gave Jacob a new name.

Jacob's son, Joseph, had compassion on his mean-spirited brothers and reconciled with them. Their journeys prepared God's people for their slavery in Egypt and the great Exodus. This in turn set the stage for the leadership of Moses. He provided the people with the instructions for how to participate in a covenant relationship.

BIBLICAL ACCOUNT (CA. 2075–1800 BCE)

Here is a little more about Abraham and Isaac. With each circumstance the patriarchs faced, they either deepened their relationship with God or were subjected to godly discipline. For example, God established His covenantal structure with Abraham. God asked Abraham to leave his familial and safe surroundings and follow a voice into the wilderness. Abraham was referred to as the father of many nations, but God wanted his undivided attention. Abraham assumed that he and his wife, Sarah, would have a son in their younger years. That did not happen. Unfortunately, late in life, Sarah took matters into her own hands and insisted that Abraham sleep with her handmaiden. This was not God's plan. The plan hatched by Sarah and Abraham would forever be a thorn in the side of the Hebrews, in the person of Abraham's son by the handmaid Hagar, Ishmael. Isaac would be God's blessing to Abraham and Sarah, in God's way.

God desired Abraham's dependence on His sovereignty. God wanted Abraham to learn to wait on Him. This would become great struggle for humanity: discontentedness results when people are not satisfied with the way God has ordered their lives. Satan uses this malady to control human circumstances. Lot's wife was an example of this lack of contentedness. She loved her past life and was punished for it.

Abraham's trust in God's sovereignty was tested. Abraham discerned wicked and evil people in Sodom and Gomorrah. God punished Sodom and Gomorrah because of immorality, homosexual behavior, and unrighteousness—behaviors outside of God's wholesomeness.

Nothing can come before God, not even a child. If you worship a child more than God, the profound relationship does not lie within you. Yes, this sounds harsh, but if you understand our God, then you know cruelty is not a part of Him. His thoughts are higher than our thoughts. This is the basis of *God-serving leadership*.[142]

Abraham was not perfect, but this trial provided a great lesson about God's protection. In the company of a king, Abraham referred to his wife, Sarah, as his sister, because he feared for his life. He did not trust that God was his great shield. Nevertheless, God delivered Abraham from harm and his wife from illicit behavior.

The covenant extended to Abraham's son, Isaac. Interestingly, there was deceit and underhandedness in this family despite the fact that God's intervention had been all blessings for them. God's blessings were passed to Isaac, who remained faithful to God.

Abraham sent his servant to get a wife for Isaac. God did as the servant requested and presented him with Rebekah. Rebekah bore twins, Jacob and Esau. She and Isaac played favorites with the boys. Rebekah's meddling harmed Jacob's relationship with his brother, Esau, and his father, Isaac. Jacob lived in fear of his brother because Rebekah assisted Jacob in stealing Esau's blessing from Isaac through deceitful leverage. Jacob ran in fear from Esau for many years. Isaac, also in fear, had committed the same deception as his father, Abraham, and had lied about his beautiful

---

[142] Isaiah 55:9.

wife Rebekah to a king.[143] In a dream, God reminded Isaac that He would protect and bless.[144]

The covenant extended to Isaac's son, Jacob, and the intrigue continued.[145] The trickery and the deception continued. His uncle Laban lied to Jacob, who was in pursuit of Laban's daughter Rachel, in order to receive God's continued blessings on Laban's farm. Laban deceived Jacob by replacing Rachel with Leah on Jacob's wedding night. Laban required another commitment from Jacob to gain Rachel as a second wife.

Jacob, a farmer and a driller of wells, was blessed. His sons worked the herds and fields. Jacob wrestled with God's messenger and was renamed Israel. There was bitter rivalry between the sons of Rachel and the sons of Leah. Jacob's youngest son, Joseph, was his favorite. Joseph's eleven brothers hated his arrogance and his dreams from God. Joseph was sold by his brothers to nomadic traders. Through a set of God-ordained actions, Joseph became a leader in Egypt. A famine forced Jacob to send his sons to Egypt for food. The quarreling brothers were reunited with Joseph. Joseph showed great love and mercy for his brothers. Jacob's family was reunited and remained in Egypt. Eventually, the Hebrews become slaves to the Egyptians.

What God is teaching through His covenant relationship is more than submission. It is about dependence. Submission is about yielding to a superior force, but dependence is about relying on someone or something for support. Dependence has a relational quality.

> [W]e humans are firmly placed within the natural order. As God's creatures, we are dependent upon God's sustaining power, moment by moment. This dependence upon and allegiance to God alone frees us from bondage to anybody's word, except to those found in God's books.[146]

---

[143] Genesis 26:5–9.

[144] Genesis 26:24: "That night the LORD appeared to him and said, "I am the God of your father Abraham. Do not be afraid, for I am with you; I will bless you and will increase the number of your descendants for the sake of my servant Abraham."

[145] Genesis 28:13–15.

[146] David G. Myers and Malcolm A. Jeeves, *Psychology: Through the Eyes of Faith* (Christian College Coalition and HarperCollins Publishers, 1987), 3.

God has established through His patriarchs a binding, covenantal relationship. Throughout the Old Testament, the identifying codification "the God of Abraham, Isaac, and Jacob" confirms a covenant leadership and family identification the Hebrews are to follow. The familial bonding birthed by the patriarchs of the chosen people existed from generation to generation.[147]

THE STORY OF JOB

There is another critical motif that epitomizes our God-serving relationship with Him. That's the story of Job.[148] It is the very beginning of this story that is so startling: God releases His protection of Job to Satan. First, Satan is given an audience with God. Second, God gives this righteous man over to Satan. Third, Satan is allowed to torment Job as he pleases (but not take his life). Fourth, God proves His point regarding the steadfast faith of Job. Finally, Job is rewarded greatly by God.

This is the true mark of a man right with God: he serves God and knows that God controls *all* things. Job's faith transcends the ungodly words of his "friends." Job lives at a greater level of faith that understands human experience *with a sense of the sacred or divine.*[149] Truly understanding our relationship with God is the mystery, for in our weakness is our strength.[150]

TRIALS

God's method of instruction for His leadership and people are trials. Each trial possesses a special object lesson that makes it unique and wonderful. For instance, Joseph's arrogance and pride pit him against his brothers. Keep in mind that this was a blended family with serious sibling rivalry. Joseph was blessed by God, but God had to help Joseph with a lack of self-control.[151] In prison, Joseph learned a critical lesson about a vision built on humility.

---

[147] Genesis 12:1–3.
[148] Job 1:1-42:17.
[149] Meyers and Jeeves, *Psychology*, 112.
[150] 2 Corinthians 12:9.
[151] Genesis 37:2–50:26.

Engaging trials with the perspective that God is maturing you can be extremely beneficial. In the Old Testament (OT), the patriarchs and God's leaders learned through trial and error the intent of God as well as His love for them. God used His prophets to give fair warning regarding sinful behavior or rebellion. Leadership that did not live by biblical principles was punished, but most profited from God's chastisement.

James 1:2 says, "Consider it pure joy ... whenever you face trials of many kinds." Embrace the truth that the God of the universe is raising you up to be His leadership.

DEVELOPING A PROFOUND AWARENESS

Like Abraham, we require safety and security. However, Abraham was called upon to trust God only. His son Isaac, through a trial for his father, learned an incredible lesson about his God. Yet additional trials were undertaken before Isaac understood who God was as his great shield. His son Jacob, despite all that God had done in the lives of his father and grandfather, was presented with his own trials to learn about this covenantal relationship that he possessed. Jacob's son Joseph was falsely accused and ended up in prison. There he experienced a trial that taught him dependence on Yahweh.

As human beings, we are faced with being alone in this very large universe. According to the existentialists, no matter how many friends we have, we are still alone. We may find people to hold our hands, but in reality, every day we are existentially alone. We leave this world alone. Our soul-vision connects us supernaturally with God. God is our great shield too. This must be a pivotal part of our vision. Our vision must build on the truth that God is the King of the universe, and He is with us. *This truth must permeate our souls.*

The Abrahamic covenant was extended to Isaac, Jacob, and Joseph. They were Abraham's covenant people. Wholesome behavior taught by God lends itself to being fruitful and multiplying, or thriving and nourishing. Godly behavior is a significant confirmation of God in us. God has made it very clear that the work He has begun in us will not be defeated.[152] God

---

[152] Philippians 1:6.

will not be thwarted in His pursuit of His people. You are either for Him or against Him.[153]

In the garden, God began teaching us what it means to be His people.[154] Trust in God for your spouse! Abraham believed that God had chosen a woman for his son, Isaac. Abraham sent his servant to find the woman for Isaac. The servant's trust in God was great, and God answered his prayer.

Jacob finally reconciled with Esau. In his reunion with his brother, Esau showed compassion to Jacob. Despite Jacob's trickery, God saw what happened. And because Esau was also a member of this covenant, God blessed him. Wrestling with God prepared Jacob for the reunion.

Likewise, when Joseph was reunited with his brothers in Egypt, he showed them great compassion. God used this very difficult circumstance for Joseph's character development.[155] As a part of our relationship with God, He is always working for the good character of godly men and women. Embrace the trials God has for us. See His intervention as an everlasting love to make you more like His Son.

---

[153] Matthew 12:30: "Whoever is not with me is against me, and whoever does not gather with me scatters."

[154] Philippians 1:6: "[Be] confident of this, that he who began a good work in you will carry it on to completion until the day of Christ Jesus."

[155] Genesis 50:20: "You intended to harm me, but God intended it for good to accomplish what is now being done, the saving of many lives."

10

GOD IS WITH HIS PEOPLE: THE EVERLASTING COVENANT OF FAMILY

THE LEADERSHIP IN EGYPT CHANGED AFTER THE DEATH OF JOSEPH, AND the new leadership did not have compassion or understanding for the Hebrews.[156] The Egyptians feared the growing number of Hebrews. They did not hold the history of Joseph's leadership in their hearts. Consequently, the Hebrews became slaves for the Egyptian building programs. The pharaohs were brutal. God heard the prayers of His people and sent Moses to bring them out of bondage and captivity. God had to prepare His man. Never forget, this is our heritage as the people of God through Jesus.

PRE-CREATION PLANNING

I can only imagine developing their plan whereby God would introduce Himself to humanity. Moses would meet the great I Am! Moses would flee from his Egypt upbringing to live as a herdsman. This was a significant moment in all of time! The plan was to address Moses from a burning bush. God sent Moses back to his adopted country to demand freedom for the Hebrew people from Pharaoh.

Making matters more difficult, Moses was reluctant when God called. The plan was for the Hebrews to remain as slaves in Egypt until the day that God came to lead them. They were under harsh rule. God called a man from among the Egyptians to request their release. Pharaoh refused. God demonstrated His power. It was more than the Egyptians could bear.

---

[156] Exodus 1:8.

In celebration with the Egyptian people, the Hebrews left Egypt, guided by God.

God renewed His covenant with His chosen people through Moses. In the covenant, God provided them with rules for behavior that were written on tablets, defining their relationships with Yahweh and with each other. The people needed those commandments to live in a wholesome and thriving kingdom. Moses gave these commandments to the chosen people. Moses led the chosen people to live as a testimony to their God. God would always be known as the God who led them out of bondage.

There would be many trials for His people to learn from, but unbelief would continually be their challenge. They had moments of greatness and other moments of deep disappointment. They even chose to have a king. They so badly harmed the purposes of God that they did not recognize Jesus as their Savior. They took God's blessings to themselves and were not a light on the hill.

All their enemies recognized that the God of the People of the Book was a powerful God. Moses struggled with these stiff-necked people. Moses had questions about God's plans. God shared an everlasting love with him. Moses taught God's people to depend on Him through law and worship.

BIBLICAL ACCOUNT (CA. 1445–1405 BCE)

Moses begins his life not as a Hebrew, but as an Egyptian. Through a chain of events, he discovered his true heritage. When he realized who he was, he ran. He lived in a land called Midian, where he met his family. He became a successful sheep herder and married. Forty years later, he encountered a burning bush not consumed by fire. Out of the burning bush came a voice that directed him to lead the people of God.

> When the Lord saw that he had gone over to look, God called to him from within the bush,
> "Moses! Moses!" And Moses said, "Here I am."
> "Do not come any closer," God said. "Take off your sandals, for the place where you are standing is holy ground." Then he said, "I am the God of your father, the God of Abraham, the God of Isaac and the God of Jacob."

79

At this, Moses hid his face, because he was afraid to look at God. The Lord said, "I have indeed seen the misery of my people in Egypt. I have heard them crying out because of their slave drivers, and I am concerned about their suffering. So I have come down to rescue them from the hand of the Egyptians and to bring them up out of that land into a good and spacious land, a land flowing with milk and honey— the home of the Canaanites, Hittites, Amorites, Perizzites, Hivites and Jebusites. And now the cry of the Israelites has reached me, and I have seen the way the Egyptians are oppressing them. So now, go. I am sending you to Pharaoh to bring my people the Israelites out of Egypt."

But Moses said to God, "Who am I that I should go to Pharaoh and bring the Israelites out of Egypt?"

And God said, "I will be with you. And this will be the sign to you that it is I who have sent you: When you have brought the people out of Egypt, you will worship God on this mountain."

Moses said to God, "Suppose I go to the Israelites and say to them, 'The God of your fathers has sent me to you,' and they ask me, 'What is his name?' Then what shall I tell them?"

God said to Moses, "I am who I am. This is what you are to say to the Israelites: 'I am has sent me to you.'" God also said to Moses, "Say to the Israelites, 'The Lord, the God of your fathers—the God of Abraham, the God of Isaac and the God of Jacob—has sent me to you.' "This is my name forever, the name you shall call me from generation to generation. "Go, assemble the elders of Israel and say to them, 'The Lord, the God of your fathers—the God of Abraham, Isaac and Jacob—appeared to me and said: I have watched over you and have seen what has been done to you in Egypt. And I have promised to bring you up out of your misery in Egypt into the land of the Canaanites, Hittites, Amorites, Perizzites, Hivites and Jebusites—a land flowing with milk and honey.' "The elders of Israel will listen to you.

Then you and the elders are to go to the king of Egypt and say to him, 'The Lord, the God of the Hebrews, has met with us. Let us take a three-day journey into the wilderness to offer sacrifices to the LORD our God.' But I know that the king of Egypt will not let you go unless a mighty hand compels him. So I will stretch out my hand and strike the Egyptians with all the wonders that I will perform among them. After that, he will let you go. And I will make the Egyptians favorably disposed toward this people, so that when you leave you will not go empty-handed. Every woman is to ask her neighbor and any woman living in her house for articles of silver and gold and for clothing, which you will put on your sons and daughters. And so you will plunder the Egyptians."

Moses answered, "What if they do not believe me or listen to me and say, 'The Lord did not appear to you'?"

Then the Lord said to him, "What is that in your hand?"

"A staff," he replied.

The Lord said, "Throw it on the ground."

Moses threw it on the ground and it became a snake, and he ran from it. Then the Lord said to him, "Reach out your hand and take it by the tail."

So Moses reached out and took hold of the snake and it turned back into a staff in his hand. "This," said the Lord, "is so that they may believe that the Lord, the God of their fathers—the God of Abraham, the God of Isaac and the God of Jacob—has appeared to you." Then the Lord said, "Put your hand inside your cloak." So Moses put his hand into his cloak, and when he took it out, the skin was leprous—it had become as white as snow. "Now put it back into your cloak," he said. So Moses put his hand back into his cloak, and when he took it out, it was restored, like the rest of his flesh. Then the Lord said, "If they do not believe you or pay attention to the first sign, they may believe the second. But if they do not believe these two signs or listen to you, take some water from the Nile and pour it on the dry ground. The water you take from the river will become blood on the ground."

Moses said to the Lord, "Pardon your servant, Lord. I have never been eloquent, neither in the past nor since you have spoken to your servant. I am slow of speech and tongue."

The Lord said to him, "Who gave human beings their mouths? Who makes them deaf or mute? Who gives them sight or makes them blind? Is it not I, the LORD? Now go; I will help you speak and will teach you what to say."

But Moses said, "Pardon your servant, Lord. Please send someone else."

Then the Lord's anger burned against Moses and he said, "What about your brother, Aaron the Levite? I know he can speak well. He is already on his way to meet you, and he will be glad to see you. You shall speak to him and put words in his mouth; I will help both of you speak and will teach you what to do. He will speak to the people for you, and it will be as if he were your mouth and as if you were God to him. But take this staff in your hand so you can perform the signs with it."[157]

There are several key issues to unpack in this discussion between God, referred to as the Lord, and Moses. Moses was shepherding his flock when he came upon a burning bush. God's relationship with Moses began with an apprehensive Moses. Moses was not sure about anything God was asking him to do.

Before we review these critical themes, let's look at another conversation in which God instructed Moses what to tell the Israelites when he initially met with them.

God also said to Moses, "I am the Lord. I appeared to Abraham, to Isaac and to Jacob as God Almighty, but by my name the Lord I did not make myself fully known to them. I also established my covenant with them to give

---

[157] Exodus 3:4–4:17.

them the land of Canaan, where they resided as foreigners. Moreover, I have heard the groaning of the Israelites, whom the Egyptians are enslaving, and I have remembered my covenant. "Therefore, say to the Israelites: 'I am the Lord, and I will bring you out from under the yoke of the Egyptians. I will free you from being slaves to them, and I will redeem you with an outstretched arm and with mighty acts of judgment. I will take you as my own people, and I will be your God. Then you will know that I am the Lord your God, who brought you out from under the yoke of the Egyptians. And I will bring you to the land I swore with uplifted hand to give to Abraham, to Isaac and to Jacob. I will give it to you as a possession. I am the Lord.'"[158]

These were powerful words being shared with a people discouraged under hard labor. Despite their lack of understanding, this was a message of change in their lives that they had dreamed of and prayed for. This moment in time would forever change the world. Specifically, it set the stage for announcing the family of God!

Let's continue with our review of Moses being called by God. First, Moses answered God's voice. It is clear he had heard the stories of this God of the Israelites. God established that He is holy and that Moses must respond with appropriate holy-honoring behavior, but Moses turned away.

Second, God immediately declared His purpose. He had heard the cries of His people and was going to rescue them from their oppressors. Moreover, He would free His people to a land of their own. And He would send Moses. Moses responded with alarm, saying, in effect, "Who? You talking to me?" This is almost humorous. God reassured him that He was with him, and Moses would worship Him. Moses was still reluctant and asked further about who this voice was, so that Moses could tell the Israelites whom he was representing. God made a now-famous response: "I am who I am." Nothing more needed to be said. He is the God of their covenants, King of the universe, the Great I Am. This is critical for all believers to bury deep in their hearts. God is the sovereign Creator of the universe, the one and only I Am.

---

[158] Exodus 6:2–8.

Third, God continued to instruct Moses about what he was to do. He added that there would be a great reward for the people of Israel. If the elders were reluctant, they would come around.

Fourth, God informed Moses that Pharaoh would resist, but that God had a plan for unbelief. Moses hesitated again. "What if they don't believe me?" Moses didn't say that to God, but God knew what he was thinking. Moses was very familiar with the Egyptians. He knew that Pharaoh was a very powerful man and could strike Moses dead on the spot. So the Lord demonstrated His power to Moses with a staff and a hand.

Finally, Moses once more questioned God's instruction, putting forward a self-confidence issue regarding his public speaking ability. God was not happy with Moses's continued hesitation. God instructed him to call on his brother Aaron. Aaron would be the mouthpiece. Aaron would speak Moses's words.

With Moses, a covenant renewal occurred. The Mosaic covenant, which we'll discuss in the next chapter, extended the covenant relationship with some new amenities for the chosen people. Covenant renewal is the guardrails of our vision.

DEVELOPING A PROFOUND AWARENESS

We find several critical recurring themes essential to a vision of restoration to a gardenlike relationship with our Creator God. Believing this in your heart and mind leads to the profound awareness of living in your true identity in God. These themes involve leadership, individual spiritual growth, trusting God, and God's sovereignty.

First, to experience the presence of God, each believer must know that God is holy. God is establishing a relationship with you. Deep within your soul, you must believe that God is holy.

Second, we see that God rescues His people from oppression. Your soul-vision must believe that you are being restored to relationship with Him. Like most of us, Moses was reluctant to take on this responsibility. Do what He has asked you to do!

Third, God also instructed Moses to take his elders and Pharaoh's staff (leadership) to worship together before discussions regarding the release of the Hebrew people. The Israelite elders met together in worship and prayed for a successful mission for Aaron and Moses. Worship and pray before any significant decisions.

Finally, Moses hesitated momentarily regarding God's instructions, claiming he was not a public speaker. I am sure God heard the fear in Moses's voice. Moses wasn't sure that God would have his back. He feared that he would look foolish before Pharaoh. Early in Moses's days of leadership, he struggled to trust God.[159] After many years in this role, Moses's leadership became more perceptive and discerning. Moses's vision and soul-understanding improved by believing God's Word, trusting God's actions, and pursuing God's purpose with submission and surrender.

ACCOUNT SUBSTORIES

I've included these substories, if you will, for your reading pleasure. They are great stories that will add to your understanding.

- Exodus 2:1–25: The early life of Moses and his heritage
- Exodus 3:1–22, 4:1–9: Moses's meeting with God and the establishment of who the Great I Am is

---

[159] Genesis 3:1–17.

PART V

Mosaic Covenant: The Law of Love and Worship

11

COVENANT PROTECTION: REVERENCE FOR GOD

MOSES MET WITH PHARAOH. PHARAOH DID NOT LISTEN. GOD SENT plagues to weaken Pharaoh's resolve. Finally, the death of Pharaoh's son, as part of the plague on the firstborn, moved Pharaoh to release the Hebrews. Moses led the Hebrews to safety in the wilderness. God's covenant was renewed through Moses. God led the Israelites to the Promised Land. They are the people of God!

PRE-CREATION PLANNING

I can only imagine the trinitarian plan for the Exodus. God hardened Pharaoh's heart to accomplish His purpose of teaching the Hebrews about His everlasting love that began with the Creation of the universe.[160] The plagues sent by God did not weaken Pharaoh's resolve until the firstborn were taken. This event became known as the Passover. The blood theme continued: the blood of a lamb spread on the doorposts saved the firstborn of His people.[161] Blood remains a theme to save them. Pharaoh relented. Unfortunately, he changed his mind and chased after the Israelites.

God led the Israelites to the Red Sea. The sea opened for them and closed upon the Egyptians ready to attack. The Hebrews were not happy with the I Am who led them out of Egypt and into a wilderness. They revealed their fear of this God who had left them alone for four hundred years. Despite their wavering trust, God provided them with food and water. God provided them with many opportunities to grow strong as His people. Despite God's

---

[160] Exodus 7:3.
[161] Exodus 11:1–12:13.

protection and the food and water they needed, the Hebrews squandered the opportunities to grow and trust God because they were discontented. God would make it possible for His Son to visit them as a messenger of the Lord. The theme of discontent continued, humanity's great Achilles heel.

I can only imagine a trinitarian moment in which they decided the covenantal rules and actions of worship, which included a sacrificial system for His people. The Passover to this day is an annual festival celebrated by the Jews as a sign that I Am is their God and they are His people. This became an important time as they learned His precepts of how to be a holy, thriving, and flourishing people, just like Adam and Eve in Eden.

These are the secrets to living a joyful life in which people can be fruitful and multiply. Our Creator God is leading the bride through the wilderness and back to Eden—back to an intimate relationship with all believers, as it was in the garden.[162] God planned for Jesus to go down and help them. God gave them the Law and, more importantly, the tabernacle for worship. The Law and worship are critical themes.

BIBLICAL ACCOUNT (1450–1390 BCE)

The part of the God Story that presents the Exodus is crucial to understanding our Judeo-Christian heritage. Pharaoh had huge building projects in progress. The Hebrews were his slave laborers. Pharaoh provided them with shelter and food. The Hebrews prayed daily for God's help. God sent Moses to negotiate a release of God's people, but Pharaoh refused. God used plagues to convince Pharaoh that the Hebrew God was all-powerful and meant what He said.

PASSOVER

The final plague in Egypt was the plague of the firstborn, who died in the night (ca. 1445 BCE). Pharaoh had a firstborn son. His son, like the others, died in the night, and Pharaoh released the Hebrews. The Passover became a festival of commemoration of what God did for His people that announced the coming of a Messiah. The Messiah would shed blood to remove the

---

[162] Revelation 22.

rebellion of man. The Passover in the God Story is the foreshadowing of a Lamb to come who will remove the sins of our rebellion and restore all who believe to an authentic and personal relationship with the Father.

Then Moses summoned all the elders of Israel and said to them, "Go at once and select the animals for your families and slaughter the Passover lamb. Take a bunch of hyssops, dip it into the blood in the basin and put some of the blood on the top and on both sides of the doorframe. None of you shall go out of the door of your house until morning. When the Lord goes through the land to strike down the Egyptians, he will see the blood on the top and sides of the doorframe and will pass over that doorway, and he will not permit the destroyer to enter your houses and strike you down. "Obey these instructions as a lasting ordinance for you and your descendants. When you enter the land that the Lord will give you as he promised, observe this ceremony. And when your children ask you, 'What does this ceremony mean to you?' then tell them, 'It is the Passover sacrifice to the Lord, who passed over the houses of the Israelites in Egypt and spared our homes when he struck down the Egyptians.'" Then the people bowed down and worshiped. The Israelites did just what the Lord commanded Moses and Aaron.

At midnight the Lord struck down all the firstborn in Egypt, from the firstborn of Pharaoh, who sat on the throne, to the firstborn of the prisoner, who was in the dungeon, and the firstborn of all the livestock as well. Pharaoh and all his officials and all the Egyptians got up during the night, and there was loud wailing in Egypt, for there was not a house without someone dead.

During the night Pharaoh summoned Moses and Aaron and said, "Up! Leave my people, you and the Israelites! Go, worship the LORD as you have requested. Take your flocks and herds, as you have said, and go. And also bless me."

The Egyptians urged the people to hurry and leave the country. "For otherwise," they said, "we will all die!" So the people took their dough before the yeast was added, and carried it on their shoulders in kneading troughs wrapped in clothing. The Israelites did as Moses instructed and asked the Egyptians for articles of silver and gold and for clothing. The Lord had made the Egyptians favorably disposed toward the people, and they gave them what they asked for; so they plundered the Egyptians.[163]

The Hebrews were guided by God on a trek to the Red Sea. Pharaoh had a violent change of heart and went after the Israelites. God did a miracle and opened the Red Sea for His people to cross. The Egyptians followed and were swallowed up by the sea. The Hebrews were freed of their bondage.

Despite their newly enjoyed freedom from bondage and all that God had done, the Hebrews began to complain. As a consequence of the many challenges the people had experienced, they complained loudly. Often, the people looked back at what they had had in Egypt and wanted to go back. They complained about having no water; God provided water. The Israelites complained about having no bread and meat; God provided manna and quail. As they traveled farther into the wilderness, the people again complained about water. God instructed Moses to bring forth water from a rock.[164] God defeated the Amalekite marauders. The chosen people grew, and Moses took good advice from his father-in-law, Jethro.

TEN COMMANDMENTS

God called Moses to the top of Mt. Sinai and gave him the Ten Commandments—precepts for the people of Israel to live by in harmony and peace.[165] Until this time, the Hebrews had had no guidelines or statutes to give their lives order. God taught Adam and Eve, but that process was cut short. God chose Abraham, Isaac, and Jacob to lead His chosen people. Then it became Moses's responsibility to organize this family with precepts of worship and governance.

---

[163] Exodus 12:21–36.

[164] Exodus 17:1–7.

[165] I.e. the Ten Commandments, Exodus 20:1–20.

[1] "I am the Lord your God, who brought you out of Egypt, out of the land of slavery. "You shall have no other gods before me.

[2] "You shall not make for yourself an image in the form of anything in heaven above or on the earth beneath or in the waters below. You shall not bow down to them or worship them; for I, the Lord your God, am a jealous God, punishing the children for the sin of the parents to the third and fourth generation of those who hate me, but showing love to a thousand generations of those who love me and keep my commandments.

[3] "You shall not misuse the name of the Lord your God, for the Lord will not hold anyone guiltless who misuses his name.[166]

[4] "Remember the Sabbath day by keeping it holy. Six days you shall labor and do all your work, but the seventh day is a sabbath to the Lord your God. On it you shall not do any work, neither you, nor your son or daughter, nor your male or female servant, nor your animals, nor any foreigner residing in your towns. For in six days the Lord made the heavens and the earth, the sea, and all that is in them, but he rested on the seventh day. Therefore the Lord blessed the Sabbath day and made it holy.

[5] "Honor your father and your mother, so that you may live long in the land the Lord your God is giving you.

[6] "You shall not murder.

---

[166] The Third Commandment has been seriously misinterpreted. The commandment refers to a believer's followership. God is instructing the Hebrews not to refer to themselves as followers of Yahweh if they were not going to authentically walk life out with Him. The verse does not refer to coarse language or using God's name inappropriately, even though it would be included in the actual meaning.

[7] "You shall not commit adultery.

[8] "You shall not steal.

[9] "You shall not give false testimony against your neighbor.

[10] "You shall not covet your neighbor's house. You shall not covet your neighbor's wife, or his male or female servant, his ox or donkey, or anything that belongs to your neighbor."

When the people saw the thunder and lightning and heard the trumpet and saw the mountain in smoke, they trembled with fear. They stayed at a distance and said to Moses, "Speak to us yourself and we will listen. But do not have God speak to us or we will die." Moses said to the people, "Do not be afraid. God has come to test you, so that the fear of God will be with you to keep you from sinning."[167]

The first four commandments focus on the people's relationship with their God, and the remaining six commandments focus on believers' relationships with one another. These are the godly precepts taught to Adam and Eve in the garden that led to fruitfulness and multiplication. They remain the principles of a fully functioning and wholesome society. God created us, and He knows what we need as people to thrive.

The Mosaic covenant is established through the Law as well as through worship.[168]

> Then the Lord said to Moses, "Come up to the Lord, you and Aaron, Nadab and Abihu, and seventy of the elders of Israel. You are to worship at a distance, but Moses alone is to approach the Lord; the others must not come near. And the people may not come up with him."

---

[167] Exodus 20:1–17.
[168] Exodus 24:1–11.

When Moses went and told the people all the LORD's words and laws, they responded with one voice, "Everything the Lord has said we will do." Moses then wrote down everything the Lord had said.

He got up early the next morning and built an altar at the foot of the mountain and set up twelve stone pillars representing the twelve tribes of Israel. Then he sent young Israelite men, and they offered burnt offerings and sacrificed young bulls as fellowship offerings to the Lord. Moses took half of the blood and put it in bowls, and the other half he splashed against the altar. Then he took the Book of the Covenant and read it to the people. They responded, "We will do everything the Lord has said; we will obey." Moses then took the blood, sprinkled it on the people and said, "This is the blood of the covenant that the Lord has made with you in accordance with all these words."[169]

An angel of the Lord[170] was sent ahead of Moses and the Israelites to prepare the way for their arrival in the land promised to Abraham, Isaac, and Jacob.[171] The angel provided leadership and confidence for the people. The angel was a warrior for the people of God. God informed Moses that the people in that land were a godless people and must be annihilated. God added that He would send His terror ahead to throw confusion into every nation the Israelites encountered.

Following the covenant renewal, the Israelites began work on the tabernacle and the worship process they were to follow. The tabernacle was the dwelling place of God.[172] Unfortunately, Moses's staff, Aaron and Miriam, became fearful because Moses had not returned from his meeting with God on Mt. Sinai. The people wanted something to worship because

---

[169] Exodus 24:1–8.

[170] Exodus 23:20–33. God is adamant that the Israelites take the land. Theophany: the angel of the Lord is Jesus—notice verse 21, "my Name is in him."

[171] Exodus 23:20–33. God's instructions for Moses are very clear regarding what Moses must do in the Promised Land; Moses must pay attention to the angel and not rebel against him.

[172] Exodus 25–31.

they had heard nothing from Moses or God. They made an idol. This rebellion resulted in God bringing down severe punishment upon Moses's staff and annihilating the people. Moses pleaded with God to spare them, and God relented. Punishment was nonetheless given. Moses grasped the vision God gave him in the same way that Abraham did as the father of many nations. Moses knew his steps continued that covenant established by God.

Here is an excerpt from John and Lisa Bevere's book regarding the critical place of vision, *The Story of Marriage* (as quoted by H. Norman Wright):

> Vision could be described as foresight, with the significance of possessing a keen awareness of current circumstances and possibilities, and of the value of learning from the past. Vision can also be described as seeing the invisible and making it visible. It's having a picture held in your mind of the way things could be or should be in the days ahead. Vision is also a portrait of conditions that don't yet exist. It's being able to focus more on the future than getting bogged down with past or present. Vision is the process of creating a better future with God's empowerment and direction.[173]

A SIGNIFICANT TRIAL

God instructed Moses to leave the place the people were in and go to the place God had promised to Abraham, Isaac, and Jacob. Moses's patience with the people had worn thin. In a moment of weakness, he forgot to honor God and took the glory for himself. The people had become thirsty in their new destination and were complaining to Moses. Moses in frustration went to God.

> Moses and Aaron went from the assembly to the entrance to the tent of meeting and fell facedown, and the glory of the Lord appeared to them. The Lord said to Moses, "Take the staff, and you and your brother Aaron gather the

---

[173] H. Norman Wright, *The Secrets of a Lasting Marriage* (Regal Books, 1995), 70.

assembly together. Speak to that rock before their eyes and it will pour out its water. You will bring water out of the rock for the community so they and their livestock can drink."

So Moses took the staff from the Lord's presence, just as he commanded him. He and Aaron gathered the assembly together in front of the rock and Moses said to them, "Listen, you rebels, must we bring you water out of this rock?" Then Moses raised his arm and struck the rock twice with his staff. Water gushed out, and the community and their livestock drank.

But the Lord said to Moses and Aaron, "Because you did not trust in me enough to honor me as holy in the sight of the Israelites, you will not bring this community into the land I give them." These were the waters of Meri bah, where the Israelites quarreled with the Lord and where he was proved holy among them.[174]

God told Moses they needed water and how to get it. Unfortunately, in a moment when he lacked self-control, Moses took the glory of this miracle for himself.

This story has always had a profound effect on me. Despite all the good that Moses had done, he was punished for his lack of self-control in honoring God. Moses had an authentic relationship with God. He had enough influence with God that he was able to influence God's decision on several issues. With God's guidance, Moses dealt with the issues presented by the Hebrews and guided them through the wilderness. Then, in one moment, Moses forgot who he was as a man of God.

THE GREAT UNBELIEF

Moses and the Israelites, a little over a year after leaving Egypt, arrived at the Promised Land. They were on the doorstep of the land promised to Abraham, a place flowing with milk and honey. Moses sent in men to explore

---

[174] Numbers 20:6–13. God does *not* tolerate a man or woman taking glory for His blessings. We give God *all* the glory for what He has done in through His people. Gratitude is honoring God for what He has done.

the land and determine a strategy for entrance. He sent one man from each of the twelve tribes. They returned, and only two of the twelve were in favor of entering the land. It is interesting that only 17 percent believed victory was theirs.

This caused great dissent among the people. They were fearful and rebellious, desiring to return to Egypt. After a year in the wilderness, when they were dependent upon God, a lack of deepening trust and maturing faith became evident. Joshua and Caleb made a case for taking the land. Both young men knew God had given them that land. Again, God's anger with the Israelites was great for not trusting in Him. This was a great gift He was giving His people, but they rejected it because of fear. Moses persuaded God to forgive them.

The scene was ugly! Because the people lacked faith, God returned them to the wilderness for forty years, with the single goal of allowing the rebellious adults, the ones who did not support Caleb and Joshua, to die. No Hebrew over age twenty would see the Promised Land except Joshua and Caleb.[175] They possessed a fearless and God-ward vision that rested on surrender and submission to His Word, sovereignty, and purpose. The punishment for the unbelief of the elders was very great. The rebellion was led by the elderly. They had not developed a trust in God.

DEUTERONOMY

The book of Deuteronomy has several key parts to it. First, Moses reminded the Israelites of where they had come from to get to the threshold of the land promised to the Hebrew patriarchs. Second, Moses exhorted them to follow the Law and worship Yahweh. Third, Moses encouraged them to be fearless and faithful, remembering their restoration. Fourth, the book focuses on the transfer of leadership to Joshua with song and a blessing. However, the Lord made it clear to Israel that He knew who they were:

> But if from there seek the Lord your God, you will find him
> if you seek him with all your heart and with all your soul.[176]

---

[175] Numbers 13 and 14. Only Caleb and Joshua survived the forty years, because they trusted God's Word.
[176] Deuteronomy 4:29.

This encouragement became a foundation to the life of Judaism, then and now. Referred to as the Shema prayer, it is the anchor of the Jewish faith and is recited when a believer rises and when they go to sleep.[177]

> Hear, O Israel: The Lord our God, the LORD is one. Love the Lord your God with all your heart and with all your soul and with all your strength.[178]

DEVELOPING A PROFOUND AWARENESS

In each biblical event, the Story of God reveals something about our Creator God and us. In the Deuteronomy account, we learn more about God molding our hearts and minds—shaping us to be known as the People of the Book, a peculiar people, a holy nation or a royal priesthood, and obviously dependent upon Him.[179] I know I am repeating myself on this point, but it is vital that we understand that, from the beginning to the end of the covenants, He is creating a vision in us. That vision is holy and right. A vision that is anchored in everything we see and do must reflect His everlasting love. *A people with no vision will perish.*[180]

The initial covenant with Abraham revealed God's desire to be in relationship with His people. It was extended to Isaac and Jacob. The Mosaic covenant revealed a deepening of that relationship, a renewing of God's purpose. It was a covenant relationship that required all to believe His Word, His sovereignty, and His purpose for His people. To thrive, people must surrender and submit their hearts and minds to these principles of godly and righteous living.

Unfortunately, humankind is unable to create guidelines for human behavior that lead to thriving and joy. Becoming the people of God lies within the spiritual dimension of existence. The choice humans must

---

[177] "Shema Prayer," https://www.chabad.org/library/article_cdo/aid/705353/jewish/The-Shema.htm.

[178] Deuteronomy 6:4–5.

[179] 1 Peter 2:9: "But you are a chosen people, a royal priesthood, a holy nation, God's special possession, that you may declare the praises of him who called you out of darkness into his wonderful light."

[180] Proverbs 29:18 NASB: "Where there is no vision, the people are unrestrained, But happy is he who keeps the law."

make—to surrender and submit to God—lies deep within their being. The transformation is one of profound transcendence. Each person must travel their own path, but it begins with a choice to disconnect from one's rebellious, pride-filled autonomy to a childlike innocence—to make God the Lord of your life in all things.

In Deuteronomy, God had the attention of His people in the wilderness. Water and food were provided. He instructed them to build a tabernacle, which was His home among His people. They were dependent upon him. The precepts of God, the Ten Commandments, were absolutely necessary and foundational in the development of a holy vision, the cornerstone of their covenant relationship with God. God had not forgotten what happened in the garden and made it clear that He is the great I Am.

The word *idols* refers to anything that distracts one's attention from a relationship with God. Anything on earth that distorts your vision or relationship with Him is an idol. His name and Sabbath are holy; honor them. The remaining six commandments focus on the social environment of the family of God.

As we learned earlier, the boundaries in a relationship are there for a reason. They are there to protect us. Throughout the OT, God clearly defined the boundaries. Be very clear: the vision is built on surrendering and submitting our lives to believing His Word, trusting His sovereignty, and seeking His purpose for our lives.

I must add a critical note. The third commandment has a different and more significant emphasis from its common interpretation. Taking the "Lord's name in vain" is not necessarily condemning something by using His name or cursing. Taking the Lord's name in vain is more closely interpreted as referring to yourself a "follower of God" when your behavior and actions do not reflect a godly life. This is the chasm between the Lord God and the people who talk the talk but do not walk the walk.

A new Barna Research study indicates that only 17 percent of those who claim to be followers of Jesus Christ practice weekly worship, daily prayer, and daily Bible reading, and believe that God is intimately intervening in their lives.[181] This is the mystery of the profound awareness possessed by God's people—to live in the presence of God.

[181] "Competing Worldviews Influence Today's Christians," Barna Research, May 2017, https://www.barna.com/research/competing-worldviews-influence-todays-christians/.

At the threshold of the Promised Land, the Hebrews did not believe in what He had promised Abraham. They did not trust God to protect them, and they did not want to pursue God's will for the Hebrews. Let's be very clear about the issues here. First, they failed on all four faith counts and were sent back to the wilderness! Second, God sent them back to the wilderness explicitly to wait for the older people to die! No one older than twenty would see the Promised Land

TRIALS AND LESSONS LEARNED

Trials can be for nonbelievers. Pharaoh did not listen; he ruled with his pride.[182] In the departure of the Israelites from Egypt, there was a poignant moment when God instructed Moses about what to do next. God led the people, not via the easy road, but along a more difficult mountain route. God's reasoning was that if the Israelites faced war, they might change their minds and return to Egypt. Wow! The God of the chosen people understood their weakness and led them to a sea, where His power was demonstrated.[183]

There were many trials in the wilderness. Deuteronomy is a story about the Hebrews establishing themselves as a nation, and their awful and fateful rebellion in choosing not to trust God.[184]

Moses accepted advice from Jethro regarding judicial procedures. Moses accepted the wisdom of another.[185] Moses provided instructions for the spiritual lives of the Hebrews, the Ten Commandments.[186]

Let's reframe Moses's failed trial. In a subtle form of humanistic self-deception, older Christians too often fall into a trap and believe their life experiences have led them to a comfortable place in their old age. They foolishly believe they are responsible for their favorable results. The truth is that God has blessed their lives, and they are doing as Moses did—taking the glory for themselves. Don't be misled! I've seen too many elders and trustees leading a church in their own strength, trusting in their life success and not trusting God. Please, my older brothers and sisters, seek God and do

---

[182] Exodus 7:1–12, 12:51.
[183] Exodus 13:17–18.
[184] Exodus 13:16–35:13.
[185] Exodus 18:1–27.
[186] Exodus 20:1–22:30.

not trust your ways. Hearing God becomes more difficult as you get older. Profound awareness requires living in the here and now of His presence.[187]

Deuteronomy is the account of the Hebrews in the wilderness for forty years. At the end, before entering the land promised to Abraham, Moses made a grievous error, and Joshua was called to lead the Israelites.[188]

ACCOUNT SUBSTORIES

- Exodus 4:27–31: Moses's report to the elders of what God called him to do
- Exodus 4:10–17: Moses's lack of confidence or fear of what God asked him to do
- Numbers 1:1–13:33: The journey of the Hebrews as Moses led them through the wilderness, seeking the land promised to Abraham
- Numbers 20:1–13: Moses's grievous error
- Deuteronomy 1:1–34:12: Moses's narrative and instruction to the Hebrews and the passing of the mantle of leadership

---

[187] Numbers 20:1–13.
[188] Deuteronomy 1:1–34:12.

12

COVENANT FAMILY ARRIVES HOME: THE PROMISED LAND

FOR A SECOND TIME, THE HEBREWS RETURNED TO THE THRESHOLD OF the land promised to Abraham and his descendants. They were at the end of the forty years they had spent in the wilderness as a consequence of their *not* trusting God. Never forget that God allowed a generation of followers to die because they lacked trust in His sovereignty. This is a critical issue with God.

Israel had become large in number, and God had taken them through one situation after another. Moses was punished for his lack of gracious honor for Yahweh. Moses had been an advocate for God's people and received many blessings from God.

Let's not miss the important issue here: God is not to be defeated in carrying out His plan. Abraham, Isaac, Jacob, Joseph, and Moses had to contend with their human nature as men of God. They were God's men, but they also possessed a human nature. However, God used each trial to teach them about being in a covenant relationship with Him. They all learned what it meant to love the Lord their God. Despite their failings, God's plan of salvation for mankind would continue.

PRE-CREATION PLANNING

I can only imagine the plan for establishing the covenant relationship and family. Moses built a tabernacle, a house of worship. And he ensured the Law was enacted for a wholesome people. The Law outlined the ways of right living. The Law was necessary for a people to be nourished and thriving. The Law enabled a vision of who they were and how they were to live.

Unfortunately, Moses would not lead them into the land that God promised to Abraham. Moses wrote a great letter, Deuteronomy, about his time with the Hebrews and provided final instructions before passing leadership off to Joshua.

I can only imagine what the Trinity had planned as they returned the Hebrews to the wilderness for forty years. Once again, the lack of trust in God's sovereignty was a critical theme in the life of His believers. Eventually, they would enter the land promised to Abraham. Only an Israelite under sixty years of age would see the land. Only the oldest among them would remember the failed unbelief of their dearly departed families. God removed the unbelieving adults from the entry cohort and called a new leader, Joshua.

I can only imagine what the Trinity experienced as they saw Moses standing on the mount, watching the people cross the Jordan into the Promised Land. God's Son would also face a very challenging moment.[189]

Faith is made up of believing God's Word, trusting His decisions, and pursuing His will. Surrender and submission are required to engage His vision. Moses organized the people. He taught them about Yahweh. Moses led them well in the wilderness. Moses led them in conquering kings who did not fear God. Joshua led them across the Jordan and took the land God promised to Abraham.

I can only imagine the excitement for the Trinity as they prepared the Hebrew people. The Hebrews possessed God's vision. They were the people who would announce the coming of the Savior who would make it possible for humanity to return to the Eden relationship with God. The Hebrew people struggled with that responsibility. Again, they took it to themselves and believed it was all about them.

Joshua was a good leader. There were bitter disputes regarding God's Word. Many did not understand the vision they were to teach. The believers pursued their relationship with God in the same way the Israelites entered and took the Promised Land. There were wonderful moments of celebration as they sought Yahweh. Their enemies feared the Hebrews because they recognize that the Hebrews followed a powerful God. That fear remains to this day for Islam.

---

[189] Luke 22:42: "Father, if you are willing, take this cup from me; yet not my will, but yours be done."

BIBLICAL ACCOUNT (CA. 1405–1373 BCE)

Deuteronomy is a review of where Israel had come from and its call to make a choice to follow God. Moses emphasized the covenant relationship God had with His people, which required a devoted and steadfast people. The covenant narrative urged worship and righteous behavior from the people to Yahweh. The Shema prayer[190] became the foundation of Israel's expression of their love of God, as well as a central theme for Christianity.[191] God has an everlasting love for the Hebrews, and where He led, they must go.

Joshua was a strong leader. He had watched for a lifetime God's faithfulness to His people. The oldest of the people were sixty. God was very clear that the Hebrews and those traveling with them were going to enter the Promised Land. Moreover, those traveling along would obey the Israelites' God.[192]

Joshua led the people across the Jordan River and into the land promised to Abraham. God provided protection as they entered the land and headed for Jericho. Circumcision was a seal for the men who participated in the Mosaic covenant. The Mosaic covenant was renewed with Joshua.[193]

God's command to Joshua was twofold. First, he was to be strong and courageous. Second, he was to obey the Law Moses had given him. If he followed these instructions, no enemy would stand against Joshua. God would be with the Hebrews wherever they went.[194] From the crossing of the Jordan River through battles and to the division of the land, God went with them and did not forsake them.

Joshua led the people through a seven-year campaign to take the Promised Land for God and His people. They were successful because Joshua maintained the covenant with the Law.

The closure of Joshua's leadership was very focused and purposeful. He called the people to obedience. These verses set the stage for a people to be ruled by God as a nation of believers. Joshua made it clear as he spoke to the Hebrews regarding their allegiance to the Mosaic covenant. The Lord had

---

[190] Deuteronomy 6:4–5.

[191] Matthew 22:36–37.

[192] Joshua 1:18: "Whoever rebels against your word and does not obey it, whatever you may command them, will be put to death. Only be strong and courageous!"

[193] Joshua 8:31.

[194] Joshua 1:4–9.

prepared his words, and he made no mistakes in reminding them of their history and what God had done.

> Now fear the Lord and serve him with all faithfulness. Throw away the gods your ancestors worshiped beyond the Euphrates River and in Egypt, and serve the Lord. But if serving the Lord seems undesirable to you, then choose for yourselves this day whom you will serve, whether the gods your ancestors served beyond the Euphrates, or the gods of the Amorites, in whose land you are living. But as for me and my household, we will serve the Lord.[195]

Joshua set the stage for the Hebrew people to make a decision. They were aware of the evil forces that sought to draw people away from God. Joshua understood that. The decision was theirs, as individuals and as a nation. Joshua wanted an answer!

> Then the people answered, "Far be it from us to forsake the Lord to serve other gods! It was the LORD our God himself who brought us and our parents up out of Egypt, from that land of slavery, and performed those great signs before our eyes. He protected us on our entire journey and among all the nations through which we traveled. And the Lord drove out before us all the nations, including the Amorites, who lived in the land. We too will serve the Lord, because he is our God."[196]

The Hebrews clearly understood what was being asked of them. They knew God had led them to take this land and create a nation. He had fulfilled His promises. They would serve Him!

Curiously, Joshua pushed them harder. He knew their ways.

> Joshua said to the people, "You are not able to serve the Lord. He is a holy God; he is a jealous God.

---

[195] Joshua 24:14–15.
[196] Joshua 24:16–18.

He will not forgive your rebellion and your sins. If you forsake the Lord and serve foreign gods, he will turn and bring disaster on you and make an end of you, after he has been good to you."[197]

Joshua knew the people of Israel and was skeptical of their obedience. He reminded them what had happened to their grandparents. He took a step back and reminded them that they had not been good keepers of the covenant! A pleading voice from the people was heard:

But the people said to Joshua, "No! We will serve the Lord."[198]

Joshua remained a skeptic and cautioned them about their vow. They persisted in their allegiance.

Then Joshua said, "You are witnesses against yourselves that you have chosen to serve the Lord."
"Yes, we are witnesses," they replied.[199]

Finally, Joshua gave them commands regarding their behavior.

"Now then," said Joshua, "throw away the foreign gods that are among you and yield your hearts to the Lord, the God of Israel." And the people said to Joshua, "We will serve the Lord our God and obey him."[200]

DEVELOPING A PROFOUND AWARENESS

We are always His people, but being humble, surrendered, and dependent upon Him is our worship of who He is and our relationship with Him. God calls for a yielded heart! In the Hebrews' entry to the Promised Land, we

---

[197] Joshua 24:19–20.
[198] Joshua 24:21.
[199] Joshua 21:22.
[200] Joshua 24:23–24.

find a metaphor for our spiritual existence. Every detail of this conquering process reveals, over and over, what is necessary to return to our Eden relationship with Him.

As an example, the fall of Jericho provides instruction about our spiritual lives.[201] The Israelites followed God's instruction, and the walls fell. However, the soldiers had to go into the city and root out the enemy. In addition, God required that they kill all the inhabitants and destroy any sacred items. In the same way, as believers, we must approach God with clean hearts and minds. The relationship necessitates that we root out the rebellion that lies within. Moreover, we must destroy the idols and bury them.

Moses dealt with the golden calf, and Joshua addressed other gods. In his final address, Joshua identified Yahweh as a holy and jealous God. Yahweh would not tolerate unfaithfulness, as seen in the Israelites' first arrival at the Promised Land. Joshua made it very clear that the pivotal decision in life is deciding if you will follow God and make Him the Lord of your life. The *rebellious choice* that Adam and Eve made in the garden—to seek their own autonomy for self-determination—was the same choice the Hebrews had to make. Frankly, it is the same choice you and I must make. Idols and gods dramatically hinder a vision for His profound awareness.

Moses and Joshua acknowledged that idols and other gods distract us from surrender and submission to God. *Idols* are not only images of worship, but can be material possessions. Our lives can be distracted by desires for a car, a new set of golf clubs, a fishing boat, a house, a motorcycle, and so on. If our lives are focused on accumulating "things," then we'll struggle to hear from God.

In the same way, *foreign gods* are those thought processes that are independent of the one true God. The rebellious choice is still an option for humankind. Foreign gods include any belief system that distracts one's attention from our Creator God. These include Hinduism, Buddhism, other Eastern mystics, existentialism, humanism, naturalism, selfism, atheism, and so on. These choices are pivotal to what Joshua identified as detestable to God. Idols, other religions, and secular philosophies are disconcerting and bring confusion to the vision of God.

---

[201] Joshua 5:13–6:27.

Joshua refers to these ways of thinking as rebellious and sinful. Not choosing God's ways is clearly rebellion and leads to sin. God basically told Cain the same thing: if Cain rebelled against God's precepts, then sin was crouching at the door. This theme is critical to us as human beings, and unfortunately it is not clearly stated enough. Being restored to a garden relationship with God requires a *renouncement of our rebellion*. It is our rebellion that separated us from God. The sins followed. Man used his God-given choice to rebel against Him.

Critical to a profound relationship with God are submission and surrender to His vision. God created humanity, led them, brought the boundaries of His vision, and taught them how to worship Him as His chosen people in the land promised to Abraham, Isaac, and Jacob. God's vision must be the vision of His followers!

13

GOD-SERVING LEADERSHIP: JUDGES AND PROPHETS

THE PERIOD OF THE JUDGES FOLLOWED JOSHUA'S DEATH. THE BOOK OF Joshua covers the time between the conquest of the Promised Land and the establishment of a kingdom of Israel. The books of Samuel provide an account of the time during which the judges served as God's leadership. It didn't take long for the Hebrews to forget their vow to follow Yahweh. The stories reveal the behaviors of these stiff-necked people driven by their flesh. Israel was unfaithful to God. He delivered them into the hands of their enemies. Israel repented and asked for mercy. God raised up a leader or judge. The judge delivered the Israelites from oppression. The Israelites prospered. But soon they fell again into unfaithfulness, and the scenario repeated.

PRE-CREATION PLANNING

I can only imagine the trinitarian plan to install the leadership of judges and prophets. God's presence through the judges and prophets was most often not well received by the Israelites, but they tolerated God's messengers. Unfortunately, they didn't listen, and they found themselves seeking God when the oppressors showed up. The people forgot the vow they had made to God when Joshua was with them. They needed the judges because they had great moments of unbelief, but they called on God when they recognized they had rebelled.

Eventually, the Israelites wanted more than a judge led by Yahweh. Even the people of foreign gods knew when the Great I Am was not with the people. Over and over, they rebelled. They decided for themselves that if they had a king like other nations, it would be better than a judge or a prophet. God sent down His Son as an angel to encourage, teach, and protect the Hebrew leadership.[202]

BIBLICAL ACCOUNT (JUDGES)

After Joshua led the Israelites in the conquest of the Promised Land, his elders managed the kingdom. This leadership was weak, and enemies attacked because they believed Yahweh had forgotten the Israelites. This cycle is repeated over and over in the book of Judges.[203] God raised up a leader every time the people lost faith. These true stories reveal people who struggled to believe in their God, but He still loved them! Read and learn from them.

Othniel (1373–1334)	Jair (1126–1105)
Ehud (1316–1237)	Jephthah (1087–1081)
Shamgar (1262–1247)	Ibzan (1081–1075)
Deborah (1237–1198)	Elon (1075–1065)
Gideon (1191–1151)	Abdon (1065–1058)
Tola (1149–1126)	Samson (1069–1049)

Othniel

As a result of Hebrew transgressions against God, the king of Aram oppressed them for eight years. When they called on God, Othniel was raised up by God. Under Othniel, peace lasted for forty years.[204]

Ehud

Ehud was sent by the Israelites to the Moabite king, Eglon, to deliver the Israelites' monetary sign of allegiance. Once they met, Ehud told the king he had a secret message for him. The king allowed Ehud to meet him in private. Ehud said, "I have a message from God for you," drew his sword, and stabbed

---

[202] Genesis 32:22.
[203] Judges 1:1–21:25.
[204] Judges 3:7–11.

the king. Ehud escaped and rallied the Israelite tribes, killing about ten thousand Moabite soldiers. There was peace in the land for eighty years.[205]

Shamgar

Little is known about the judge Shamgar, who worked in the shadow of Ehud. He is said to have repelled attacks from the Philistines in the regions of Israel. History indicates that he slaughtered six hundred of the invaders. You'll find in OT history, in this case Judges 5, that Deborah and Shamgar were placed by God in the role of judges. Unlike the other judges, Shamgar is given no introduction, conclusion, or reference to the length of his reign. The only other mention of Shamgar suggests that he was present during a low period of Israelite society.

Deborah

Deborah was a judge of Israel and the wife of Lappidoth. She rendered her decisions beneath a palm tree. The Hebrews had been oppressed by King Jabin of Canaan for twenty years. Stirred by the wretched condition of Israel, Deborah sent a message to General Barak, telling him that the Lord God had commanded him to gather ten thousand troops and prepare for battle. She informed him that the Lord God would draw in the commander of Jabin's army. However, Barak would not go unless she went with him. Deborah agreed, but noted that the victory would then be credited to a woman.

Gideon

God appeared to Gideon. "The Lord turned to him and said, 'Go in the strength you have and save Israel out of Midian's hand. Am I not sending you?'"[206] God chose Gideon to free the people of Israel and to condemn their backsliding idolatry. The angel of the Lord came as a traveler who sat down in the shade to enjoy a little refreshment and to relax. He entered into conversation with Gideon regarding an upcoming battle with the Midianites. The angel of the Lord greeted Gideon with "The Lord is with you, you mighty man of valor!"

---

[205] Judges 3:12–30.
[206] Judges 6:14.

Gideon requested proof of God's will in the form of miracles: a sign from the angel of the Lord, in which the angel appeared to Gideon and caused fire to shoot up out of a rock; and two signs involving a fleece. God met his requests.

God informed Gideon that the men he had gathered were too many. If Gideon brought so many men, there would be a reason for the Israelites to claim the victory as their own instead of acknowledging that God had saved them. God first instructed Gideon to send home those men who were afraid. Gideon invited any man who wanted to leave to do so. Twenty-two thousand men returned home and ten thousand remained. Yet God told Gideon they were still too many and instructed him to bring them to the water. All those who lapped the water with their tongues, as a dog laps, were to be put to one side. All those who kneeled to drink, putting their hands to their mouths, were to be put to the other side. The number of those who lapped was three hundred; the rest of the troops knelt down to drink. Then the Lord said to Gideon, "With the three hundred that lapped I will deliver you, and give the Midianites into your hand. Let all the others go to their homes."[207]

Divided into three companies, Gideon and his three hundred men marched on the enemy camp. He instructed them to blow the trumpet, give a battle cry, and light torches, simulating an attack by a large force. As they did so, the Midianite army fled.

Tola

Of all the judges, the least is written about Tola. There is no record of his work other than the account from Judges 10:1–2: "And after Abimelech there arose to defend Israel Tola the son of Puah, the son of Dodo, a man of Issachar; and he dwelt in Shamir in mount Ephraim. And he judged Israel twenty and three years, and died, and was buried in Shamir."

Jair

Tola was followed by Jair of Gilead, who led Israel for twenty-two years. He had thirty sons, who rode thirty donkeys. They controlled thirty towns in Gilead, which to this day are called Havvoth Jair. When Jair died, he was buried in Kamon.[208]

---

[207] Ibid.

[208] Judges 10:3–5.

Jephthah

Jephthah appeared as a judge to preside over Israel for a period of six years. His father's name was Gilead, and his mother is described as a prostitute. Much is written of Jephthah. He is considered an important judge because of the length of the biblical account. However, he was a judge for only six years.

In Judges 10–12, we find that the people of Yahweh "again did what was evil in the sight of the Lord ... they forsook the Lord ..."[209] So the anger of the Lord was kindled against Israel, and He sold them into the hand of Ammon. Jephthah was asked to lead them against the Ammonites.

Ibzan

This is what we know: "Ibzan of Bethlehem led Israel. He had thirty sons and thirty daughters. He gave his daughters away in marriage to those outside his clan, and for his sons he brought in thirty young women as wives from outside his clan. Ibzan led Israel for seven years. Then Ibzan died and was buried in Bethlehem."[210]

Elon

Elon was a son of Zebulun. He was among those who came to Egypt with Jacob. From him sprang the Elonites. He judged Israel for ten years and was considered wise and fair. He died and was buried in Aijalon.

Abdon

"Abdon, son of Hillel, from Pirathon, led Israel. He had forty sons and thirty grandsons, who rode on seventy donkeys. He led Israel for eight years. Then Abdon son of Hillel died and was buried at Pirathon in Ephraim, in the hill country of the Amalekites."[211]

---

[209] Judges 10:6.
[210] Judges 12:8–10.
[211] Judges 12:13–15.

Samson

Samson was given great strength against his enemies, which allowed him to perform great feats. The stories told about him include slaying a lion with his bare hands and massacring an entire enemy army using only the jawbone of an ass. However, Samson's strength was connected to his long hair. If it was cut, then his Nazarite vow would be defiled, and he would lose his strength.

Delilah discovered Samson's secret and shared it with the Philistines. She had a servant cut Samson's hair while he was sleeping. She turned him over to his Philistine enemies, who gouged out his eyes and forced him to grind grain in a mill. While he was there, his hair began to grow again. When the Philistines took Samson into their temple, Samson asked to rest against one of the support pillars. After being granted permission, he prayed to God and miraculously recovered his strength, allowing him to bring down the columns. This collapsed the temple and killed Samson as well as all of the Philistines.

DEVELOPING A PROFOUND AWARENESS

It is interesting to note that the enemies of the Hebrews focused on their spiritual lives. If they saw chaos in the Hebrew nation, they believed Yahweh was no longer protecting the Hebrews, and they made plans to attack.

The Israelites' on-again, off-again relationship with Yahweh was very surprising. For a people to experience the direct intervention of their God and not remain steadfast is monumental. Overcoming their rebellious spirits took an everlasting love. Yet, when I look at my own spiritual formation, I see the same rebellious spirit, despite the fact that I possess a profound awareness of His presence.

In what seems like a very short time, the Hebrews forgot about Yahweh. They found themselves in trouble, so they prayed and called on Yahweh to save them. The judges were called by Yahweh to deliver His people. The judges did rescue them, and peace reigned—until the next time.

14

A TROUBLED LEADERSHIP: KINGS AND PROPHETS

WHAT IS IMPORTANT HERE, ISRAEL'S HUMAN HISTORY OR THE intervention of God? Theologian Brevard Childs clarifies the confusion that existed for Israel. It lay somewhere between their natural and supernatural existence because "Israel's history involves both divine and human agency."[212] Despite God's design to bring out His people from bondage, to teach His people what it means to be the family of God, to protect them, to give them a land filled with milk and honey, and to bless them with leadership and victories over their enemies, they failed to grasp their relationship with God. The Israelites lost the vision that Yahweh had given to them. The prophets continued to instruct the Israelites in God's ways and warn them about their rebellion.

God established the family to live in love, honor, and gratitude for what He had done for them. God's everlasting love, from Creation to the close of the OT, was absolutely amazing. From Creation, we've seen the desire of God's heart: that His people would live in a profound awareness of His loving presence. He called them to believe His Word, trust His sovereignty, and pursue His plan for their lives—to announce the Messiah.

PRE-CREATION PLANNING

I can only imagine what the Trinity faced as they considered the issues that the chosen people would present. The judges and prophets did all that God had designed. Unfortunately, the Hebrews had determined that their

---

[212] Brevard Childs, *Biblical Theology of the Old and New Testaments* (Fortress Press, 1992), 100.

troubles would be over if they had an earthly king rather than a judge or prophet. They asked Samuel to ask Yahweh. As you will see, this was not the answer for these stiff-necked people.

I can only imagine, during this time of an on-again, off-again relationship, that the judges attempted to rescue the Hebrews from their transgressions. The stiff-necked people struggled deeply to be covenant keepers. Despite the fact that a king was not a good idea for His people, God allowed it. Politics supplanted theocratic guidance, and the Hebrews became divided.

That division led them deeper into rebellion. Prophets aligned with kings to bring about peace. The prophets warned them of coming tragedy if their rebellion continued. Foreign kings attacked, and the Israelites were exiled from the Promised Land by their enemies. They would not listen to the words of the prophet Jeremiah.[213]

God withdrew from the Hebrews in preparation for His Son's arrival. Their purpose was to love God and announce the coming of their Savior, Redeemer, and Restorer—the One who would restore them to a personal and intimate relationship with God, if they believed.[214]

BIBLICAL ACCOUNT (1 AND 2 SAMUEL, 1 AND 2 KINGS, 1 AND 2 CHRONICLES, CA. 950–0 BCE)

The books of Samuel, Kings, and Chronicles provide a history of Israel from greatness to a captured and exiled people. This brief summary will reveal God's ever-increasing struggle with His chosen people.

We have seen the challenges Moses experienced as he organized the Hebrews as the people of God and brought them the Law to live and thrive by. Joshua, on the other hand, experienced a tranquil reign, with conquest as the focus. Joshua, learning from Moses, followed the Lord's instruction and drew close to Yahweh. God performed a very special miracle upon the request of Joshua: God stopped the sun and moon so Joshua could complete a battle.

Following the conquest of Canaan, Joshua turned over leadership to the elders. Unfortunately, the elders were too weak to lead, and the Israelites

---

[213] Jeremiah 29: 11–14.
[214] Jeremiah 17:9–10.

became unrighteous. God raised up a series of judges to bail them out of oppression and chaos, There were twelve different judges over 350 years. This on-again, off-again struggle the Israelites had with unbelief led to God providing a king and a prophet to lead them back to Him. They lacked the vision of what God had done. Consequently, they did not understand what He was going to do.

KINGS

The Israelites went to Samuel to ask for a king. King Saul was the first king anointed by Samuel. He was very popular but soon fell into disfavor with God for not following Samuel's instruction. This is the critical theme of being in a relational covenant with God. Making matters worse for King Saul, David slew the giant Goliath and won the hearts of the Israelites. Not long after, David was anointed by Samuel as Saul's successor. This sequence of disobedient events, with a new king in waiting, was more than Saul's mind could handle. Saul pursued David to kill him. Saul was king for thirty years. He died in battle by throwing himself on his sword (ca. 1010 BCE).

God raised up a king after his own heart.[215] David grew up in humble circumstances and was passionate about his God. David had an opportunity to take King Saul out but refused, saying, "He is God's anointed."[216]

King David's success was anchored in his vision. He was a man whose soul was grounded in Yahweh. In nine separate instances, David sought God's advice.[217] David's vision of life and living were grounded deeply in the King of the universe. He submitted and surrendered to (1) believing God's Word, (2) trusting the sovereign Yahweh, and (3) pursuing what God wanted him to do. He worshipped God with a reckless abandon.[218]

As a result, David's integrity and humility were essential parts of his life. He knew he had sinned before God with Bathsheba, and he went directly to Yahweh for forgiveness.

---

[215] 1 Samuel 13:14.

[216] 1 Samuel 24:6.

[217] Maurice Bassali, "Nine Inquiries," *Grace & Truth Magazine*, 2012.

[218] 2 Samuel 6:14.

King David was blessed and powerful[219] "because the Lord God was with him."[220] David took back Jerusalem and brought the ark of the covenant to be placed in the synagogue. The covenant was extended to King David by God.[221] He informed David, through Nathan, that David's son would build God's great house. King David prepared the ground and bought the materials.[222]

Unfortunately, there was much heartache in the city of David. Sexual immorality and revenge caused distrust and wickedness.[223] Absalom, David's third son, attempted to take the kingdom from his father. His efforts were thwarted by God. Solomon, another of King David's sons, replaced his father.

King Solomon took Israel to great prominence in the Middle East. Yahweh asked Solomon what he wanted more than anything else, King Solomon asked for the wisdom and knowledge to rule the people.[224] Without a doubt, King Solomon understood the Hebrews. With all care and passion, Solomon built the great nation and a temple for Yahweh to dwell in among His people.[225] The temple dedication was a week-long celebration. The Lord God provided warning to the king and his people, but made it clear that if they stayed away from wickedness and prayed, He would protect and heal.

"I have heard your prayer and have chosen this place for myself as a temple for sacrifices.

"When I shut up the heavens so that there is no rain, or command locusts to devour the land or send a plague among my people, if my people, who are called by my name, will humble themselves and pray and seek my face and turn from their wicked ways, then I will hear from heaven, and I will forgive their sin and will heal their land. Now my eyes will be open and my ears attentive to the prayers offered in this place. I have chosen and consecrated this temple so that my Name may be there forever. My eyes and my heart will always be there.

"As for you, if you walk before me faithfully as David your father did, and do all I command, and observe my decrees and laws, I will establish your

---

[219] 1 Kings 10:23.

[220] 2 Samuel 5:10.

[221] 2 Samuel 7:21; 1 Chronicles 17.

[222] 1 Chronicles 22.

[223] 2 Samuel 13.

[224] 2 Chronicles 1:10.

[225] 2 Chronicles 2–5.

royal throne, as I covenanted with David your father when I said, 'You shall never fail to have a successor to rule over Israel.'

"But if you turn away and forsake the decrees and commands, I have given you and go off to serve other gods and worship them, then I will uproot Israel from my land, which I have given them, and will reject this temple I have consecrated for my Name. I will make it a byword and an object of ridicule among all peoples. This temple will become a heap of rubble. All who pass by will be appalled and say, 'Why has the Lord done such a thing to this land and to this temple?' People will answer, 'Because they have forsaken the Lord, the God of their ancestors, who brought them out of Egypt, and have embraced other gods, worshiping and serving them—that is why he brought all this disaster on them.'"[226]

The wise King Solomon was able to make Israel even greater than his father had made it. His penchant for women of other lands and gods was his greatest error.[227]

Here is the wisdom of King Solomon, a truth that continues today:

The words of the Teacher, son of David, king in Jerusalem:

"Meaningless! Meaningless!" says the Teacher. "Utterly meaningless! Everything is meaningless." What do people gain from all their labors at which they toil under the sun? Generations come and generations go, but the earth remains forever. The sun rises and the sun sets, and hurries back to where it rises. The wind blows to the south and turns to the north; round and round it goes, ever returning on its course. All streams flow into the sea, yet the sea is never full. To the place the streams come from, there they return again. All things are wearisome, more than one can say.

The eye never has enough of seeing, nor the ear its fill of hearing. What has been will be again, what has been done will be done again; there is nothing new under the sun. Is there anything of which one can say, "Look! This is something new"? It was here already, long ago; it was here before our time. No one remembers the former generations, and even those yet to come will not be remembered by those who follow them ... I have seen all the things that are done under the sun; all of them are meaningless, a chasing after the wind ... Then I applied myself to the understanding of

---

[226] 2 Chronicles 7:11–22.
[227] 1 Kings 11:6–13.

wisdom, and also of madness and folly, but I learned that this, too, is chasing after the wind ... I denied myself nothing my eyes desired; I refused my heart no pleasure. My heart took delight in all my labor, and this was the reward for all my toil. Yet when I surveyed all that my hands had done and what I had toiled to achieve, everything was meaningless, a chasing after the wind; nothing was gained under the sun ... I have seen the burden God has laid on the human race. He has made everything beautiful in its time. He has also set Eternity in the human heart; yet no one can fathom what God has done from beginning to end. I know that there is nothing better for people than to be happy and to do good while they live. That each of them may eat and drink, and find satisfaction in all their toil—this is the gift of God.[228]

Ecclesiastes is one of the most fundamental books in the Bible regarding humanity and its endeavors, desires, and appetite for wisdom. I believe the words of Solomon found their way into the hands of the fourth century BCE Greek philosophers and influenced their thinking. The words could basically be the foundation of existentialism, save for the references to God. There is no doubt in my mind that the basic understanding of humanity's existence is found here, albeit with the foreboding fear of aloneness. Fear plagues humanity! In short, all the pursuits of humanity lack an inherent value—a reality that speaks to existential dread.

Two terms come to mind when considering the human predicament: *novelty* and *first impression*. We could say of Solomon's wisdom that it carries an air of novelty—it is new, original, or unusual.

I minored in philosophy as an undergraduate. There were as many strains of thought as there were philosophers. Ideas were constantly made anew by the next thinker. These thought systems received attention because, on first impression, they were considered engaging, but on further examination they revealed a lackluster significance.

I find Solomon's understanding of human wisdom in the same realm of new or unusual and shallow judgment. Human wisdom does carry a very stale and bottomless explanation. For humanity, our reality rests in a truth that value, meaningfulness, and significance are found only in God.

---

[228] Ecclesiastes 1:1–3:13.

121

DIVISION

Following the death of Solomon, the nation of Israel split into two kingdoms: Israel, the northern kingdom, and Judah, the southern kingdom. The dissection weakened both kingdoms and resulted in great friction. Due to this division, both kingdoms experience hostility with their oldest enemies. This breakup continued for almost two hundred years until the northern kingdom was defeated and taken into captivity by the Assyrian king, Shalmaneser V (ca. 720 BCE). Judah was then alone. The significance of the division wasn't only about political and social war, it was about disobedience and not following God.

Judah remained relatively intact for a while, despite losing its political independence. That political independence was lost in battle to the Babylonian king, Nebuchadnezzar. Judah was placed into captivity for seventy years until Cyrus, king of Persia, released the Israelites.

The truth about the Israelites' downfall isn't directly related to these great kings. Their defeat is due to their abandonment of God's vision for them. The Hebrews ignored the prophets whom God raised up to give warning of the coming destruction if they did not repent and turn from their wicked ways.

The division between the two kingdoms was brought about by infighting and not seeking unity. The Israelites were unable to mend fences and return to God. The division was ninety years old when God raised up Elijah, a prophet, to bring warning to the Hebrew kings regarding their behavior as well as to the foreign gods those kings worshipped. The warnings were stern, but the Israelites did not heed the advice. Israel was so weakened by its theological, political, and civil strife that invaders were able to defeat the northern kingdom of Judah and place thousands into Assyrian captivity.

Judah remained in this captive state. Eventually the southern kingdom, Israel, also weakened, was conquered, and was placed under the rule of the Babylonians. Despite the fact that God had spoken through His prophets, the Hebrews did not listen.

PROPHETS

Each of the prophets had a message for the Hebrews. All prophets created vision for His people. The prophets were called by and received a message from God through different means. They spoke the Word of God and relayed it by deed and word. They performed miracles, wrote the Word of God, and were called to minister to the people.[229] Many of the prophets focused on the Hebrews' backsliding. Some prophets said that God would rescue them from oppression. Others reminded them that Yahweh remembered who they were. Most prophets announced that their God would send a redeemer, a savior who would free them from their years of oppression.

Unfortunately, the onus of the Hebrews' misery was their hard-heartedness. Keeping covenant with their God was extremely difficult for them. At the center of their troubles, they failed in their worship.[230] Making the situations more challenging was the turmoil that came between prophet and king. Dr. Rutland said, "Sometimes—though not often, because of royal pride is a powerful obstacle—the tangential vectors of these prophet-versus-king interactions suddenly, dramatically realigned and shifted from a collision course onto a plane of agreement. The prophets who came as confronters became advisers, sometimes even valued counselors."[231]

Israel	Judah
	Elijah 859–849
	Elisha 849–800
Jonah 780–850	Obadiah 840–825
Amos 765–750	Joel 835–796
Hosea 755–715	Micah 740–690
	Isaiah 739–685[232]
	Zephaniah 635–625

---

[229] Trent Butler, ed., *Holman Bible Dictionary* (Holman Bible Publishers, 1991), 1142.

[230] William C Williams, ed., *They Spoke from God: A Survey of the Old Testament* (Gospel Publishing House, 2003), 700.

[231] Mark Rutland, *Of Kings and Prophets* (Charisma House, 2021), 13.

[232] Following Isaiah is a generation without prophets.

[233] These prophets warned of a coming Babylonian conquest and exile; as well as a future return to Israel and a coming Messiah who would be their King. It is likely that Jeremiah, Daniel, and Ezekiel lived directly under Babylonian rule.

[234] These prophets tell the people to prepare for conquest by their enemies and a separation from God if they continue in rebellion. Malachi was the last prophet prior to the intertestamental period of four hundred years, during which time God was silent in preparation for the arrival of the Messiah!

Nahum 630–612

Habakkuk 606–604

Jeremiah 627–580[234]

Daniel 606–530

Ezekiel 592–570

Haggai 520–516[3]

Zechariah 520–518

Malachi 435–415

To this day, the People of the Book believe they are the oppressed. They await a messiah who will free them from their tormentors. Without a doubt, the Israelites had their share of troubles in the world because the foreign gods considered them the image bearers of God. If they were to be victorious over their enemies and over their unbelief, the prophets would have to call them back to their covenant faith.[235]

ISAIAH

Isaiah's name means "God of salvation." He is considered the key prophet who informed Israel of the coming Messiah! On many occasions, Isaiah used his messianic prophecy to inform the Israelites who to look for.[236]

DEVELOPING A PROFOUND AWARENESS

There are many great examples of the people of God and their on-and-off relationship with the King of the universe. The wrongdoers relied on earthly means to control their destinies—in the meantime provoking God to further punishment. The people of God grew tired of the leadership God raised up. The Israelites wanted to be like other countries and have a king. Little did they realize the disastrous effect this would have on their ownership of their spiritual heritage. The infighting began and is there to

---

[235] William Dyrness, *Themes of the Old Testament* (InterVarsity Press, 1977), 215.
[236] Hunter Sherman, *The Good, Bad, and Ugly* (LWG Publications, 2019), 251.

this day. They have abandoned their God. Fortunately for them, He has not abandoned them.

I am always surprised by those who love to memorize and recite the words of Jeremiah:

This is what the LORD says: "When seventy years are completed for Babylon, I will come to you and fulfill my good promise to bring you back to this place. For I know the plans I have for you," declares the Lord, "plans to prosper you and not to harm you, plans to give you hope and a future. Then you will call on me and come and pray to me, and I will listen to you. You will seek me and find me when you seek me with all your heart. I will be found by you," declares the LORD, "and will bring you back from captivity. I will gather you from all the nations and places where I have banished you," declares the LORD, "and will bring you back to the place from which I carried you into exile."[237]

These words were for God's chosen, but a rebellious people needed to be taught a lesson. God admitted that He would *bring them back* to the place from which He carried them into exile. And He did bring them back! They did not heed the words spoken by Jeremiah, which resulted in their defeat.

More important is the verse "You will seek me and find me when you seek me with all your heart." Wow! Please understand this: to have a personal and intimate relationship with God, seek Him with all your heart. This is the crucial detail in this passage.

Jeremiah was considered "the weeping prophet" because his heart broke for the people of God. He made several references to the coming Messiah, which should have been the focus of the leadership for the Jews (see Jeremiah 11:19, 30:19, 31:31–33, 34, 33:15–16). Sad to say, it was not.

---

[237] Jeremiah 29:10–14.

PART VI

Davidic Covenant: Seeking the Heart and Vision of God

15

KING DAVID AND KING SOLOMON: WISDOM AND UNDERSTANDING

CLEARLY, GOD CREATED A RELATIONSHIP FILLED WITH MYSTERY THAT was bound by a covenant. The covenant was built on a vision, and the vision was constructed from the transcendent precepts and commitment of God. It is a vision that permeates the soul of every believer. The precepts interweave the covenant vision for both participants.

The Father and Jesus designed and carefully crafted the created to possess their image, hosting an innermost being to cultivate a vision of wholeness and thriving. When the vision is integrated into the heart and mind of the believer, a profound awareness of a joyful relationship in God is discovered. The psalms of King David and the proverbs of King Solomon provided the foundation of a sustaining *haza* (vision).

The psalms of King David speak specifically to vision development that was very different from worldly living. In short, the psalms are about the formation of perceptual being and the interpretation of that which is perceived. All of this leads to developing a vision that is in the likeness and image of God.

There isn't sufficient space here to examine all of the psalms, but those selected will accurately reflect what God sought to teach the created in the garden and in His written revelation.

The aural transmission process of hearing and speaking the God Story continued to grow over hundreds of years, in some cases deepening the allegiance of God's people. God was fully aware of the on-again, off-again nature of His people.

PRE-CREATION PLANNING

I can only imagine that the planning was more exciting the closer it came to the Messiah's arrival. The Trinity planned for every detail. The crucial goal was placing the kingdom wisdom on the hearts of His people.[238] The prophets would lead and teach them. They would teach the people the wisdom to follow the precepts taught in the garden.

So God would place His words on the tongues of the anointed. His anointed leadership would rescue the people from their unbelief. The hard-hearted people would call on God. The prophets would rise up to assist the kings. The prophets anointed with the Holy Spirit would share the heart of the God Story. Lovers of God would seek the words of King David. Those words would be written for generations to come and guide His people in all they did for those who believe. Those words would prepare the world for the Messiah's arrival.

BIBLICAL ACCOUNT (JOB 2300–2100 BCE, PSALMS 1010–930 BCE, PROVERBS 950–687 BCE)

As you read the passages from Psalms that follow, take a moment to consider how each one might influence your vision—your mindset or mental framework. I am certain you'll find great value in the words that must be at the core of your vision. Of the many chapters and verses, I have pulled those that I believe assist in understanding the pieces making up a vision. There are three categories: (1) what we learn about our vision, (2) what it takes to build the God-vision, and (3) what life is like without vision. The three categories reveal the characteristics of vision and set the foundations and boundaries of our hearts and minds. Do not ignore these passages.

A VISION DEVELOPED

Your vision is what you choose it to be. Vision development just doesn't happen on its own. Unfortunately, too many don't recognize its progress

---

[238] Deuteronomy 11:18: "Fix these words of mine in your hearts and minds; tie them as symbols on your hands and bind them on your foreheads."

within, that how you see the world becomes a personal choice. Choosing God's perspective is pivotal to possessing eternal joy.

> Whose delight is in the law of the Lord and who meditates on his law, day and night ... that person will not wither, but will prosper. And, if you delight in the Lord he will watch over you.[239]

These words are the starting point of a profound awareness. Meditating on the Word of God instructs you in your covenant relationship with Him.

> Tremble and do not sin when you are on your beds, search your hearts and be silent.[240]

God desires each of us to listen to His words of right living. Desire your heart to be in harmony with Him.

> You, the righteous God who probes minds and hearts.[241]

As you seek a deeper relationship with Him, His light will reveal your mind and heart to you and Him.

> What is mankind that you are mindful of them ... human beings that you care for them? You have made them a little lower than the angels, and crowned them with glory and honor.[242]

These words are God's valuation of you. You were built just a little lower than angels, but are God's crowning work!

> The law of the Lord is perfect, refreshing the soul. The statutes of the Lord are trustworthy, making wise the

---

[239] Psalm 1:2-4.

[240] Psalm 4:4.

[241] Psalm 7:9.

[242] Psalm 8:4–5.

simple. The precepts of the Lord are right, giving joy to the heart. The commands of the Lord are radiant, giving light to the eyes. The fear of the Lord is pure, enduring forever. The decrees of the Lord are firm, and all of them are righteous ... By them your servant is warned; in keeping them there is great reward ... who can discern their own errors? Forgive my hidden faults. Keep your servant also from willful sins; may they not rule over me. Then I will be blameless, innocent of great transgression. May these words of my mouth and this meditation of my heart be pleasing in your sight, Lord, my Rock and my Redeemer.[243]

It is unimaginable peace, joy, and love that makes you dance and sing. It is part of the mystery of the intimacy you supernaturally experience when you recognize He is your Creator and loves you. Right living is profound!

As I always told my students, "God does not play. He means what He said." The statutes are trustworthy if we learn to live by them as a people. Following His Word is a rock for us. Best of all, we will be redeemed to relationship with Him for eternity.

Yet you brought me out of the womb; you made me trust in you, even at my mother's breast. From birth I was cast on you; from my mother's womb you have been my God.[244]

This is a cornerstone of profound awareness. His love for the created came before the foundations of the earth.

Who may ascend the mountain of the Lord? Who may stand in his holy place? The one who has clean hands and a pure heart, who does not trust in an idol or swear by a false god.[245]

Just place your trust in His hands only!

---

[243] Psalm 19:7–14.
[244] Psalm 22:9–10.
[245] Psalm 24:3–4.

Show me your ways, Lord, teach me your paths. Guide me
in your truth and teach me, for you are God my Savior, and
my hope is in you all day long.[246]

As the profound awareness of your relationship with God grows, your
desire for His truth grows. This gives the victory over the pull of evil and the
corrupt nature of humanity.

Be strong and take heart, all you who hope in the Lord.[247]

While everything around you seems to be in chaos, allow your heart to
meet in peace with the Holy Spirit.

The following are some of the most powerful statements in Psalms. The
depth of understanding God through a spiritual surrender and submission
is a mystery only a true believer understands. The broken spirit and contrite
heart flow from surrender and submission. This isn't a human commitment
to loyalty. The broken spirit and contrite heart are spiritual prerequisites
uniting you to God. Too often, a momentary emotional release is confused
as a redemptive step toward God. God is calling His people away from their
pride to spiritual intimacy.

David discovered this in the fields as a shepherd. Life as a shepherd
contains few or no distractions. David's vision grew out of his night hours
gazing in wonder at the heavens and imagining the greatness of the God of
his people.

Create in me a pure heart, O God, and renew a steadfast
spirit within me.[248]

Many of these words came to David in adulthood. His words always get
to the core of his soul, his innermost being.

My sacrifice, O God, is a broken spirit; a broken and contrite
heart you, God, will not despise.[249]

---

[246] Psalm 25:4–5.
[247] Psalm 39:24.
[248] Psalm 51:10.
[249] Psalm 51:17.

David knew that a man's broken heart, when he has hit rock-bottom, reveals that his relationship with God is authentic. He recognizes that humanity is lost.

> The day is yours, and yours also the night; you established the sun and moon. It was you who set all the boundaries of the earth; you made both summer and winter.[250]

> The fear of the Lord is the beginning of wisdom; all who follow his precepts have good understanding. To him belongs eternal praise.[251]

David is so profoundly aware of God's wisdom that he coaches his son, Solomon, to always seek it.

> Give me understanding, so that I may keep your law and obey it with all my heart. Direct me in the path of your commands, for there I find delight. Turn my heart toward your statutes and not toward selfish gain.[252]

There are two paths in life: the one you want and God's. The joy of life is found in God's way, but you must pursue it.

> For you created my inmost being; you knit me together in my mother's womb. I praise you because I am fearfully and wonderfully made; your works are wonderful; I know that full well.[253]

This is one of the greatest passages in God's Word. It is the truth of our conception and our value before God.

---

[250] Psalm 74:16–17.
[251] Psalm 111:10.
[252] Psalm 119:34–36.
[253] Psalm 139:13–14.

GOD BUILDS VISION

> I will instruct you and teach you in the way you should go;
> I will counsel you with my loving eye on you.[254]

There is peace and joy when you discover that God's purpose for your life is the way you always wanted to go.

> But the plans of the Lord stand firm forever, the purposes
> of his heart through all generations.[255]

Because these words were true then, that means they are true today. He is our Savior.

> Fear the Lord, you his holy people, for those who fear him
> lack nothing.[256]

This fear is one of reverence, not one to hide from.

> The Lord is close to the brokenhearted and saves those who
> are crushed in spirit.[257]

When you have hit rock-bottom and discovered that your way doesn't result in joy, then He is there to pick you up.

> Take delight in the Lord, and he will give you the desires
> of your heart.[258]

The mystery here, as you deepen your humility, is that you discover His desires are becoming yours.

---

[254] Psalm 32:9.
[255] Psalm 33:11.
[256] Psalm 34:9.
[257] Psalm 34:18.
[258] Psalm 37:4.

The Lord makes firm the steps of the one who delights in him; though he may stumble, he will not fall, for the Lord upholds him with his hand.[259]

As a result of your love for Him, He will protect you in all things.

He says, "Be still, and know that I am God; I will be exalted among the nations, I will be exalted in the earth.[260]

It is here, in the quiet of your innermost being, your heart, that you will hear from Him.

My mouth will speak words of wisdom; the meditation of my heart will give you understanding.[261]

Humble submission and meditation on His Word give understanding to the profound awareness.

God looks down from heaven on all mankind to see if there are any who understand, any who seek God.[262]

A profound awareness will keep you seeking after God.

Your ways, God, are holy. What god is as great as our God? You are the God who performs miracles; you display your power among the peoples.[263]

Always be profoundly aware of God's holiness.

---

[259] Psalm 37:23–24.
[260] Psalm 46:10.
[261] Psalm 49:10.
[262] Psalm 53:2.
[263] Psalm 77:13–14.

Glory in his holy name; let the hearts of those who seek the Lord rejoice. Look to the Lord and his strength; seek his face always.[264]

We find a supernatural presence in His holy name!

Your hands made me and formed me; give me understanding to learn your commands.[265]

Be profoundly aware of the power and peace in understanding His commands for you and your family.

May I wholeheartedly follow your decrees, that I may not be put to shame.[266]

His truth creates within each of us a whole peace within a profound awareness.

I hate double-minded people, but I love your law. You are my refuge and my shield; I have put my hope in your word.[267]

We cannot live in both worlds. We either please God or please mankind. God's ways are *not* man's ways.

WITHOUT A VISION

Be merciful to me, LORD, for I am in distress; my eyes grow weak with sorrow, my soul and body with grief.[268]

It is a distressful place to live in separation from God.

---

[264] Psalm 105:3–4.
[265] Psalm 119:73.
[266] Psalm 119:80.
[267] Psalm 119:113–114.
[268] Psalms 31:9.

> They would not be like their ancestors—a stubborn and rebellious generation, whose hearts were not loyal to God, whose spirits were not faithful to him.[269]

A rebellious people seek their own evil ways, choosing unnatural and nefarious lifestyles.

> [F]or they did not believe in God or trust in his deliverance.[270]

A rebellious people will ignore the goodness of God.

> But they put God to the test and rebelled against the Most High; they did not keep his statutes. Like their ancestors they were disloyal and faithless, as unreliable as a faulty bow." They angered him with their high places; they aroused his jealousy with their idols. When God heard them, he was furious.[271]

God will *not* be defeated. His wrath will come.

> The 'gods' [of this earth] know nothing, they understand nothing. They walk about in darkness; all the foundations of the earth are shaken.[272]

The wisdom of man is darkness. The rich will attempt to make men live according to their rule.

> How great are your works, Lord, how profound your thoughts! Senseless people do not know, fools do not understand.[273]

A profound awareness will always seek understanding.

---

[269] Psalm 78:8.

[270] Psalm 78:22.

[271] Psalm 78:56–59.

[272] Psalm 82:5.

[273] Psalm 92:5–6.

Take notice, you senseless ones among the people; you fool, when will you become wise? Does he who fashioned the ear not hear? Does he who formed the eye not see? Does he who disciplines nations not punish? Does he who teaches mankind lack knowledge? The Lord knows all human plans; he knows that they are futile.[274]

A profound awareness will pray for the futile efforts, planning, and power of humanity.

It is better to take refuge in the Lord than to trust in humans. It is better to take refuge in the Lord than to trust in princes.[275]

Be very clear: God's ways are higher than man's.

Do not put your trust in princes, in human beings, who cannot save. When their spirit departs, they return to the ground; on that very day their plans come to nothing.[276]

Be profoundly aware of the truth that your choice to be a man or woman of God has eternal consequences.

LIVING BY THE SOUL-VISION

In Proverbs, we find statements that are the specific foundation to a vision—that is, knowledge, wisdom, understanding, and warnings due to unbelief. God asked Solomon what one gift he desired above all others. Here is their discussion:

"So give your servant a discerning heart to govern your people and to distinguish between right and wrong. For who is able to govern this great people of yours?" The Lord

[274] Psalm 94:8–11.
[275] Psalm 118:8–9.
[276] Psalm 146:3–4.

was pleased that Solomon had asked for this. So God said to him, "Since you have asked for this and not for long life or wealth for yourself, nor have asked for the death of your enemies but for discernment in administering justice, I will do what you have asked. I will give you a wise and discerning heart, so that there will never have been anyone like you, nor will there ever be. Moreover, I will give you what you have not asked for—both wealth and honor—so that in your lifetime you will have no equal among kings. And if you walk in obedience to me and keep my decrees and commands as David your father did, I will give you a long life." Then Solomon awoke—and he realized it had been a dream.[277]

King Solomon was his father's son; he understood what was important to God and His people. Solomon knew that the justice of Yahweh was much higher than the justice of humankind. He especially knew he needed to have wisdom to govern the people of God. What is sweet in this conversation is that God was so pleased with Solomon's request that He gave Solomon what Solomon did not ask for—wealth and honor. However, Solomon's long life was contingent upon his obedience to God's instruction.

In the first passage of Proverbs, King Solomon made clear his reason for writing this book of wisdom to influence the mind and the heart. Again, I have drawn out the wisdom given to King Solomon from Yahweh. Be sensitive to the proverbs, but also to the themes of knowledge, wisdom, and understanding. Much of the focus of the wisdom theme involves building the foundations of your heart and mind.

ENCOURAGEMENT FROM PROVERBS

I will not provide commentary here. Instead, I ask you to read and meditate on the words from the wisdom of Proverbs. Allow God's wisdom to penetrate your heart.

---

[277] 1 Kings 3:9–15.

These are the proverbs of Solomon, son of David, king of Israel, for gaining wisdom and discipline, for comprehending words of insight, and for receiving instruction in wise living and in righteousness, justice, and equity. To impart prudence to the simple and knowledge and discretion to the young, let the wise listen and gain instruction, and the discerning acquire wise counsel by understanding the proverbs and parables, the sayings and riddles of the wise.[278]

The fear of the Lord is the beginning of knowledge, but fools despise wisdom and instruction.[279]

For the waywardness of the simple will kill them, and the complacency of fools will destroy them.[280]

My son, if you accept my words and store up my commands within you, turning your ear to wisdom and applying your heart to understanding—indeed, if you call out for insight and cry aloud for understanding, and if you look for it as for silver and search for it as for hidden treasure, then you will understand the fear of the Lord and find the knowledge of God.[281]

For the Lord gives wisdom; from his mouth come knowledge and understanding. He holds success in store for the upright, he is a shield to those whose walk is blameless, for he guards the course of the just and protects the way of his faithful ones.[282]

Then you will understand what is right and just and fair— every good path. For wisdom will enter your heart, and

---

[278] Proverbs 1:1–6.
[279] Proverbs 1:7.
[280] Proverbs 1:32.
[281] Proverbs 2:1–2.
[282] Proverbs 2:6–8.

knowledge will be pleasant to your soul. Discretion will protect you, and understanding will guard you.[283]

Above all else, guard your heart, for everything you do flows from it.[284]

Listen, for I have trustworthy things to say; I open my lips to speak what is right. My mouth speaks what is true, for my lips detest wickedness. All the words of my mouth are just; none of them is crooked or perverse. To the discerning all of them are right; they are upright to those who have found knowledge. Choose my instruction instead of silver, knowledge rather than choice gold, for wisdom is more precious than rubies, and nothing you desire can compare with her.[285]

In their hearts humans plan their course, but the Lord establishes their steps.[286]

Whoever would foster love covers over an offense, but whoever repeats the matter separates close friends.[287]

WARNINGS FROM PROVERBS

The proverbs also provide warnings against rebellion.

Because they hated knowledge and did not choose the fear of the Lord, they would have none of my counsel and despised my every rebuke. Therefore they shall eat the fruit of their own way, and be filled to the full with their

---

[283] Proverbs 2:9–11.
[284] Proverbs 4:23.
[285] Proverbs 8:6–11.
[286] Proverbs 16:9.
[287] Proverbs 17:9.

own fancies. For the turning away of the simple will slay them, and the complacency of fools will destroy them; But whoever listens to me will dwell safely, and will be at ease, without fear of evil.[288]

Wisdom will save you from the ways of wicked men, from men whose words are perverse, who have left the straight paths to walk in dark ways, who delight in doing wrong and rejoice in the perverseness of evil, whose paths are crooked and who are devious in their ways.[289]

Trust in the Lord with all your heart and lean not on your own understanding; in all your ways submit to him, and he will make your paths straight. Do not be wise in your own eyes; fear the Lord and shun evil. This will bring health to your body and nourishment to your bones.[290]

For the lips of the adulterous woman drip honey, and her speech is smoother than oil; but in the end she is bitter as gall, sharp as a double-edged sword. Her feet go down to death; her steps lead straight to the grave. She gives no thought to the way of life; her paths wander aimlessly, but she does not know it.[291]

There are six things the Lord hates, seven that are detestable to him: haughty eyes, a lying tongue, hands that shed innocent blood, a heart that devises wicked schemes, feet that are quick to rush into evil, a false witness who pours out lies and a person who stirs up conflict in the community.[292]

Can a man scoop fire into his lap without his clothes being burned? Can a man walk on hot coals without his feet being

---

[288] Proverbs 1:29–33.
[289] Proverbs 2:12–15.
[290] Proverbs 3:5–8.
[291] Proverbs 5:3–6.
[292] Proverbs 6:16–19.

scorched? So is he who sleeps with another man's wife; no one who touches her will go unpunished.[293]

PROPHECY

The proverbs speak of what was to come. These verses fulfill the nature of a covenant. The Messiah would represent humanity in the covenant established between God and mankind. You'll recall Abraham's covenant dream in Genesis 15. When a covenant is violated, the violator may lawfully be cut to pieces. Jesus was flogged so badly that he was unrecognizable, as Isaiah prophesied:

> As many were astonished at you—his appearance was so marred, beyond human semblance, and his form beyond that of the children of mankind.[294]

> Who has believed what he has heard from us? And to whom has the arm of the Lord been revealed? For he grew up before him like a young plant, and like a root out of dry ground; he had no form or majesty that we should look at him, and no beauty that we should desire him. He was despised and rejected by men, a man of sorrows and acquainted with grief; and as one from whom men hide their faces he was despised, and we esteemed him not. Surely he has borne our griefs and carried our sorrows; yet we esteemed him stricken, smitten by God, and afflicted. But he was pierced for our transgressions; he was crushed for our iniquities; upon him was the chastisement that brought us peace, and with his wounds we are healed.[295]

---

[293] Proverbs 6:27–29.
[294] Isaiah 52:14 ESV. See also https://www.openbible.info/topics/beaten_beyond_recognition.
[295] Isaiah 53:1–12 ESV.

I gave my back to those who strike, and my cheeks to those who pull out the beard; I hid not my face from disgrace and spitting.[296]

He was despised and rejected by men, a man of sorrows and acquainted with grief; and as one from whom men hide their faces he was despised, and we esteemed him not.[297]

Therefore I will divide him a portion with the many, and he shall divide the spoil with the strong, because he poured out his soul to death and was numbered with the transgressors; yet he bore the sin of many, and makes intercession for the transgressors.[298]

He was oppressed, and he was afflicted, yet he opened not his mouth; like a lamb that is led to the slaughter, and like a sheep that before its shearers is silent, so he opened not his mouth.[299]

In that day the root of Jesse, who shall stand as a signal for the peoples—of him shall the nations inquire, and his resting place shall be glorious.[300]

And they made his grave with the wicked and with a rich man in his death, although he had done no violence, and there was no deceit in his mouth.[301]

A voice cries: "In the wilderness prepare the way of the Lord; make straight in the desert a highway for our God."[302]

---

[296] Isaiah 50:6 ESV.
[297] Isaiah 53:3 ESV.
[298] Isaiah 53:12 ESV.
[299] Isaiah 53:7 ESV.
[300] Isaiah 11:10 ESV.
[301] Isaiah 53:9 ESV.
[302] Isaiah 40:3 ESV.

DEVELOPING A PROFOUND AWARENESS

King David and his son, King Solomon, possessed relationships with God that were incredible. David began talking to his Father in heaven from a young age, as he cared for the family sheep in the fields. The *haza* was mightily developed in David and was his framework from which to approach the world of that time. King Saul was told that God had sought "a man after God's own heart."[303] On every significant decision, he inquired of the Lord. He would not move forward to battle without Yahweh's presence.

However, David was not without fault. We all know the story of Bathsheba. David failed to discipline family members for inappropriate behaviors. On a positive note, he taught his son Solomon well. Solomon grew Israel to unprecedented heights. God blessed Solomon because he asked for wisdom, not gold. However, his penchant for wives and concubines eventually led him into worship of other gods.[304]

It must be kept in mind that, despite the sinful nature of the OT leadership, God continued to lead them until their disobedience became pronounced. In each case, God used men and women to accomplish His ends, bringing salvation to all mankind. Ultimately, sin is disobedience and rebellion against God and His precepts. We are all responsible for our actions. King David was correct when he said, "Against you, you only, have I sinned and done what is evil in your sight; so you are right in your verdict and justified when you judge."[305]

This is the most powerful confession I've ever heard. King David singularly established God as his judge and jury. David faced no earthly court or judge. He faced no man and no law on the planet. He faced the Lawgiver, the King of the universe.

This is the foundation of the vision: you and I belong to the King of the universe. We are in a covenant relationship with Him. We trust His Word, His sovereignty, and His purpose for our lives.

Abraham responded to Yahweh's call to lead His people. Abraham's son Isaac and grandsons Jacob and Joseph followed. Moses responded to

---

[303] 1 Samuel 13:14 NIV.

[304] 1 Kings 11: 4–13. Solomon's heart was turned toward the gods of his wives. His idolatry resulted in the punishment of Yahweh.

[305] Psalm 51:4.

Yahweh by bringing the Law to the people of God. Joshua led the Hebrews into the Promised Land and took the land God gave them. The judges and prophets spoke and led for Yahweh. King David established Israel as an earthly kingdom. Throughout it all, the people who hated God were relentless and merciless. The tabernacle was the residence of God with His people.

Unfortunately, the Israelites continued in their disobedience, rebellion, and broken covenants, resulting in the exile of His people to a foreign land. Sadly, in approximately 400 BCE, God went quiet. Reading the final OT books of Habakkuk and Malachi reveals the damaged relationship. The good news is that God told the prophets the Messiah would come.

The Hebrew biblical educational system was very straightforward. Beit Sefer was the first level, an elementary place for children six to ten years of age to memorize the first five books of the Torah. Beit Talmud students, ages eleven through thirteen, were required to memorize the wisdom literature. Beit Mishnah students were required to memorize the prophetic literature. Those students who were most successful and displayed an outstanding grasp of their studies were called by a well-respected rabbinical school to live there and pursue further studies. The student would study while working to support the rabbi.

16

AN OT THEMATIC REVIEW: LESSONS AND TRIALS

THE GOAL IN THIS BRIEF OT SURVEY IS TO HELP YOU KNOW YOUR SOUL and a critical element within it—the vision. You must take *personal responsibility for your own vision*, because you know what happens if you are without a vision:

> Where there is no vision, the people are unrestrained,
> But happy is one who keeps the Law.[306]

The usage described in the *Theological Wordbook of the Old Testament* (TWOT) more accurately translates the Hebrew word for given here as "vision" as "revelation from God," referring to His Word. The word *unrestrained* means the people were undisciplined and get out of hand.[307] The vision is critical, as revealed by Habakkuk:

> Then the Lord said to me, "Write my answer plainly on tablets, so that a runner can carry the correct message to others. This vision is for a future time. It describes the end, and it will be fulfilled. If it seems slow in coming, wait patiently, for it will surely take place. It will not be delayed.
> "Look at the proud! They trust in themselves, and their lives are crooked. But the righteous will live by their faithfulness to God."[308]

---

[306] Proverbs 29:18 NASB.
[307] TWOT. Vol. II, usage of vision and unrestrained, 1824, p.737.
[308] Habakkuk 2:2–4 NLT.

The vision of a profound awareness understands what God is doing and believes the plan He has for humanity in the same way that Habakkuk does. God is our shield.[309]

The God Story is a story to plant deep within every aspect of your soul. The God Story is about experiencing soul liberation and living in the unimaginable joy of moment-by-moment supernatural communication with Him. The commonality for all of us is *surrender* and *submission*, which hinge on the most important commandment:

> You shall love the Lord your God with all your heart and with all your soul and with all your strength and with all your mind, and love your neighbor as yourself.[310]

This book began with a somewhat different approach. In any project, there is planning. So this book began at the beginning—not Genesis, but a planning session led by God and His Son as the Builder. We know this because it is biblically suggested in the phrase "before the foundations of the world."[311]

Understanding this has everything to do with your vision of God and your relationship with Him. Your understanding of God's method of planning—with the end in mind—affects your interpretation of His Word and, ultimately, your relationship with Him.[312] Every biblical story, truth, trial, and purpose goes back to a pre-creation planning session. So we began there, with an imagined conversation between God the Designer and Jesus the Builder.

As a reminder, the pre-creation planning meeting was about creating humans in the *imago Dei*, image of God. It was followed by a season of teaching the image-bearing created about their relationship with Him. In these lessons, God taught key precepts of this relationship: believe what God says, trust that He is sovereign, and pursue His goals for your life. He even gave them the choice to accept a relationship with Him and dominion over the earth.

Unfortunately, a rogue angel lured the created away with an alternative choice: independence. The deceiver was successful, but God knew he would

---

309 Genesis 15:1.
310 Luke 10:27.
311 Ephesians 1:4.
312 Revelation 21.

be. This began the battle of drawing the created back unto Himself. God's work is to call us back into a relationship with Him.

From that beginning, God has demonstrated His everlasting love for us. The work of God in you begins with the building of your vision or your worldview that is centered on Him.

We examined vision through the lives of Abraham, Jacob, Joseph, Moses, and King David. Despite their value as *God-serving leaders*, they struggled in their trials. They often failed in the struggle, but from each trial, they learned a greater level of surrender and submission to God, which deepened their relationship with Him. The power of our trials to shape and change us can never be overstated. If understood correctly, trials will create in us a oneness with God. To participate as God's own requires a choice—a choice that makes God the Lord of your life.

Vision development is critical to the soul. The culmination of the soul-work is our character. Vision includes the God Story embedded in the hearts of believers.

In chapters 1-6, we examined a topic of little to no discussion in theological circles or in the local church: the pre-creation planning. This was a moment in time and space that is biblically referred to as "before the foundations of the world." Several biblical accounts reveal that a discussion occurred between God the Designer and Jesus the Builder, planning with the end in mind. Understanding God's design provides an excellent starting point for your vision.

We can only imagine what God may have instructed Jesus to build. I suggested an imagined dialogue between God and Jesus derived from the divine inspiration of biblical revelation. Angels abounded who cried, "Holy, holy, holy!" Eden was beyond our imagination, and a perfect place for a loving relationship between the Creator and the created.

We saw the work of God in the image-bearing created. His created, made in His likeness, were male and female. He established a relational agreement, or covenant, with the created. The foundational basis of society was marriage, and a critical expectation was that the created would work.

The theme and emergence of evil was expected. Lucifer was the guardian cherub and highly anointed by God. The God-vision understands the evil of pride. Its independence and choices are lures.

The Eden tragedy is a heartbreaking story of Adam and Eve's rebellion and disobedience. Perceived discontent was their thoughtful downfall. They were offered an alternative lifestyle not offered by their Creator. They chose the alternative and were summarily dismissed from the garden, dead in their sin and separated from God. The thematic covenant moved forward.

In chapters 7 and 8, we saw the first family of the earth toiling for subsistence. Adam and Eve had two sons, also successful farmers. We saw their deadly sibling rivalry. Adam and Eve taught their grandchildren about God and their great sin against God. The progeny of these great leaders listened and lived by the words of Adam and Eve. On the basis of those stories, they lived as men and women of God. Eventually the stories were told to Noah and on down to Abram, and likewise filled their souls with a desire to be righteous men.

In chapters 9 and 10, we examined Abraham's life and calling by God to establish His family. That family became the chosen people, who were stiff-necked. Their dependence on God was critical to their covenant relationship. Abraham practiced a new leadership approach, one in which he served God alone. This *God-serving leader*, in the trial of his existence, proved his faith in God to the point of sacrificing his only son.

This wasn't only about Abraham, but also about his progeny—Isaac, Jacob, and Joseph—to whom God extended His covenant. These are great stories about the trials God initiated to teach His leaders about the need for trusting His sovereignty. These trials contained critical lessons about honor, truth, submission, family, and possession of a vision aligned to God. Abraham was called to establish the family of God. The mantle of this patriarchal leadership was passed to Isaac, Jacob, and Joseph. This journey set the stage for the Egyptian captivity and the Exodus.

Chapters 11-14 was about the reluctant leader, Moses. Moses was called by God to lead the Israelites. Unfortunately, Moses knew all too well how the Egyptians lived and led. God walked Moses through trials to teach him about their relationship. Each trial grew Moses's soul-vision and faith. The Israelites arrived at the Promised Land. Unfortunately, because of their failure to trust God, they were sent back to the wilderness to die. No one who was older than twenty at the time of the Exodus saw the Promised Land.

God was not to be defeated. He established His people with a set of divine precepts that set them apart from other nations. God taught His people how to worship Him. As a consequence, they grew and were blessed. But Moses and Aaron had erred and would not enter the Promised Land.

151

Led by Joshua, the Israelites' conquest of the Promised Land was successful. Joshua was a good leader. He learned much through the trials experienced by Moses. Joshua made the Israelites promise that they would follow God's ways. With a resounding affirmative, they agreed to follow God.

Yet the Israelites forgot their promise to God and Joshua and returned to their old ways. Their soul-vision was weak. Faith cannot be a knowledge of God; it must be a soul-vision grounded in God. God brought the Israelites back to Him by sending them judges to rescue them from the problems of their unbelief. If we don't develop a relationship with God that permeates our souls and a vision that allows God to work through us, then we are doomed to repeat a shaky faith in God, like the Israelites.

In chapters 15 and 16, the Israelites made the big ask! They wanted to be like other countries, so they asked to have a king. God granted their request. King Saul was the first to be anointed. The soul-vision was waning. The Israelites' dependence fell on a king. King David and his son Solomon followed King Saul. King David and King Solomon both honored and failed God. They were blessed by God and grew Israel into a mighty nation. Sadly, the Israelites forgot about God and depended on their kings. Solomon, while growing Israel, was distracted by his foreign wives. Israel was broken. The kingdom was divided upon Solomon's death.

These two kings were wise and provided critical psalms and proverbs for their readers. They told an important Story of God: of truth, of love, and of broken covenants. From the pre-creation planning session to the end of the intertestamental period, God's plan was to live in a personal and intimate relationship with His created. Every circumstance and trial was designed to build within their hearts and minds a preparation to live out a thriving and flourishing life with Him.

> You shall love the Lord your God with all your heart and
> with all your soul and with all your strength and with all
> your mind, and love your neighbor as yourself.[313]

The recurring theme was the discontent of God's people. The chosen people committed their lives to living and leading as God instructed them, but they forgot quickly, despite the fact that He was their very great reward.

---

[313] Luke 10:27.

Their discontent centered on their desire for something else; they were not content with what God provided to them. This malady had been seen in Adam and Eve and led them down a tragic path. This continued. The Israelites failed to celebrate what God provided.

Next, we will find the culmination of God's design: the trinitarian plan for restoring all believers to a new earth, a new Eden, and a new Jerusalem where God will rule. The new covenant in Christ will allow all believers to enter the Promised Land of eternity with our Creator!

The blood that was shed in Eden to cover the created's shame and guilt is a critical theme found also in the Passover. The blood, for all Christians, is a continuing theme running through the covenants. Today, that theme remains for the people of God in Christ's death on the cross, which we celebrate in the Eucharist and communion.

The challenge is that we still suffer from discontent. Our desire is to be in control of our own lives. Individually, we must learn submission to God's rule in our lives. Lucifer seduced humanity (and still does) into believing that we can find contentment and peace in our own choices. Considering the state of our world today, it is obvious that we are *not* good in our decision-making.

Our prayer of salvation is *not* only about our sins being forgiven, but more importantly about returning to our relationship with God and giving back control of our lives to Him. Our sins are forgiven in order that we can approach God's holiness and return to a wholesome relationship of innocence with God. The critical part is seeking that supernatural relationship with Him in earnest. He has desired an intimate relationship with us from *before the foundations of the world*. We must slow our lives down to be in communion and follow His purpose for our lives.

PART VI

A New Covenant
for Eternity

JESUS RESTORES US TO THE FATHER: WILDERNESS AND SERMON ON THE MOUNT

KING SOLOMON WAS DEAD (CA. 930 BCE). JUDEA WAS BROKEN. THE great kingdom split through political turmoil. There was bitter rivalry between the ten tribes of the northern and the two tribes of the southern kingdoms. The prophets gave warning that this feud dishonored Yahweh and would result in victory for the enemies overwhelming them.

Their enemies knew when their God was not with Israel. The people believed their kings would defeat their enemies. Prior to his death, Solomon left a letter for his people. In this letter, he shared what he had learned about reality. He identified life as being without real value. He described that in living, all pursuits were futile and filled with frustration. However, he had a very dignified picture of a deep soul covenant. Not surprisingly, he ended with this statement, the truth of which remains to this day:

> Now all has been heard; here is the conclusion of the matter: Fear God and keep his commandments, for this is the duty of all mankind. For God will bring every deed into judgment, including every hidden thing, whether it is good or evil.[314]

As I have shared here, deep in our souls must be an unequivocal belief in Scripture, an unwavering trust in God's sovereignty, and a relentless pursuit of God's plan for our lives. Solomon knew what he was talking about regarding the essence of living.

---

[314] Ecclesiastes 12:13–14.

INTERTESTAMENTAL PERIOD

Unfortunately, the people did not listen. For more than two hundred years, Israel was divided. The northern tribes were taken into captivity circa 720 BCE. Jerusalem was destroyed, and its people went into exile or were put under house arrest.

The prophets continued to give warning to the Southern Kingdom, but to no avail. The southern tribes were placed in captivity for seventy years, 605–530 BCE. Jerusalem was sacked. The Temple built by King Solomon was destroyed in 586 BCE. The Israelites returned and rebuilt the Temple under Nehemiah's direction in 445 BCE.

As Israel rebuilt, it found itself without a relationship with Yahweh by the late fifth century BCE. In the next four hundred years, a power struggle took among the Persians, Macedonians, Babylonians, and Egyptians. Alexander the Great brought them all under his dominion by 320 BCE.

Making matters more difficult, the great thinkers of the Hellenistic period, beginning with Socrates, Plato, and Aristotle, influenced the way humanity saw itself. Humanity entered a new era of self-importance. Alexander the Great's son, Alexander IV, never participated in his father's success, and new alliances were formed among the Macedonians, Egyptians, and Persians. Maccabean Israel was in the shadow of the Syrians until the Roman conquest began in approximately 70 BCE. The prophet Daniel wrote about all of that.

The Jews have experienced the favor as well as the displeasure of God. They were called His chosen people and given the task of announcing the coming Messiah to all the world. Unfortunately, they believed the Messiah would come and destroy their oppressors. They missed the point! The Messiah was coming to restore the Jews and all believers to an intimate relationship with the Father, as it was in Eden.[315]

PRE-CREATION PLANNING

I can only imagine the excitement of this stage of the planning. Four hundred years passed before the silence came to an end. The time had come for the Bridegroom, the Messiah, the Son of God to make right what the Trinity

[315] Revelation 21:1–7.

began before the foundations of the world. In that time, mankind had lifted themselves up to great heights—the work of Lucifer, the deceiver. Mankind trusted their own wisdom and leaned on their own understanding. Jesus would be born to a virgin from His people.

The prophets announced the coming of the Messiah. A written revelation informed the people of a new covenant. It was a very dangerous time. God sent word to Mary and Joseph of Jesus's arrival. His earthly parents taught Jesus much, and God gave Jesus great understanding and wisdom. Jesus was called by a righteous and loving teacher (rabbi) who taught the love the Father offered.[316] Jesus studied with him for many years and then went to teach His followers.

Jesus teaches those who love His Father, if they believe. They must understand and believe in the great sacrifice made for their sins, so they might be made holy and blameless in order to be in covenant relationship with their Creator God. The followers will be His bride. Most will be glad to have their sins forgiven and enter into communion with the Trinity. The Messiah made them holy through His death, and He will be in the new covenant relationship with them for eternity.

Living was very different for believers in Jesus's time. They were no longer in a sacrificial system. They were made right with the Father. The Father sent Jesus's cousin to baptize believers. He baptized Christ as well.

The created made the wrong choice in Eden. Jesus is the way, the truth, and the life. Believers will be the bride of Jesus. Jesus met Lucifer in the wilderness. The deceiver had taken the created away from God, but Jesus brought them back home. Lucifer attempted the same deception he used in Eden on Jesus. Jesus gave him the truth.

Jesus will always be in prayer with His Father.

---

[316] This teaching would have occurred in the House of Hillel. It has not been confirmed that Hillel the Elder knew Jesus, but they shared a similar perspective; see https://www.learnreligions.com/hillel-the-elder-4771507. After his encounter with the teachers (Luke 2:41–52), it is possible Jesus spent many years in this school until beginning His ministry.

NEW TESTAMENT (NT) BIBLICAL ACCOUNT (AD 0–26)

The entire God Story is about God communing with his created. In the OT, God chose His people to announce the coming of the Messiah. He focused on developing a soul-vision through trials that shape our humility and understanding of the God-reality in which we live as kingdom people. The vision included principles and precepts that enable humanity to thrive and flourish, creating for the image bearers a wholeness to live by. Trials would be the divine, lived experience that would shape the believers. The covenants would guide their relationship.

In addition, God used His prophets to announce the coming of the Messiah. He established the great nation of Israel. Unfortunately, His chosen people failed in keeping the covenants. They believed the coming Messiah would conquer their enemies and they would be the ruling people.

In the New Testament (NT), the new covenant was revealed as a vision of adjustment and fulfillment. The Messiah was not coming to fight an earthly war. The Messiah arrived to fulfill the ancient covenants. Then He established a covenant for intimate and personal relationship with God. Jesus taught that He is the perfect Lamb of sacrifice, once and for all. Through Him, believers could commune with His Father directly. This relationship is for every person who believes the God Story.

Jesus taught the disciples, but they would struggle to understand His teaching. We'll continue to discuss the themes that carry over from the OT to the NT, as well as examine the new themes of the new covenant.

God broke His silence with a favored priest, Zechariah, in the Holy of Holies. God informed Zechariah that he would have a son, who would be called John. John would announce a time for preparation, rebirth, and baptism for the coming of the Savior.[317] A short time later, Gabriel appeared to a young girl named Mary. She was told that she was blessed among women.[318]

Jesus was born in Bethlehem. Herod the Great was out to get the One who had been prophesied to become the King of the Jews. God protected Jesus and His parents, and they fled to Egypt.

---

[317] Luke 1:5–25.
[318] Luke 1:26–38.

They returned to Nazareth after Herod died. Jesus grew up, attended His Torah classes, and learned a trade from His earthly father. Around the age of thirteen or fourteen, He was one of a few called by a rabbi to attend a school of greater theological study. This has much to do with why we do not hear or see anything from Jesus following His visit at age twelve to the Temple in Jerusalem, where rabbis marveled at His gift.[319]

The next level of deep study involved being called by a learned rabbi and living with the rabbi's family, as well as working for them to pay His way. Jesus's skill as a carpenter was likely His means to pay for this education.

JOHN THE BAPTIST

Many years later, everything changed when the itinerant evangelist John, referred to as John the Baptist, encouraged preparation through baptism. He announced the coming of the Jews' Savior.[320] The vision now included a Messiah, the One sent by God to save the world. Jesus referred to John in great terms: "[T]here has not risen anyone greater than John the Baptist."[321]

In the Gospels (Matthew, Mark, Luke, John), we find the birth of Jesus, the work of John the Baptist, and Jesus's ministry, which fulfilled the prophecy of the OT. We learn from Luke that the angel Gabriel said this about the birth of John:

> He will be a joy and delight to you, and many will rejoice because of his birth, for he will be great in the sight of the Lord. He is never to take wine or other fermented drink, and he will be filled with the Holy Spirit even before he is born. He will bring back many of the people of Israel to the Lord their God. And he will go on before the Lord, in the spirit and power of Elijah, to turn the hearts of the parents to their children and the disobedient to the wisdom of the righteous—to make ready a people prepared for the Lord.[322]

---

[319] Luke 2:41–52.
[320] Lawrence O. Richards, *Every Man in the Bible* (Thomas Nelson Publishers, 1999), 193.
[321] Matthew 11:11.
[322] Luke 1:14–17.

The work of Jesus began with the preaching of a Spirit-filled John, who was compared to Elijah, on the shores of the Jordan River. It was an incredible scene as Jesus presented Himself to John for baptism:

> Then Jesus came from Galilee to the Jordan to be baptized by John. But John tried to deter him, saying, "I need to be baptized by you, and do you come to me?"
>
> Jesus replied, "Let it be so now; it is proper for us to do this to fulfill all righteousness."

Then John consented.

> As soon as Jesus was baptized, he went up out of the water. At that moment heaven was opened, and he saw the Spirit of God descending like a dove and alighting on him. And a voice from heaven said, "This is my Son, whom I love; with him I am well pleased."[323]

The next verse indicates that the Spirit led Jesus into the wilderness. Be clear: the Spirit of God led Jesus into the wilderness to starve for forty days. The only thing made available to Him was water. In Luke's account, Jesus was tested during this time and given trials like the OT patriarchs.

WILDERNESS

This miraculous moment in all of time and space was interrupted by a trial that *only* Jesus could withstand. The Spirit landed on Him like a dove and escorted Him into the wilderness. Lucifer, Satan, devil, the deceiver—whatever he is called by you—was waiting. On the fortieth day, when Jesus was weakest, Lucifer appeared. Three temptations occurred:

> Then Jesus was led by the Spirit into the wilderness to be tempted by the devil. After fasting forty days and forty nights, he was hungry. The tempter came to him and said,

---

[323] Matthew 3:17.

"If you are the Son of God, tell these stones to become bread."

Jesus answered, "It is written: Man shall not live on bread alone, but on every word that comes from the mouth of God."

Then the devil took him to the holy city and had him stand on the highest point of the temple. "If you are the Son of God," he said, "throw yourself down. For it is written: 'He will command his angels concerning you, and they will lift you up in their hands, so that you will not strike your foot against a stone.'"

Jesus answered him, "It is also written: 'Do not put the Lord your God to the test.'"

Again, the devil took him to a very high mountain and showed him all the kingdoms of the world and their splendor.

"All this I will give you," he said, "if you will bow down and worship me."

Jesus said to him, "Away from me, Satan! For it is written: 'Worship the Lord your God, and serve him only.' Then the devil left him, and angels came and attended him."[324]

Jesus used God's Word to respond to Satan three times:

1. Satan attempted to diminish the Word of God. However, Jesus reminded Satan, using Scripture, that for man to live, the Word of God is more important than food.
2. Satan attempted to leverage Jesus to force God's hand in saving Him. However, Jesus again used Scripture to make it clear that we are not to trifle with the sovereignty of God. If Jesus needed saving, God would send an army. Jesus knew Satan's request was designed to minimize God's sovereignty.
3. Satan showed Jesus the world and offered Him power and control over His destiny. Once again, Jesus used His relationship with the

---

[324] Matthew 4:1–11.

Father to make it clear to Satan that His Father came first. Jesus's goal in life was to pursue *only* the Father's plan for His life. Jesus commanded this relentless fallen angel out of His presence. He was then served by the angels.

Do the temptations in this wilderness event look familiar? This was the same strategy used by Lucifer in the garden with Adam and Eve: get them to doubt the Word of God, get them to doubt the sovereignty of God, and place discontent in their hearts for something better than what God had given them. Lucifer persuaded Adam and Eve to believe they were independent of God and had control over their destiny.

No doubt Jesus saw Lucifer in the garden, leading Adam and Eve into sin. This remains Satan's strategy to this day: to create doubt about the Word of God, to undermine belief that God is who He has said He is, and to deceive with lies about autonomy through freedom of choice.

A NEW COVENANT VISION

In the same way that Moses revealed a vision of a chosen people in relationship with God through the Law and worship, Jesus demonstrated a soul-vision for victory over Satan's way of deception. We can walk through the wilderness with power to defeat the deceiver. We can have victory through a faith that is anchored in belief in His Word, trust in His sovereignty, and pursuit of His will for our lives.

Jesus called His disciples. Understanding the steps to defeat Satan means understanding the steps to spiritual formation. Do not miss what is happening here. Jesus was a teacher who was second to none. First, Jesus was baptized and filled with the Holy Spirit as a seal. Second, Jesus maintained His commitment of faith. The Sermon on the Mount, often referred to as the Beatitudes, was His first teaching:

> Blessed are the poor in spirit, for theirs is the kingdom of heaven.
> Blessed are those who mourn, for they will be comforted.
> Blessed are the meek, for they will inherit the earth.
> Blessed are those who hunger and thirst for righteousness, for they will be filled.

Blessed are the merciful, for they will be shown mercy.

Blessed are the pure in heart, for they will see God.

Blessed are the peacemakers, for they will be called children
of God.[325]

Each statement of blessedness is a step in one's spiritual transformation and not necessarily individual groups. Jesus destroyed Satan's attacks on Him. Then He taught His followers the process for growing in a transformed soul.

As His first teaching following the wilderness event, the Beatitudes are vitally important in the whole of God's Word. While it isn't widely discussed, I take the position here, as I did in my first book, that the statement made by Jesus lays out a progressive sequence for us to attend to in our faith-walk. Our soul-vision will change as we are led by the Spirit.

A prayer of salvation is the first step. The prayer of salvation means you repent and are turning away from your old life and independent choices. In the garden, we used our choice to follow a life guided by independent thinking and our own selfish, fleshly desires. In the prayer of salvation, we ask for forgiveness for turning away from God and for a life of unrighteousness. This prayer reestablishes your choice to have God as the Lord of your life, to seek forgiveness of your sins, and to depend on Him in your one-on-one covenantal relationship.

The challenge we all face when we are reborn to new life in Christ is tumultuous and exhilarating. The transition from one's habitual and self-operated hubris to a self that is guided by the Holy Spirit requires spiritual mentorship. There is a difference, spiritually and humanly. A self-guided person believes in their own subjective reality. The Spirit-guided person sees truth and reality as a product of God. To experience unswerving spiritual growth, a believer's relationship with a confidant is essential. Those who experience a dynamic and authentic transformation do so under the guidance of a God-serving leader. Progressive spiritual growth is proportional to your submission and surrender to God's will.

---

[325] Matthew 5:3–9.

165

BLESSED ARE THE POOR IN SPIRIT

The poor in spirit have arrived at the rock-bottom of life. They understand that they are in a very powerless state and separated from God. Such a person attempts to make sense of the world through a human-contrived reality. They can be deceived by the wise, but something is tugging on their heart, indicating that their soul is adrift and not buying the world's truth. The mystery that God reveals to the poor in spirit is pure, wholesome, and right.

You were born with a nature of selfishness. You have lived your life making your own choices, but your heart is broken. Now God is calling you to turn away from your self-determined independence and to allow Him to become the Lord of your life. The Holy Spirit is revealing two very different realities to you. One is a reality created by secular humanism; the other is a spiritual truth given by God.

I clearly recall how fearful it was to release control of my life through a prayer of confession to the unknown. My understanding of these two realities and this decision was very real. God gave us a choice to live in an eternity of love, joy, and peace, or in an eternity of torment. In my garage, I decided to trust God because the world and its ways were untrustworthy.

> My sacrifice, O God, is a broken spirit; a broken and contrite heart you, God, will not despise.[326]

This is the turning point: to recognize that you have no *real* control over your life. God is in control and pursuing you. Allow your broken and contrite heart to be restored to your Creator. Ask God for the vision He wants you to live in your faith-journey. The best part is that you will experience within your soul a supernatural and indescribable liberation.

The church family is responsible for assisting you in your growth. Pastors and fellow believers should be checking in on your progress and encouraging you. Get involved in a small group or find a believer who you discern has a heart after God.

There is a caution here: don't count on your brothers and sisters to be perfect. Even though they might be spiritually mature, they are going to

---

[326] Psalm 51:17.

make mistakes. Stay focused on the Holy Spirit. The journey is anchored in the God-man relationship.

BLESSED ARE THOSE WHO MOURN

The mourners are those who choose to turn away from their autonomy (independence) and turn their hearts back to God (dependence). This is pivotal. After your prayer of confession and belief that Jesus died for your sin of rebellion, there is something discomfiting and frightening about leaving your old self to become dependent on a God you know very little about. There is second-guessing of your decision. Stay vigilant! Shake those doubts and ask God for His intervention in growing you in the fruit of the Spirit. You will miss the old life and come up with a thousand reasons why you should return to it. Ask God for encouragement. Persevering through the trials will lead to a supernatural comfort.

Lot, Abraham's brother, was married to a woman who was deeply attached to her old life. Two men—angels, in fact—came to help the family leave Sodom and Gomorrah before it was destroyed by God:

> When he hesitated, the men grasped his hand and the hands of his wife and of his two daughters and led them safely out of the city, for the Lord was merciful to them. As soon as they had brought them out, one of them said, "Flee for your lives! Don't look back, and don't stop anywhere in the plain! Flee to the mountains or you will be swept away!"[327]
>
> But Lot's wife looked back, and she became a pillar of salt.[328]

Lot's wife couldn't help but look back to see what was happening to her old life. Leave the past in the past. Your old life can make you mourn what you loved in your flesh. King David said this about our old lives:

> The Lord is compassionate and merciful, slow to get angry and filled with unfailing love.

---

[327] Genesis 19:16–17.
[328] Genesis 19:26.

He will not constantly accuse us, nor remain angry forever. He does not punish us for all our sins; he does not deal harshly with us, as we deserve. For his unfailing love toward those who fear him is as great as the height of the heavens above the earth. He has removed our sins as far from us as the east is from the west.[329]

When you study your behaviors and recognize a consistent pattern to please the self, you'll realize that you must detach from that old self and pursue right living in God.

The apostle Paul speaks clearly about this challenge from our fleshly nature (*sarx*: desires for material and sexual objects). The self seeks after what it desires.[330]

Those who live according to the flesh have their minds set on what the flesh desires; but those who live in accordance with the Spirit have their minds set on what the Spirit desires. The mind governed by the flesh is death, but the mind governed by the Spirit is life and peace. The mind governed by the flesh is hostile to God; it does not submit to God's law, nor can it do so. Those who are in the realm of the flesh cannot please God.[331]

Paul knew you would discover that self-concern and self-reliance have been the drivers of your life, and independence your enemy.[332] Dependence on God is frightening but has a mystery of freedom with it.

Mourning is the most critical time in your growth. Count on your church family to help you through your addiction to the world. You are vulnerable! *The greatest weapons are prayer and study.* Be real with God, yourself, and your accountability partner.

---

[329] Psalm 103:8–12 NLT

[330] *Theological Dictionary of the New Testament, sarx*... flesh becomes bad when one builds on it. Vol. 7, pg. 135. 1968. Strong's G4561, the sensuous nature of man, "the animal nature."

[331] Romans 8:5-8 NIV.

[332] D. Martin Lloyd-Jones, *Sermon on the Mount* (Eerdmans Publishing, 1971), 74.

I believe the church loses more believers during this stage of spiritual growth than any other. Even though you may feel good about your journey, beware of your feelings. By now you should be accountable to a trusted brother or sister (girls with girls, boys with boys).

BLESSED ARE THE MEEK

The meek begin to realize there is a change taking place in their souls from the inside out. Meekness is an undeterred humility filled with reverence for God. Humbleness results as you realize the work of the Spirit is authentic, but you can't explain the supernatural transformation. Meekness is *not* natural to us.[333] Our selfish goal is to be noticed or take the lead or be promoted. The meek are no longer interested in being noticed; they just work every day as if Jesus is the Boss. They stay out of God's way.

> That is why, for Christ's sake, I delight in weaknesses, in insults, in hardships, in persecutions, in difficulties. For when I am weak, then I am strong.[334]

Developing meekness and humility reveals the intervention of the Holy Spirit. Humility involves a vision that is moving away from personal distractions and focusing on the things of God. Best of all, no longer do the pangs of mourning interfere with your thoughts. Those around you notice the peace within you because you are letting God be God. You no longer need to have your own way. So you begin to serve others without concern for recognition. You just want to honor Jesus. You'll discover a new, supernatural vigor for God's call.

BLESSED ARE THOSE WHO HUNGER
AND THIRST FOR RIGHTEOUSNESS

As you continue to recognize that God is changing you from the inside out, you come to value righteous living. Righteous behavior means living out

---

[333] Lloyd-Jones, *Sermon on the Mount*, 67.
[334] 2 Corinthians 12:10.

your faith-journey through the Word of God. In your growth, you discover within yourself the pull to seek happiness. You've been happy, but it's been fleeting. Being blessed is more appealing than happiness because it carries joy with it. Those who hunger and thirst recognize the wisdom of God's precepts and engage in deeper understanding of God's Word. They employ behaviors that honor Him: "[F]or he satisfies the thirsty and fills the hungry with good things."[335]

The *Theological Dictionary of the New Testament* (TDNT) passionately reflects about hunger and thirst:

> The hungry are men who both outwardly and inwardly are painfully deficient in the things essential to life as God meant it to be, and who, since they cannot help themselves, turn to God on the basis of His promise. The men, as these alone, find God's help in Jesus ... in basic unity with the promise of the Psalm ... The hungry who are blessed are not beggars. They are believers who seek help from Jesus because of their own helplessness.[336]

When you read the Bible, no longer are you thinking, "This would be good for my friend." Your concern is for the plank in your eye, and God is speaking to you.

BLESSED ARE THE MERCIFUL

The merciful have a new perspective about other people. The merciful see others like Christ does: in their lostness. What the merciful can see is heartbreaking for them. God's Word reveals a depth of understanding of what has happened to humanity. We cry out to the lost regarding their eternal consequence.

Be merciful, just as your Father is merciful.[337]

---

[335] Psalm 107:9.
[336] *Theological Dictionary of the New Testament*, 1968, Vol. 6, pg. 18.
[337] Luke 6:36.

> Speak and act as those who are going to be judged by the law that gives freedom, because judgment without mercy will be shown to anyone who has not been merciful. Mercy triumphs over judgment.[338]

Grace is shown to men in their sins, but mercy is applied to humanity in the misery of their existential dread. Mercy is pity coupled with a desire to relieve suffering.[339] Mercy comes from within the soul. It isn't an attitude developed, but a disposition from the inmost part, the heart. You may experience a strong emotional reaction when considering the lost, especially the lost from your own family, as you witness their rebellious nature leading them toward the abyss. The lost are headed to eternal torment, having not responded to the pursuit of God.

BLESSED ARE THE PURE IN HEART

The pure in heart have matured to a point where their singular life-focus is the work of God. They can easily discern the plight of the lost but can also see the joy of abundant life. The pure in heart know that the only job of the believer is calling on the lost.

King David knew the pain of an unclean heart best. He cried out to God to change it:

> Create in me a pure heart, O God, and renew a steadfast spirit within me.[340]

A pure heart "consists in full and unreserved self-offering to God which renews the heart and rules out any acceptance of what is against God. Those who are pure in heart in this way are called to participate in the kingdom of God."[341] Said another way, the pure in heart are singularly focused on the purposes of God. Yes, you can have a secular job; however, your work is in support of your ministry, not the reverse.

---

[338] James 2:12–13.

[339] Lloyd-Jones, *Sermon on the Mount*, 99.

[340] Psalm 51:10.

[341] TDNT. Vol. 3, pg. 425.

BLESSED ARE THE PEACEMAKERS

The peacemakers are God's own. They live within the fruit of the Spirit. Peace, love, and joy fill the soul of the peacemaker. They recognize humanity's existential dread and understand the damage it does to humankind. The peacemaker is not the outgoing, charismatic leader whom the world loves to see. But their God-serving leadership is seen by others.

> Take my yoke upon you and learn from me, for I am gentle and humble in heart, and you will find rest for your souls.[342]

The only other time the word *peacemaker* is used in the NT is by James:

> Peacemakers who sow in peace reap a harvest of righteousness.[343]

James recognized the power of making peace.

D. Martin Lloyd-Jones asks, "Why are peacemakers blessed? ... [B]ecause they are so absolutely unlike everybody else. The peacemakers are blessed because they are the people who stand out as being different from the rest of the world."[344] I can challenge you in this: if you sow peace in your workplace, it will change your workplace. Lloyd-Jones hits the nail on the head when he states that peacemakers are "absolutely unlike everybody else." This results from the full measure of the peacemaker possessing the fruit of the Spirit. They see the world from God's perspective—a world with the kingdom of God well-planted.

BLESSED ARE THE PERSECUTED

The last couple of beatitudes speak specifically to the persecuted. It isn't a transformational step; it is about what to expect as a result of your transformation. The greater you grow in your relationship with God, the more persecution you can expect to experience.

---

[342] Matthew 11:28–30.
[343] James 3:18.
[344] Lloyd-Jones, *Sermon on the Mount*, 119.

The characteristics of the deepening soul-vision are reflected through the heart. According to Lloyd-Jones, all Christians should manifest these characteristics, none of which come naturally to secular humanity.[345]

> Blessed are those who are persecuted because of righteousness, for theirs is the kingdom of heaven. Blessed are you when people insult you, persecute you and falsely say all kinds of evil against you because of me. Rejoice and be glad, because great is your reward in heaven, for in the same way they persecuted the prophets who were before you.[346]

In the final two words of blessedness, we leave the logical sequence of the previous seven. Here we have Jesus stating that taking back your soul is going to result in pain and suffering. You will be persecuted for your right living. Nonbelievers will throw insults at you and say all sorts of bad things about you. It is the same thing that happened to the prophets, but you will be rewarded in heaven.

Most important here and throughout the NT is the source. These scoffers and evildoers are attacking the Jesus inside you, so don't buckle at the knees. You will be compared to prophets! Know that your reward is eternity in heaven with Him.

DEVELOPING A PROFOUND AWARENESS

You may need to read this chapter again. The new covenant is the fulfillment of the previous covenants. Interestingly, like a good teacher, Jesus provided examples of how the mature believer interacts with the world around them with a reborn perspective. A people *must* possess a wholesome attitude to thrive and flourish as a society! There are no shortcuts or selfish choices.

---

[345] Lloyd-Jones, *Sermon on the Mount*, 33–35.
[346] Matthew 5:10–12.

Your soul should now make sense of what these examples mean:

- "the salt of the earth" means your soul should shine for Jesus, always![347]
- the Ten Commandments are still the basis of society[348]
- issues should be resolved quickly; do not allow issues to fester with your adversary[349]
- your eyes reveal your heart—get control of your lust[350]
- divorce only in cases of infidelity, and always try to work it out first—God hates divorce[351]
- love your enemies and pray for them[352]
- be humble in giving to the needy[353]
- protect the sacredness of prayer—pray with adoration, confession, thanksgiving, and seeking (ACTS)[354]
- fasting is sacred; do so in humble privacy[355]
- your rewards are in heaven; be humble[356]
- do not worry; trust in God's sovereignty[357]
- be discerning, but do not judge others—you have no idea where God has them[358]
- knock on the door and seek from Him[359]
- the way of secular man is wide and headed to destruction—be very clear about this journey and its difficulty[360]

---

[347] Matthew 5:13–16.
[348] Matthew 5:17–20.
[349] Matthew 5:21–26.
[350] Matthew 5:27–30.
[351] Matthew 5:31–32.
[352] Matthew 5:43–48.
[353] Matthew 6:1–4.
[354] Matthew 6:5–15.
[355] Matthew 6:16–18.
[356] Matthew 6:19–24.
[357] Matthew 6:25–34.
[358] Matthew 7:1–6.
[359] Matthew 7:7–12.
[360] Matthew 7:13–14.

- recognize true prophets by their good fruit—you will be able to discern[361]
- some church leaders will disappoint you—do not gossip or get even, because God will deal with them[362]

I want to discuss this last example. I purposely left it for last. Your newly acquired soul-vision makes an authentic difference in your life. All the examples we just discussed culminate in your new soul-vision. You know that you know that there is a supernatural work going on within you, creating a new way of viewing the world around you. This vision is driven by the Holy Spirit, who gives comfort and counsel.

This is how God intended that we live our lives: thriving and flourishing with each other and depending on Him. This is our firm foundation! Living our lives according to these precepts and principles will allow us to withstand any storm. We are responsible to the Holy Spirit to submit to these truths in our souls. This is the solid footing that we are to live on as wise builders of our soul-vision. This is the conclusion to His sermon.

Let's be clear! It is vitally important that we understand what is happening as we turn our hearts to home with God. We were created for relationship with Him. That's why we are in His image and likeness, *imago Dei*. The created were given a choice. *If* we desire relationship with our Creator, *then* we must choose to willingly stay away from the fruit of the tree of the knowledge of good and evil. Failure to keep this covenant will result in death.

Humanity will seek knowledge to answer all its questions in its lived experiences. They failed in the garden and opted to choose independence from God. Their discontent, disobedience, and rebellion resulted in death—spiritual separation from God.

When we pray a prayer of confession, we are using our gift of choice to:

- turn away from the choice made in the garden and ask God for the forgiveness of our sins that have resulted from our rebellion

[361] Matthew 7:15–20.
[362] Matthew 7:21–23.

- ask God to be the Lord of our lives, meaning that we return to dependence on Him
- ask for a personal and intimate relationship with Him

To do this, you will:

- believe the Word of God
- trust the sovereignty of God in your life
- pursue God's will for your life

God is serious about your choice! No matter what you see in other people, the church, or the world, lean into Him! Trust in Him to lead you in growing your vision. This choice has eternal consequences.

18

THE NEW COVENANT MINISTRY: THE CRUCIAL THEMES

THE OT PROPHETS MADE IT CLEAR THAT A MESSIAH WAS COMING. IT WAS the prayer of the people. Most of the rabbis believed that a messiah was coming to relieve them of their oppression. We know they understood His coming this way because it was a specific request in their prayer lives: "How long O Lord, shall I call for help?"[363]

Unfortunately, a significant part of the religious leadership didn't see it anymore. They did not announce to all mankind that the Messiah would restore them to relationship with God. Only the chosen would be privy to the Savior's victories. They thought they were wise in their own eyes. The Jewish leadership was sure that the Savior would defeat their oppressors on earth, and they would rule.

Jesus established from the very beginning of His ministry that the process of spiritual formation culminated in go and teach. He was baptized and received the Holy Spirit. He was challenged in the wilderness to overcome the taunts of evil, lead the disciples, become the blood sacrifice to remove sin of rebellion, and return humanity to an authentic relationship with our Creator God.

PRE-CREATION PLANNING

I can only imagine what discussions prevailed as the Trinity prepared for the ministry of Jesus. The disciples were given all the qualities that Jesus needed in His work. They were all taught to memorize the Torah. They saw Jesus as the One they awaited.

---

[363] Habakkuk 1:2 NLT.

Yet His disciples struggled to understand their purpose. Once they understood who Jesus was, they wanted miracles to deal with their oppressors. In their lack of understanding, the work was difficult—but they grew. At times they tested Jesus's patience. They retreated when their lives were at stake—for a while. But Jesus helped their understanding. Believers struggle until the Holy Spirit comes upon them. The disciples became stronger as time went on.

From Jesus's role in the pre-creation planning session to His involvement in the creative process to His overcoming Lucifer in the wilderness. the Father was well pleased in His Son.

NT BIBLICAL ACCOUNT

Each disciple was called by Jesus to follow Him. It was not an uncommon experience to be called by a rabbi to follow him for more training. Two issues are surprising here. First, these young men had already passed the usual recruitment age following their compulsory Hebrew schooling. If a young man was passed over, then he was destined for a trade, farming, fishing, or some other profession. Second, they were already established in these alternative professions. They had not shown themselves to be stellar students of the Torah. But Jesus wasn't calling a bunch of misfits—each of them possessed an incredible work ethic. This was what Jesus required: people who would work at becoming His followers.

The NT describes numerous miracles done by Jesus. The disciples' faith journeys had highs and lows. Jesus turned water into wine, healed a man with leprosy, healed a Roman soldier's son, cast out demons, healed a paralyzed man, raised an allegedly dead girl, healed a blind man, enabled a mute to talk, fed thousands, and on and on it goes. Of particular note was an experience the disciples had with their rabbi.

Matthew shared the story. Jesus sent the disciples to the other side of the Sea of Galilee and told them He would meet them there. The disciples crossed the sea by boat. As they crossed, a wild storm developed, with lightning, thunder, and rain. The waves grew larger and larger. Fear broke out. The disciples argued about what to do.

Then they saw a figure walking across the water. After a few moments, they realized it was Jesus. Peter, the brash disciple, asked Jesus to prove who

He was and allow Peter to walk on water too. Jesus affirmed His identity and said, "Come." Peter was successful for the first few steps but began to sink as fear took over. Jesus reached out and caught him. "You of little faith," Jesus said, "why did you doubt?"[364]

Several questions come to mind here. First, Peter and the other disciples had just witnessed Jesus feeding the five thousand. What an incredible event! Second, they had already experienced a storm on the sea during which they panicked. Jesus on that occasion was in the boat and asleep, and they awakened him. Jesus calmed the waves and asked them, "Why are you so afraid? Do you still have no faith?"[365]

The disciples had witnessed miracle after miracle, but, when they were under stress, they buckled at the knees. Some of the disciples were seasoned fishermen. Yet the peril of losing their lives weakened their resolve.

Let's recall what Jesus asked them:

"But what about you?" he asked. "Who do you say I am?"
Peter answered, "God's Messiah."[366]

They had witnessed all of the miracles, experienced churning seas with Him, and acknowledged that He was the Son of God. They had walked with, talked with, and been taught by Him! Clearly, their faith-journey required something more than just a soul-vision. They believed Jesus, understood His sovereignty, and were walking out the plan with Him. Something was happening in the episode of the walk on water. Loving and committed friends of Jesus stumbled in their faith. Jesus did not chastise them; He gave them grace. They used His grace as their personal conviction to keep trying.

One thing has become evident to me as I have considered the struggles in my own faith-journey. There have been times when I have lapsed in my walk with God—actually, too many. Those lapses were very embarrassing or downright disobedient. I know what King David meant when he said:

---

[364] Matthew 14:22–31.
[365] Mark 4:35–41.
[366] Luke 9:20.

> Against you, you only, have I sinned and done what is evil
> in your sight; so you are right in your verdict and justified
> when you judge.[367]

This wouldn't be the last time when fear struck at the hearts of the disciples. We don't see a great deal written about their spiritual growth during Jesus's time of ministry, which is as it should be. The focus of the ministry was on Jesus and preparing His bride, the church. Jesus was seeking the attention of Jews and Gentiles, urging them to repent from their ways and be forgiven for their sin-stained rebellion. The healings gain their attention to His power and authority. The sermons and the parables were meant to teach what the heart of God looks like in His kingdom.

However, there are a few examples of the growth of disciples.

JOHN

John, the brother of James and son of Zebedee, was considered the beloved of Jesus. The trials in his faith-journey built up the disciple Jesus loved. One event found John in anger over the way in which he, Jesus, and the disciples were being treated by the Samaritans. He requested the authority of Jesus to rain down fire on these godless people.[368] On another occasion, John wanted to raise an issue with someone else—not a disciple—casting out demons. John was aggravated when Jesus told him to leave it alone because the man was not against them.[369] In addition, in a self-serving mood, John asked Jesus if he and James could sit on His right and left hand in His kingdom. The other disciples were incensed. This resulted in a rebuke and teaching from Jesus.

> Not so with you. Instead, whoever wants to become great
> among you must be your servant, and whoever wants to be
> first must be slave of all.[370]

---

[367] Psalm 51:4.
[368] Luke 9:51–56.
[369] Mark 9:38–41.
[370] Mark 10:43–44.

Despite these obvious issues, John went on to write the gospel of John and three short epistles. He also received the vision from God described in the book of Revelation.[371]

THOMAS

Thomas's life was filled with doubt. He was always in need of proof. It took Jesus offering His hands to Thomas, to feel the scars left by the crucifying nails, before Thomas believed Jesus had been resurrected.[372]

PETER

No one misses the cowboy of the group, brash and forthright. Peter walked on the water, but Peter, under stress, also denied knowledge of Jesus. His denial came just hours after he vowed to go to prison or death with Him. Yet, in the same breath, we know that Peter became a powerful preacher and leader after Pentecost.

The trials went on and on. Following the Last Supper communion, the disciples argued among themselves about who was the greatest.[373] Such trials and rivalries reveal the struggle in your spiritual transformation being a faith-journey to grow your soul-vision. Luke recorded an incredible conversation between Jesus and an expert in the Law.

The expert asked, "What must I do to inherit eternal life?"

Jesus asked, "What is written in the Law?"

The expert responded, "'Love the Lord your God with all your heart and with all your soul and with all your strength and with all your mind'; and, 'Love your neighbor as yourself.'"

Jesus responded, "You have answered correctly. Do this and you will live forever."[374]

---

[371] Lawrence O. Richards, *Every Man in the Bible* (Thomas Nelson Publishers, 1999), 186–188.

[372] Richards, *Every Man in the Bible*, 190–191.

[373] Luke 22:24.

[374] Luke 10:25–28.

Wow! "Do this and you will live forever"! The words are profound. The experience of eternal life is for those whose hearts are surrendered and humbled before God.

The theme most prevalent in all of Jesus's teaching is the love of the Father. It is surprising that the disciples missed the everlasting love of God and were more focused on miracles, supernatural healings, and their status in heaven. We will not go into all the events of the arrest, judgment, Crucifixion, and Resurrection here. However, we will discuss some poignant issues and the fifty days of waiting for the arrival of the Holy Spirit.

HIS MINISTRY

Over Jesus's three years with the disciples, His ministry was filled with teaching them about how to bring the kingdom of God to earth. Jesus taught all who would listen through preaching sermons and parables, healing the sick and lame, casting out demons, and performing other miracles, all of which established His authority. The Gospels contain well-documented stories of His work. Most are in agreement and confirm their truth. Here are just a few of the substories that lead to the truth of Jesus as the Son of God and also reveal that He is the authentic Servant of His people:

- Jesus heals a man with leprosy[375]
- Jesus heals the centurion's servant[376]
- Jesus casts out demons[377]
- Jesus teaches the Twelve before sending them out[378]
- Jesus teaches the parable of the pearl[379]
- Jesus teaches disciples about faith and walks on water[380]
- Jesus teaches the Pharisees and Sadducees[381]

---

[375] Matthew 8:1–4.
[376] Matthew 8:5–13.
[377] Matthew 8:28–34.
[378] Matthew 10.
[379] Matthew 13:44–46.
[380] Matthew 14:22–36.
[381] Matthew 16:1–4.

- Jesus teaches the disciples who He is[382]
- Jesus teaches about the importance of every person[383]
- Jesus teaches the way[384]
- Jesus heals a possessed boy who is deaf-mute[385]
- Jesus teaches about dependence on material well-being[386]
- Jesus teaches about someone forgiven who does not forgive[387]
- Jesus teaches love for enemies[388]
- Jesus heals the widow's son[389]
- Jesus teaches the disciples about faith, calming the storm[390]
- Jesus feeds the five thousand[391]
- Jesus teaches the Pharisees about who He is[392]

My personal favorite is the story of Jesus raising Lazarus from the dead.[393] This was the most critical miracle because it set the stage for His Crucifixion. The grave location was a short distance from Jerusalem. At this point, a miracle resurrection happened. We can only imagine the reaction when the news reached the city.

ARREST AND CONVICTION

Jesus's arrest took place just hours after His final supper with the disciples. Jesus led the disciples to the garden of Gethsemane. There He asked eight disciples to remain and wait, while He took Peter, John, and James farther on with Him. Jesus became sorrowful and troubled:

---

[382] Matthew 16:13–20.
[383] Matthew 18:10–14.
[384] Mark 8:34–38.
[385] Mark 9:14–29.
[386] Mark 10:17–31.
[387] Matthew 18:21–35.
[388] Luke 6:27–36.
[389] Luke 7:11–17.
[390] Luke 8:22–25.
[391] Luke 9:10–17.
[392] John 10:1–21.
[393] John 11:1–43.

> Then he said to them, "My soul is overwhelmed with sorrow to the point of death. Stay here and keep watch with me."[394]

What has been translated as "overwhelmed with sorrow" might better be said as "deeply grieved" to the point of death. I have no ability to understand how heavy this time was for Jesus. He and the Father had set the stage for this to come. Jesus had known this was coming before the foundations of the world. Now the hour had come upon Him. He had lived as a human being on this planet, preparing for thirty-three years for these days. His grief was clear:

> Going a little farther, he fell with his face to the ground and prayed, "My Father, if it is possible, may this cup be taken from me. Yet not as I will, but as you will."[395]

He could no longer walk and fell prostate on the ground. He asked the Father to take this responsibility from Him. He was profoundly aware of the agony and pain He would bear. He knew that bearing the sin of rebellion and the world's disobedience meant carrying a heavy weight.

I confess, I imagine this moment often. Who did Jesus consider He was going to endure such pain and agony for? I can only imagine that He asked His Father, "Do you mean that I have to die for that womanizing, pleasure-seeking, pot-smoking Eric Palmu?"

I hope the Father's response was along the lines of "I love him too."

Jesus accepted the Father's will for His life. We must all keep this in mind: what Jesus was about to experience was with you and I on His heart. His soul was ready. The pain that awaited Him would be excruciating. Approximately 750 years before Christ, the great Jewish prophet, Isaiah, foretold the Crucifixion:

> He was despised and rejected by mankind, a man of suffering, and familiar with pain. Like one from whom people hide their faces he was despised, and we held him in low esteem. Surely he took up our pain and bore our suffering, yet we

---

[394] Matthew 26:38.
[395] Matthew 26:39.

considered him punished by God, stricken by him, and afflicted. But he was pierced for our transgressions, he was crushed for our iniquities; the punishment that brought us peace was on him, and by his wounds we are healed. We all, like sheep, have gone astray, each of us has turned to our own way; and the Lord has laid on him the iniquity of us all. He was oppressed and afflicted, yet he did not open his mouth; he was led like a lamb to the slaughter, and as a sheep before its shearers is silent, so he did not open his mouth. By oppression and judgment he was taken away. Yet who of his generation protested? For he was cut off from the land for the transgression of my people he was punished. He was assigned a grave with the wicked, and with the rich in his death, though he had done no violence, nor was any deceit in his mouth. Yet it was the Lord's will to crush him and cause him to suffer, and though the Lord makes his life an offering for sin, he will see his offspring and prolong his days, and the will of the LORD will prosper in his hand. After he has suffered, he will see the light of life and be satisfied; by his knowledge my righteous servant will justify many, and he will bear their iniquities. Therefore I will give him a portion among the great, and he will divide the spoils with the strong, because he poured out his life unto death, and was numbered with the transgressors. For he bore the sin of many, and made intercession for the transgressors. [396]

We are healed! No longer are we broken, lost, alone, and separated from our Creator. Jesus restored us to His Father. Isaiah was given a word of knowledge to prophesy that the long-awaited Messiah would be despised by the Israelites.

The psalmist recognized the coming Crucifixion, saying:

Dogs surround me, a pack of villains encircles me; they pierce my hands and my feet. [397]

---

[396] Isaiah 53:3–12.
[397] Psalm 22:16.

They divide my clothes among them, and cast lots for my garment.[398]

This passage is critical to understanding the Story of God and God's covenants. You'll recall that in the Abrahamic covenant, the bonding factor was a commitment of both parties to the agreement. If one party violated the covenant, the other could tear that party to pieces like the meat alongside the path. My position is that the participants were God as the smoking oven and Jesus as the flaming torch. Jesus represented humanity and kept the covenant for all believers.

The covenant between man and God was broken. Adam could not keep it. We were separated from our Creator, and the Messiah would be the sacrifice for us. He would be torn to pieces as the covenant required.

[T]here were many who were appalled at him—his appearance was so disfigured beyond that of any human being and his form marred beyond human likeness.[399]

Jesus walked in your place. The covenant is filled with His grace and mercy for us!

Jesus said, "Father, forgive them, for they do not know what they are doing." And they divided up his clothes by casting lots.[400]

Jesus was not done. There was another horrifying moment in all of this, more painful than the nails in His hands and feet:

About three in the afternoon Jesus cried out in a loud voice, "*Eli, Eli, lema sabachthani?*" (Which means "My God, my God, why have you forsaken me).[401]

This is considered the moment when the sin of the world was imparted to Jesus. The world's sins are so wicked and evil that His Father could not

---

[398] Psalm 22:18.
[399] Isaiah 52:13.
[400] Luke 23:34.
[401] Matthew 27:46.

look upon His Son. For the first time in His life, Jesus experienced separation from His Father. This was emotionally overwhelming and gut-wrenching. For humanity to be with the Father, Jesus sacrificed.

AFTER RESURRECTION

Following His Resurrection, Jesus appeared amid the disciples to remind them of what He had taught. But He had to open their minds.

> Jesus himself stood among them and said to them, "Peace be with you."
>
> They were startled and frightened, thinking they saw a ghost. He said to them, "Why are you troubled, and why do doubts rise in your minds? Look at my hands and my feet. It is I myself! Touch me and see; a ghost does not have flesh and bones, as you see I have."
>
> When he had said this, he showed them his hands and feet. And while they still did not believe it because of joy and amazement, he asked them, "Do you have anything here to eat?" They gave him a piece of broiled fish, and he took it and ate it in their presence.
>
> He said to them, "This is what I told you while I was still with you: Everything must be fulfilled that is written about me in the Law of Moses, the Prophets and the Psalms."
>
> Then he opened their minds so they could understand the Scriptures.[402]

After three years of working alongside Jesus, they thought they had seen another ghost! They still failed to grasp the truth of what was happening. They knew Jesus was the Son of God.

Later they witnessed His departure:

> On one occasion, while he was eating with them, he gave them this command: "Do not leave Jerusalem, but wait for the gift my Father promised, which you have heard me

---

[402] Luke 24:36–45.

speak about. For John baptized with water, but in a few days you will be baptized with the Holy Spirit."

Then they gathered around him and asked him, "Lord, are you at this time going to restore the kingdom to Israel?"

He said to them: "It is not for you to know the times or dates the Father has set by his own authority. But you will receive power when the Holy Spirit comes on you; and you will be my witnesses in Jerusalem, and in all Judea and Samaria, and to the ends of the earth."

After he said this, he was taken up before their very eyes, and a cloud hid him from their sight.[403]

The disciples were to be used by God to grow His kingdom! The Holy Spirit will give you the power to do what God has called you to do, just as the Spirit enabled the disciples. New believers have a path to follow that was given by Jesus:

Thomas said to him, "Lord, we don't know where you are going, so how can we know the way?" Jesus answered, "I am the way and the truth and the life. No one comes to the Father except through me. If you really know me, you will know my Father as well. From now on, you do know him and have seen him."[404]

This is the process. It is interesting to notice how John seems to capture the words and nuances that other writers miss. All are called to believe:

Then Jesus cried out, "Whoever believes in me does not believe in me only, but in the one who sent me."[405]

Spiritual transformation begins with belief in God: His Word, His sovereignty, and His plan for our lives. This includes His Son's work on the cross with repentance and forgiveness of sins:

---

[403] Acts 1:6-9.
[404] John 14:5–7.
[405] John 12:44.

He told them, "This is what is written: The Messiah will suffer and rise from the dead on the third day, and repentance for the forgiveness of sins will be preached in his name to all nations, beginning at Jerusalem. You are witnesses of these things. I am going to send you what my Father has promised; but stay in the city until you have been clothed with power from on high."[406]

None of this—the belief we call Christianity—is possible if you do not believe in the bodily resurrection of Jesus Christ. Paul met this challenge of an unbelief in Christ's resurrection head-on:

And if Christ has not been raised, your faith is futile; you are still in your sins. Then those also who have fallen asleep in Christ are lost. If only for this life we have hope in Christ, we are of all people most to be pitied.[407]

Paul said we are to be pitied if Jesus's resurrection never happened. For new covenant believers, our faith-journey begins with submission and surrender to God through our belief in the work of Jesus on the cross. Jesus forgives and allows us to meet the Father in an intimate covenantal relationship.

PENTECOST

Fifty days after the resurrection of Jesus, something miraculous happened where the disciples and many others were gathered. It was the promised Holy Spirit:

If you love me, keep my commands. And I will ask the Father, and he will give you another advocate to help you and be with you forever—the Spirit of truth. The world cannot accept him, because it neither sees him nor knows

---

[406] Luke 24:46–49.
[407] 1 Corinthians 15:17–19.

him. But you know him, for he lives with you and will be in you. I will not leave you as orphans;

I will come to you. Before long, the world will not see me anymore, but you will see me. Because I live, you also will live. On that day you will realize that I am in my Father, and you are in me, and I am in you.

Whoever has my commands and keeps them is the one who loves me. The one who loves me will be loved by my Father, and I too will love them and show myself to them.[408]

Jesus announced that the Holy Spirit would be sent by God to all who have accepted Him to be our on-earth Advocate and Comforter for followers.

Making your commitment was made all the sweeter as Jesus prayed not only for His followers, but also for all those who would believe in the days to come:

My prayer is not for them alone. I pray also for those who will believe in me through their message, that all of them may be one, Father, just as you are in me and I am in you. May they also be in us so that the world may believe that you have sent me. I have given them the glory that you gave me, that they may be one as we are one—I in them and you in me—so that they may be brought to complete unity. Then the world will know that you sent me and have loved them even as you have loved me.

Father, I want those you have given me to be with me where I am, and to see my glory, the glory you have given me because you loved me before the creation of the world.[409]

God's plan for relationship with Him has been moving forward since the creation of the world!

And this is my prayer: that your love may abound more and more in knowledge and depth of insight, so that you may be

---

[408] John 14:15–21.
[409] John 17:20–24.

able to discern what is best and may be pure and blameless for the day of Christ, filled with the fruit of righteousness that comes through Jesus Christ—to the glory and praise of God.[410]

Paul gets it. Paul understands the Story of God. He knows it is all about drawing believers into a relationship with the Father. He knows the work of the Father and Jesus is about a perfect love—a perfect love that drives out the fear of existential dread. Because we *know* this reality and are God's own, we are supernaturally filled with love.

DISCERNMENT

Bina (pronounced bean-aw) is translated in the OT as "understanding" in most cases. *Wisdom* advises one to go in the way of righteous behavior, and *understanding* is why one should.[411] In the NT, understanding is rendered as deep thinking. Strong's indicates a movement from one side (the wisdom) to the other (understanding) to reach a place of critical thinking.[412]

The only time we find the word for *discernment* used specifically is in the NT of the New American Standard Bible, where it is translated as "perception"—not only as sense, but by intellect.[413] The beauty of this passage is the picture it paints of understanding. The definition of *discernment* is an ability in the character of a spiritual person. Interestingly, in the New International Version, the translation of the word for *discernment* is "depth of insight."[414]

The fruit of righteousness is not of right moral conduct, as in human effort. It results as one submits to the heavenly gift of godly character.[415] In

---

[410] Philippians 1:9–11.

[411] TWOT. *bina*. Vol. I. pg. 239b.

[412] "Understanding," *Strongs Concordance. Dianoia*. G1271. https://biblehub.com/greek/1271.htm.

[413] "Discernment," NASB95, Philippians 1:9, https://www.blueletterbible.org/lexicon/g144/nasb95/mgnt/0-1/.

[414] "Discernment," NIV, Philippians 1.9, https://www.blueletterbible.org/niv/phl/1/9/t_conc_1104009.

[415] TDNT. Vol. 2, pg. 210.

each passionate faith-journey, when guided by the Holy Spirit, thoughts, feelings, desires, and understanding change the soul to reflect a unity with God, the Oneness.

KEY NT ACCOUNTS

Jesus and the disciples were faced with not only making a great announcement of restoration with God, but also confronting the angry Jewish leadership, because that leadership was wrong. Jesus had incredible gifts of mercy, grace, and love for the Israelites and the nonbelieving Gentiles. Yet the legalistic leadership were hateful toward Jesus's message. The prophecies were pretty clear about who they were waiting for:

> Who has believed our message? To whom has the Lord revealed his powerful arm? My servant grew up in the Lord's presence like a tender green shoot, like a root in dry ground. There was nothing beautiful or majestic about his appearance, nothing to attract us to him. He was despised and rejected—a man of sorrows, acquainted with deepest grief. We turned our backs on him and looked the other way. He was despised, and we did not care. Yet it was our weaknesses he carried; it was our sorrows that weighed him down. And we thought his troubles were a punishment from God, a punishment for his own sins!
>
> But he was pierced for our rebellion, crushed for our sins. He was beaten so we could be whole. He was whipped so we could be healed. All of us, like sheep, have strayed away. We have left God's paths to follow our own. Yet the Lord [God] laid on him the sins of us all. He was oppressed and treated harshly, yet he never said a word. He was led like a lamb to the slaughter. And as a sheep is silent before the shearers, he did not open his mouth.
>
> Unjustly condemned, he was led away. No one cared that he died without descendants, that his life was cut short in midstream. But he was struck down for the rebellion of my people. He had done no wrong and had never deceived

anyone. But he was buried like a criminal; he was put in a rich man's grave.

But it was the Lord [God's] good plan to crush him and cause him grief. Yet when his life is made an offering for sin, he will have many descendants. He will enjoy a long life, and the Lord's good plan will prosper in his hands. When he sees all that is accomplished by his anguish, he will be satisfied. And because of his experience, my righteous servant will make it possible for many to be counted righteous, for he will bear all their sins. I will give him the honors of a victorious soldier, because he exposed himself to death. He was counted among the rebels. He bore the sins of many and interceded for rebels.[416]

Even to the end, it was clear who Jesus was. This passage reveals that Jesus fulfilled His covenant position in Abraham's dream. He was cut to pieces as the covenant is understood. Humanity belonged in that position, but Jesus received our punishment.

But many were amazed when they saw him. His face was so disfigured he seemed hardly human, and from his appearance, one would scarcely know he was a man.

And he will startle many nations. Kings will stand speechless in his presence. For they will see what they had not been told; they will understand what they had not heard about.[417]

I have felt that the following account by Matthew of the period early in their ministry is profound in many ways. The discussion took place following an encounter with the Pharisees. Jesus and the disciples sailed to the other side of the sea and begin walking toward Caesarea Philippi:

The Pharisees and Sadducees came to Jesus and tested him by asking him to show them a sign from heaven.

---

[416] Isaiah 53:1–12 NLT.
[417] Isaiah 52:14 NLT.

He replied, "When evening comes, you say, 'It will be fair weather, for the sky is red,' and in the morning, 'Today it will be stormy, for the sky is red and overcast.' You know how to interpret the appearance of the sky, but you cannot interpret the signs of the times. A wicked and adulterous generation looks for a sign, but none will be given it except the sign of Jonah." Jesus then left them and went away.[418]

Jesus informed the Jewish leadership that they lack *discernment*. He used a natural event to reveal a lack of supernatural sight. He informed them that His death and resurrection would be similar to that of Jonah in the belly of a fish.[419]

This motif of discernment continued to be a challenge for the disciples. They just didn't seem to understand what Jesus was talking about. Matthew recorded a similar situation in which the disciples lacked understanding and Jesus called them out:

When they went across the lake, the disciples forgot to take bread. "Be careful," Jesus said to them. "Be on your guard against the yeast of the Pharisees and Sadducees."

They discussed this among themselves and said, "It is because we didn't bring any bread."

Aware of their discussion, Jesus asked, "You of little faith, why are you talking among yourselves about having no bread? Do you still not understand? Don't you remember the five loaves for the five thousand, and how many basketfuls you gathered? Or the seven loaves for the four thousand, and how many basketfuls you gathered? How is it you don't understand that I was not talking to you about bread? But be on your guard against the yeast of the Pharisees and Sadducees." Then they understood that he was not telling them to guard against the yeast used in bread, but against the teaching of the Pharisees and Sadducees.

---

[418] Matthew 16:1-12.

[419] "Sign of Jonah," Got Questions.com, https://www.gotquestions.org/sign-of-Jonah.html.

For some reasons, the disciples continued to bicker about forgetting the bread. Again, Jesus must remind them that He was not worried about food. He was able to feed the five thousand; why would He be concerned about forgetting bread? The disciples bickered about bread, which clouded their thoughts about the main concern at hand.

> When Jesus came to the region of Caesarea Philippi, he asked his disciples, "Who do people say the Son of Man is?"
>
> They replied, "Some say John the Baptist; others say Elijah; and still others, Jeremiah or one of the prophets."
>
> "But what about you?" he asked. "Who do you say I am?"
>
> Simon Peter answered, "You are the Messiah, the Son of the living God."
>
> Jesus replied, "Blessed are you, Simon son of Jonah, for this was not revealed to you by flesh and blood, but by my Father in heaven. And I tell you that you are Peter, and on this rock I will build my church, and the gates of Hades will not overcome it. I will give you the keys of the kingdom of heaven; whatever you bind on earth will be bound in heaven, and whatever you loose on earth will be loosed in heaven." Then he ordered his disciples not to tell anyone that he was the Messiah.[420]

What Jesus said to Peter is extraordinary! Jesus revealed an incredibly important clue for believers. As humans, we are capable of thinking and judgment. More significant is listening for God's wisdom. This is clear evidence of God's intervention in the minds of believers. God revealed to Peter the true identity of Jesus.

The following is an example of clouded or emotional thinking, when we don't allow God to lead our thoughts. Matthew recorded what was, to the disciples, very frightening. They began thinking out of a state of fear.

> From that time on Jesus began to explain to his disciples that he must go to Jerusalem and suffer many things at the hands of the elders, the chief priests and the teachers of

---

[420] Matthew 16:20.

the law, and that he must be killed and on the third day be raised to life.

Peter took him aside and began to rebuke him. "Never, Lord!" he said. "This shall never happen to you!" Jesus turned and said to Peter, "Get behind me, Satan! You are a stumbling block to me; you do not have in mind the concerns of God, but merely human concerns."

Then Jesus said to his disciples, "Whoever wants to be my disciple must deny themselves and take up their cross and follow me. For whoever wants to save their life will lose it, but whoever loses their life for me will find it. What good will it be for someone to gain the whole world, yet forfeit their soul? Or what can anyone give in exchange for their soul? For the Son of Man is going to come in his Father's glory with his angels, and then he will reward each person according to what they have done. Truly I tell you, some who are standing here will not taste death before they see the Son of Man coming in his kingdom."[421]

Jesus responded to the group regarding Peter's remarks, which were in contrast to His previous statement of Peter's revelation. Jesus saw Peter's remonstrance not as genuine concern, but as thoughts generated by fear. We are to deny these humanistic traits and, with all our strength, establish a new way to live. Disciples must be prepared to give their lives to this mission.

These are the themes of Jesus's ministry found throughout the NT: to understand and believe the Word of God, to trust completely that God is in control, and to believe that our purpose is found in seeking God's purpose for our lives. The ultimate goal is to bring the great things of heaven to earth. We are to embrace our Eden innocence and live in the fruit of the Spirit.

The messages and themes are the same throughout the NT. Paul and the disciples were driven to teach that our lives on this planet are supposed to mimic Eden and heaven. We are to die to all the distractions we find ourselves in and rejoice in a new way of seeing and being in the world.

The mission was established in the pre-creation planning. Jesus, the Messiah, restored us to relationship with God from whence our power

---

[421] Matthew 16:1–20.

comes to bring heaven to earth. We are to *discern*—not like the disciples, but seeing and praying for the supernatural work that God is bringing to earth.

Jesus spoke to our lack of understanding and made a loving request: "Father, forgive them, for they know not what they are doing."[422]

Let's look deeper into the Story of God. Several critical themes meet here. First, *the blood is shed to remove our sin.* No longer does it cover sin; it removes sin as far as the east is from the west.[423]

Second, Jesus's work on the cross restored all believers to *an intimate and personal relationship with God.* Not only are our past and future sins forgiven and eternal life given, but our belief makes us holy and able to enter a deepened relationship with our Creator God.

Third, the entire sin of humanity was laid on Jesus. The Father couldn't look at Jesus because the sin of humanity so defiled Him. That's why Jesus said, "My God, My God, why have you forsaken me?"[424]

Fourth, within the Temple was the Holy of Holies—a place where God resided and only a high priest could enter. A large curtain in the Temple kept common worshippers from entering the Holy of Holies. At the moment of Jesus's last breath, that curtain tore from top to bottom, signifying that God was now available to all humanity if they believe.

Finally, a significant part of the God Story ended here: "When he had received the drink, Jesus said, 'It is finished.' With that, he bowed his head and gave up his spirit."[425] Clearly, the journey from the Eden tragedy to Jesus's final words had come to an end. God planned for this trek to cover approximately four thousand years, ending with His Son's Crucifixion, Resurrection, and return to heaven.

In the ministry of Jesus following the Sermon on the Mount, He focused on bringing the kingdom of God to earth. The kingdom of God resembles the Garden of Eden. Jesus called all believers to return to an intimate and personal relationship with God. In the same way God taught OT characters through trials, the NT characters learned about their covenantal relationship with God. We'll focus on key characters and their trials and suffering.

---

[422] Luke 23:34.

[423] Psalm 103:12 NLT.

[424] Mark 15:34.

[425] John 19:30.

I see no real distinction between a trial and suffering other than that suffering may involve physical distress. I will mention the miracles in passing, but my focus is on the soul-vision character of each disciple—or lack thereof.

DEVELOPING A PROFOUND AWARENESS

In the trials of the men and women used by God, we have seen spiritual transformation. Too often, biblical characters went sideways, but God's purposes were not defeated. The very fact that God has called me to write this book is a testament that God can use whomever He desires. In each case, including mine, the character loved God.

We are *not* to get tied up in our sinful behavior or thoughts. We are to get up after each failure, ask for forgiveness, and then ask God, "What am I missing here?" God-given discernment gives us the ability to see the world in the context of the truth of our spiritual heritage. Our vision is grounded in the Story of God and provides us with the fruit of the Spirit.

When we recognize that we are at rock-bottom, that we are at the end of self, that we really don't have control of our lives, and that our lives independent of God are not working—*then* we repent of our choice to do it our own way. We choose to accept the freedom of dependence on God.

Christ's work on the cross gave us forgiveness of sin and, more importantly, an authentic relationship with the Father. You see, Jesus said He is the way, the truth, and the life. This means that only in this choice will you gain access to the Father and eternal life. You will discover the truth that is God intervening in your life. You will begin to experience the mystery of love, joy and peace in your life that comes from Him.

19

BRIDE OF CHRIST: A GALILEAN WEDDING AND THE BRIDEGROOM

THIS MOTIF OF THE BRIDE OF CHRIST IS AN IMPORTANT ONE THAT BUILDS upon the ceremonial steps of a Galilean wedding. These steps bear a striking resemblance to a theme interwoven in the NT. We have referred to Jesus as the Bridegroom; however, we have not made mention of the bride. The church is a bride in waiting. The wedding theme is powerful; however, the disciples would be challenged if they did not figure out what Jesus's mission really was.

PRE-CREATION PLANNING

I can only imagine a trinitarian discussion to weave Jesus's mission into the steps of a Galilean wedding ceremony. The wedding in Cana implied that another wedding would begin as the Bridegroom looked for the bride.

Understanding that the wedding was interwoven in Jesus's ministry is important. This theme is used as an example of how believers are to be ready for the return of Jesus. The church is the bride. God's Son is the Bridegroom. God desires that His believers understand the significance of we, the church, preparing ourselves for the Lamb.[426] A time will come when the worldly wise will attempt to push us out of their world because of what we believe. God knew this from the very beginning and has planned our exit. Fear not, for Jesus overcame the world. There will be great chaos and pain. If believers abide in God, they will not live in fear. Then it will be time. Seek the fruit of the Spirit!

---

[426] Revelation 21:9.

NT BIBLICAL ACCOUNT

Keep in mind, John describes a wedding that Jesus attended.[427] This is a prominent theme in the NT. The wedding description is often referred to as foreshadowing the return of Jesus. In a Galilean wedding ceremony, the bride and bridegroom, as well as the attendees, prepare for the sacred occasion before the father of the groom instructs his son to go get his bride. The process of the Galilean wedding ceremony is symbolism for the return of Christ.[428]

The wedding ceremony has a special significance that needs to be shared. There are many instances when Jesus used cultural experiences to make a point, such as farming analogies and animal behaviors. The Galilean wedding ceremony operates in the same way as a look into the work of the church (bride), Jesus (Bridegroom), and God (Father).

The wedding ceremony begins with a reading of the marriage conditions by the father of the bridegroom to the future bride. She makes a verbal acceptance of the written arrangement. They drink wine together as a seal of the arrangement. The future bridegroom pours a cup of wine and passes it to his future bride. If she pushes the cup back, then there will be no wedding. However, if she drinks from it, she accepts the proposal of marriage. As he drinks from this cup which is his commitment to her, he vows not to drink from the vine again until they are married. At that point, the bridal pair exchange gifts and wait. Sound familiar? It should.

> I tell you, I will not drink from this fruit of the vine from
> now on until that day when I drink it new with you in my
> Father's kingdom.[429]

This sets into motion a lengthy process of wedding preparation. The bridegroom is responsible for preparing a place for the two of them to live, and for making arrangements for the wedding feast. Often, the groom's work is to build an addition to his father's house. Again, we see a parallel in Jesus's words:

---

[427] John 2:1-12.
[428] *Before the Wrath*, https://tubitv.com/movies/700890/before-the-wrath: a documentary regarding the roles of the bride, groom, and Father.
[429] Matthew 26:29.

And if I go and prepare a place for you, I will come again and receive you to Myself; that where I am, there you may be also.[430]

It is important to note here the theological relationship between the bride and the Bridegroom:

The imagery and symbolism of marriage is applied to Christ and the body of believers known as the church. The church is comprised of those who have trusted in Jesus Christ as their personal Savior and have received eternal life. Christ, the Bridegroom, has sacrificially and lovingly chosen the church to be His bride ... Just as there was a betrothal period in biblical times during which the bride and groom were separated until the wedding, so is the bride of Christ separate from her Bridegroom.[431]

The apostle Paul stated clearly that the relationship between husband and wife mirrors that of Christ and the church:

For the husband is the head of the wife as Christ is the head of the church, his body, of which he is the Savior. Now as the church submits to Christ, so also wives should submit to their husbands in everything. Husbands, love your wives, just as Christ loved the church and gave himself up for her.[432]

In the same way the Galilean bridegroom goes to prepare a place for the bride, the bride, with the assistance of her closest friends, prepares herself. There is a very clear passage in the Gospels that speak to this preparation and the fact that you don't want to be ill-prepared upon the return of Jesus.

---

[430] Matthew 14:3.
[431] Got Questions, 2023, https://www.gotquestions.org/bride-of-Christ.html.
[432] Ephesians 5:23–25.

> At that time the kingdom of heaven will be like ten virgins who took their lamps and went out to meet the bridegroom. Five of them were foolish and five were wise. The foolish ones took their lamps but did not take any oil with them. The wise ones, however, took oil in jars along with their lamps. The bridegroom was a long time in coming, and they all became drowsy and fell asleep. At midnight the cry rang out: "Here's the bridegroom! Come out to meet him!" Then all the virgins woke up and trimmed their lamps. The foolish ones said to the wise, "Give us some of your oil; our lamps are going out." "No," they replied, "there may not be enough for both us and you. Instead, go to those who sell oil and buy some for yourselves." But while they were on their way to buy the oil, the bridegroom arrived. The virgins who were ready went in with him to the wedding banquet. And the door was shut. Later the others also came. "Lord, Lord," they said, "open the door for us!" But he replied, "Truly I tell you, I don't know you." Therefore keep watch, because you do not know the day or the hour.[433]

Both the bride and bridegroom must prepare for the big ceremony. He is ready, and she is in waiting. So when does it take place?

The most unique detail regarding the Galilean wedding is the responsibility of the father of the bridegroom. It is the father who initiates the time and action for his son. It begins when the father says, "Go get your bride." Neither the son, the bride, nor anyone else in the town knows when that time will be!

What prompts the father? There are no predetermining rules for the father; no one knows that day or hour. The Boy Scout motto applies: always be prepared.

> The overall and easily seen thrust of the parable is that Christ will return at an unknown hour and that His people must be ready. Being ready means preparing for whatever contingency arises in our lives and keeping our eyes fixed

---

[433] Matthew 25:1–13.

on Jesus at all times while we eagerly await His coming. As seen in the fact that all the virgins were sleeping when the call came indicates that it doesn't matter what we are doing when Christ returns. We may be working, eating, sleeping, or pursuing leisure activities.[434]

Jesus put His followers on notice that He had no idea when His Father would send Him back for His bride. Our focus should be our preparation. Jesus said:

> But about that day or hour no one knows, not even the angels in heaven, nor the Son, but only the Father.
> As it was in the days of Noah, so it will be at the coming of the Son of Man. For in the days before the flood, people were eating and drinking, marrying and giving in marriage, up to the day Noah entered the ark; and they knew nothing about what would happen until the flood came and took them all away. That is how it will be at the coming of the Son of Man.[435]

Paul described this event in very clear terms:

> After that, we who are still alive and are left will be caught up together with them in the clouds to meet the Lord in the air. And so we will be with the Lord forever.[436]

Two passages use the wording "a thief in the night":

> Understand this: If the owner of the house had known at what time of night the thief was coming, he would have kept watch and would not have let his house be broken into.[437]

---

[434] Got Questions, 2023, https://www.gotquestions.org/bride-of-Christ.html.

[435] Matthew 24:36–38.

[436] 1 Thessalonians 4:17.

[437] Matthew 24:43.

> You know very well that the day of the Lord will come like a thief in the night.[438]

As he neared the completion of Revelation, exiled on the island of Patmos, John wrote:

> Let us rejoice and be glad and give him glory! For the wedding of the Lamb has come, and his bride has made herself ready.[439]

At some point, Jesus' Father will make that decision, based upon the bride and the Bridegroom being ready.

> The bride belongs to the bridegroom. The friend who attends the bridegroom waits and listens for him, and is full of joy when he hears the bridegroom's voice. That joy is mine, and it is now complete.[440]

Keep in mind what Jesus said about paying attention and being prepared. Luke recorded what Jesus said:

> Be dressed ready for service and keep your lamps burning, like servants waiting for their master to return from a wedding banquet, so that when he comes and knocks they can immediately open the door for him. It will be good for those servants whose master finds them watching when he comes. Truly I tell you, he will dress himself to serve, will have them recline at the table and will come and wait on them. It will be good for those servants whose master finds them ready, even if he comes in the middle of the night or toward daybreak. But understand this: If the owner of the house had known at what hour the thief was coming, he would not have let his house be broken into. You also must

---

[438] 1 Thessalonians. 5:2. These two passages are pointed out on the website Got Questions, accessed April 20, 2023, https://www.gotquestions.org/thief-in-the-night.html.
[439] Revelation 19:7.
[440] John 3:29.

be ready, because the Son of Man will come at an hour when you do not expect him.[441]

DEVELOPING A PROFOUND AWARENESS

This chapter should be a positive wake-up call to our responsibilities as believers and members of local churches. Can you grow watching services online? Yes, but not without the accountability you should receive within your local church. If you believe you are ready, which I pray that you are, then you should be in your local church, helping others prepare.

As your soul-vision grows, so does a Christlike character within you. Your daily trial is becoming ready for the return of Christ. The faith-journey is one that deepens your belief in the Word of God, strengthens your trust in the sovereignty of God, and has you on fire to pursue God's steps for your life. The things of this world can crowd out our time of waiting. A profound awareness of God releasing His Son to go and receive the bride should every day be our most significant thought. *Our lives are built around the truth of this endeavor.*

Every action and decision we make as Christ-followers should *not* be one of personal ambition or familial interests. Every act should be one in which we center our preparation for His return. Our grandchildren will miss His arrival if we fail to honor this truth with our lived experiences. Pursuit of God will *not* clutter your lives!

Be part of a congregation that readies its families for this intense moment in all of time. Parents are the leaders in the same way that Adam and Eve were for their progeny prior to the Flood. Despite the Eden tragedy, Adam and Eve's impact on their children was so profound that it impacted Noah and his commitment to follow God's instruction—a thousand years later!

Possessing a profound awareness of God's moment-by-moment actions in this world is our calling. In the same way that Adam and Eve taught their children and grandchildren, we should prepare our children. Let each of us seek such a relationship with the God of the universe that we are profoundly aware of God's love for His people and the coming arrival of His Son.

---

[441] Luke 12:31–40.

20

A NEW WINE: SPIRITUAL FORMATION, HOLY SPIRIT, THE GREAT COMMISSION

JESUS'S MINISTRY WAS INCREDIBLE. THE GOD STORY BEGAN WITH JESUS'S baptism and a forty-day trek in the wilderness, where He was tempted by Satan. Satan's deception did not work with the Son of God. Jesus's public ministry began with the teaching of the *progressive nature of spiritual formation* in the Sermon on the Mount and ended with His Resurrection and Ascension. As a result of His work, we were given all we need to live abundant lives in oneness with God, the way He intended in Eden.

In the OT, God placed His Spirit on men and women for a specific purpose: to accomplish His will.[442] King David was so profoundly aware of the Holy Spirit in his life that when he had an extramarital affair with Bathsheba, he pleaded with God not to take His Spirit from him.[443] A few of God's leaders experienced the Holy Spirit mightily on different occasions.[444] Clearly, God was sending His Spirit for His purposes.

Sending the Holy Spirit to believers was critical. Unlike in the OT, where the Holy Spirit was given to a select few, in the NT the Holy Spirit was given to all who believe. Wisdom and understanding come from the Holy Spirit. Believers who earnestly submitted their lives and sought the Holy Spirit were the anointed by God.

---

[442] Joshua (Numbers 27:18), Othniel (Judges 3:10), Gideon (6:34), King David (1 Samuel 16:13–14), Jephthah (Judges 11:29), the Seventy Elders (Numbers 11:16–26), Balaam (Numbers 24:1–6), Isaiah (Isaiah 59:21), Amasai (1 Chronicles 12:18), Jahaziel (2 Chronicles 20:14).

[443] Psalm 51:11.

[444] King Saul (Samuel 10:10, 11:6), Samson (Judges 13:25, 14:6), Ezekiel (Ezekiel 2:2, 3:24).

PRE-CREATION PLANNING

I can only imagine God, Jesus, and the Holy Spirit discussing the ministry of the Holy Spirit. Leading the disciples would be a challenging process, but Jesus's work would complete the Story for all to read, learn, and understand.

The Comforter would help believers to walk in the faith and to remember their one hope. He would be a free gift to all who believe. The Holy Spirit would work in and through believers as they learned submission and humility. Nonbelievers would know believers by the fruit of the Spirit and their love. Believers would become like Jesus, clothed in the fruit of the Spirit.

NT BIBLICAL ACCOUNT

In the NT, the Holy Spirit was part of God's plan from the start. Matthew wrote:

> Then Jesus came from Galilee to the Jordan to be baptized by John. But John tried to deter him, saying, "I need to be baptized by you, and do you come to me?" Jesus replied, "Let it be so now; it is proper for us to do this to fulfill all righteousness." Then John consented. As soon as Jesus was baptized, he went up out of the water. At that moment heaven was opened, and he saw the Spirit of God descending like a dove and alighting on him. And a voice from heaven said, "This is my Son, whom I love; with him I am well pleased."[445]

Wow! What a powerful description. Heaven was opened, and He saw the Spirit of God land on Him. This scene is critical to understanding the role the Holy Spirit was to have in the new covenant. We see its place at the very beginning, and we'll hear of the Holy Spirit as He departed the earth.

I love the American Standard Version translation of Jesus's announcement of the coming Comforter, recorded by John:

---

[445] Matthew 3:13–17.

> And I will pray the Father, and he shall give you another
> Comforter, that he may be with you forever.[446]

> But the Comforter, *even* the Holy Spirit, whom the Father
> will send in my name, he shall teach you all things, and
> bring to your remembrance all that I said unto you.[447]

> But when the Comforter is come, whom I will send unto you
> from the Father, *even* the Spirit of truth, which proceedeth
> from the Father, he shall bear witness of me.[448]

> Nevertheless I tell you the truth: It is expedient for you that
> I go away; for if I go not away, the Comforter will not come
> unto you; but if I go, I will send him unto you.[449]

The Comforter is a giver! There is giving of comfort, spiritual gifts, truth, and the fruit of the Spirit. Jesus said, "It is expedient for you that I go away." Only those whom God specifically called on in the OT received the Holy Spirit. In the new covenant, *all* would receive the Holy Spirit through a confession of faith in Jesus and baptism!

Let me say again: the arrival of the Holy Spirit was critical. Near the end of the gospel of Luke, the disciples had not experienced the baptism in the Holy Spirit, sometimes referred to as "the second baptism." It was a moment when it all became clear for them through the Spirit, and that was why Jesus instructed them to wait for it.

> Then he opened their minds so they could understand the
> Scriptures. He told them, "This is what is written: The
> Messiah will suffer and rise from the dead on the third day,
> and repentance for the forgiveness of sins will be preached
> in his name to all nations, beginning at Jerusalem. You are
> witnesses of these things. I am going to send you what my

---

[446] John 14:16 ASV.
[447] John 14:26 ASV.
[448] John 15:26 ASV.
[449] John 16:7 ASV.

Father has promised; but stay in the city until you have been clothed with power from on high."[450]

Let's see how that conversation started. Jesus had just predicted His death. Where He was going, the disciples could not follow, at least at that time. There was obvious concern among the disciples. Peter asked where He was going and added that he would give his life to follow. Well, you know what happened then: Jesus predicted that Peter would deny Him three times. Jesus attempted to comfort them:

> Do not let your hearts be troubled. You believe in God; believe also in me. My Father's house has many rooms; if that were not so, would I have told you that I am going there to prepare a place for you? And if I go and prepare a place for you, I will come back and take you to be with me that you also may be where I am. You know the way to the place where I am going.

Still bewildered, Thomas pressed Him:

> Thomas said to him, "Lord, we don't know where you are going, so how can we know the way?"
>
> Jesus answered, "I am the way and the truth and the life. No one comes to the Father except through me. If you really know me, you will know my Father as well. From now on, you do know him and have seen him."
>
> Philip said, "Lord, show us the Father and that will be enough for us."

This is stunning to me. These men had been with Jesus for three years. And still they remained seemingly faithless.

> Jesus answered: "Don't you know me, Philip, even after I have been among you such a long time? Anyone who has seen me has seen the Father. How can you say, 'Show us the

---

[450] Luke 24:45–49.

209

Father'? Don't you believe that I am in the Father, and that the Father is in me? The words I say to you I do not speak on my own authority. Rather, it is the Father, living in me, who is doing his work. Believe me when I say that I am in the Father and the Father is in me; or at least believe on the evidence of the works themselves. Very truly I tell you, whoever believes in me will do the works I have been doing, and they will do even greater things than these, because I am going to the Father. And I will do whatever you ask in my name, so that the Father may be glorified in the Son. You may ask me for anything in my name, and I will do it."

Again Jesus told them He is One with the Father. They may not have been allowed to see the Father, like Moses did, but they certainly knew who Jesus was.

Jesus added that they were not alone:

"If you love me, keep my commands. And I will ask the Father, and he will give you another advocate to help you and be with you forever—the Spirit of truth. The world cannot accept him, because it neither sees him nor knows him. But you know him, for he lives with you and will be in you. I will not leave you as orphans; I will come to you. Before long, the world will not see me anymore, but you will see me. Because I live, you also will live. On that day you will realize that I am in my Father, and you are in me, and I am in you. Whoever has my commands and keeps them is the one who loves me. The one who loves me will be loved by my Father, and I too will love them and show myself to them."

Then Judas (not Judas Iscariot) said, "But, Lord, why do you intend to show yourself to us and not to the world?"

Jesus replied, "Anyone who loves me will obey my teaching. My Father will love them, and we will come to them and make our home with them. Anyone who does not love me will not obey my teaching. These words you hear are not my own; they belong to the Father who sent me.

All this I have spoken while still with you. But the Advocate, the Holy Spirit, whom the Father will send in my name, will teach you all things and will remind you of everything I have said to you. Peace I leave with you; my peace I give you. I do not give to you as the world gives. Do not let your hearts be troubled and do not be afraid.

"You heard me say, 'I am going away and I am coming back to you.' If you loved me, you would be glad that I am going to the Father, for the Father is greater than I. I have told you now before it happens, so that when it does happen you will believe. I will not say much more to you, for the prince of this world is coming. He has no hold over me, but he comes so that the world may learn that I love the Father and do exactly what my Father has commanded me. Come now; let us leave."[451]

Then Jesus gave them instruction on how the Holy Spirit would abide with them:

When the Advocate comes, whom I will send to you from the Father—the Spirit of truth who goes out from the Father—he will testify about me. And you also must testify, for you have been with me from the beginning.

All this I have told you so that you will not fall away. They will put you out of the synagogue; in fact, the time is coming when anyone who kills you will think they are offering a service to God. They will do such things because they have not known the Father or me. I have told you this, so that when their time comes you will remember that I warned you about them. I did not tell you this from the beginning because I was with you, but now I am going to him who sent me. None of you asks me, "Where are you going?" Rather, you are filled with grief because I have said these things. But very truly I tell you, it is for your good that I am going away. Unless I go away, the Advocate will

---

[451] John 13:36–14:31.

not come to you; but if I go, I will send him to you. When he comes, he will prove the world to be in the wrong about sin and righteousness and judgment: about sin, because people do not believe in me; about righteousness, because I am going to the Father, where you can see me no longer; and about judgment, because the prince of this world now stands condemned. "I have much more to say to you, more than you can now bear. But when he, the Spirit of truth, comes, he will guide you into all the truth. He will not speak on his own; he will speak only what he hears, and he will tell you what is yet to come. He will glorify me because it is from me that he will receive what he will make known to you. All that belongs to the Father is mine. That is why I said the Spirit will receive from me what he will make known to you.[452]

Along with this encouragement and assurance came a warning regarding persecution:

If the world hates you, keep in mind that it hated me first. If you belonged to the world, it would love you as its own. As it is, you do not belong to the world, but I have chosen you out of the world. That is why the world hates you. Remember what I told you: "A servant is not greater than his master." If they persecuted me, they will persecute you also. If they obeyed my teaching, they will obey yours also. They will treat you this way because of my name, for they do not know the one who sent me. If I had not come and spoken to them, they would not be guilty of sin; but now they have no excuse for their sin. Whoever hates me hates my Father as well. If I had not done among them the works no one else did, they would not be guilty of sin. As it is, they have seen, and yet they have hated both me and my Father. But

---

[452] John 15:26–16:15.

this is to fulfill what is written in their Law: "They hated me without reason."[453]

The disciples were waiting in their hidden place. What they were waiting for, they did not know. About 120 in all remained together in one place. Then this happened:

> Suddenly a sound like the blowing of a violent wind came from heaven and filled the whole house where they were sitting. They saw what seemed to be tongues of fire that separated and came to rest on each of them. All of them were filled with the Holy Spirit and began to speak in other tongues as the Spirit enabled them.
>
> Now there were staying in Jerusalem God-fearing Jews from every nation under heaven. When they heard this sound, a crowd came together in bewilderment, because each one heard their own language being spoken. Utterly amazed, they asked: "Aren't all these who are speaking Galileans? Then how is it that each of us hears them in our native language? Parthians, Medes and Elamites; residents of Mesopotamia, Judea and Cappadocia, Pontus and Asia, Phrygia and Pamphylia, Egypt and the parts of Libya near Cyrene; visitors from Rome (both Jews and converts to Judaism); Cretans and Arabs—we hear them declaring the wonders of God in our own tongues!" Amazed and perplexed, they asked one another, "What does this mean?"[454]

Peter took the leadership role and explained to all who were present:

> In the last days, God says, I will pour out my Spirit on all people. Your sons and daughters will prophesy, your young men will see visions, your old men will dream dreams. Even on my servants, both men and women, I will pour out my

---

[453] John 15:18–25.
[454] Acts 2:2–12.

Spirit in those days, and they will prophesy. I will show wonders in the heavens above and signs on the earth below, blood and fire and billows of smoke. The sun will be turned to darkness and the moon to blood before the coming of the great and glorious day of the Lord. And everyone who calls on the name of the Lord will be saved.[455]

The Holy Spirit had given Peter a word to share with all the onlookers. Peter went on to reveal the truth of what had happened and why the Israelites should pay attention.

You may recall that, in the heat of the moment when Jesus was arrested, Peter ran. He was seen by many and asked about his association with Jesus. He denied any knowledge of Jesus. When the rooster crowed, he realized what he had done. He wept bitterly.[456]

In this moment, armed with the Holy Spirit, Peter was on fire for his Savior. Three thousand repented, were baptized, and indwelt with the Holy Spirit as a seal of the new covenant in Christ. The work of the Holy Spirit was to accomplish the will of God.[457] Believers were given gifts by the Spirit to complete His work. Their souls were filled with God's power to go and make disciples.

Then Jesus came to them and said, "All authority in heaven and on earth has been given to me. Therefore go and make disciples of all nations, baptizing them in the name of the Father and of the Son and of the Holy Spirit, and teaching them to obey everything I have commanded you. And surely I am with you always, to the very end of the age."[458]

This is referred to as the Great Commission. It was a final instruction from Jesus to those meeting with Him on the mountain. This same authority now lies within the soul of every believer who believes, submits to His sovereignty, and does *only* the Father's will.

---

[455] Acts 2:17–21.
[456] John 18:25–27.
[457] Acts 1:7–8.
[458] Matthew 28:18–20.

DEVELOPING A PROFOUND AWARENESS

The lack of understanding among pre-Pentecost disciples can be surprising to Christ-followers, including me. However, years after I first encountered it, I am no longer surprised by it. The spiritual walk of the disciples was like that of many self-proclaimed Christ-followers: they just don't get it! Too many have walked out their faith in their own striving. They treat Christianity like a social club full of nice people. This can be a real frustration for some.

The frustration they experience is seen in all believers early in their faith-journey. Unfortunately, if spiritual growth stalls, then this "ye of little faith" is experienced far longer than it should be. If all church attendees submitted to the Holy Spirit's leading, then a more victorious church would overwhelm the world.

Let's be very clear about this growing level of spiritual maturity: understanding your transformation is critical to your growth as a believer. It means you are recognizing that God is intervening in your life.

I've previously mentioned these benchmarks in our transformation. If we lose sight of what God is doing in and through us, we potentially inhibit our continuing growth. Sometimes these inhibiting factors are not easily discerned and require the help of a spiritual mentor to uncover.

Here are two verses that take a positive look at deep waters as a refreshing and life-giving source of wisdom[459]:

> The words of the mouth are deep waters, but the fountain of wisdom is a rushing stream.[460]

> The purposes of a person's heart are deep waters, but one who has insight draws them out.[461]

I believe our progressive growth will coincide with the growth taught by Jesus in the Sermon on the Mount as benchmarks that lead to a full measure of joy (*pleroo*).[462]

---

[459] "Deep waters," *Moody Bible Commentary*, 932.
[460] Proverbs 18:4.
[461] Proverbs 20:5.
[462] John 17:13.

The Hebrew word *shalom* is in the same vein as "full measure of joy."[463] "Peace to you" is the most common translation. Peace comes with completeness or a wholeness in God.

We saw in the OT stories a spiritual connection between God and His leaders. They were speaking and listening relationships of a dynamic nature. In the NT, this spiritual connection was new and improved, a consequence of Pentecost. The transactions were powerful and secure and sometimes deadly. They were powerful communications, as if an inferno were flowing down a supernatural river of connectedness with God. The disciples didn't see it coming, and it overwhelmed them. The firestorm made them whole and at peace. Their knowledge turned them into emboldened preachers of God, reaching out to every Jew and Gentile they met.

Here is a brief review of our progressive spiritual transformation (sanctification) as we submit to the work of the Holy Spirit within us.

Blessed are the poor in spirit, for theirs is the kingdom of heaven

The nonbeliever or seeker recognizes that existential dread is separation from God. They have no *real* control over their destiny. Their aloneness and spiritual separation from God is not understood in the world. This is often referred to as hitting rock-bottom. The seeker surrenders to experience unexplainable, supernatural love, joy, and peace. The focus must be on prayer and submission. Embrace your epiphany of freedom. *Believe His Word*. Find a mentor!

Blessed are those who mourn, for they will be comforted

At this point, a Christ-follower realizes that the Holy Spirit is revealing the truth about their old life, friends, personal decisions, and godless activities that seemed like fun. Separation from your old circles is painful and lonely. The Spirit is reaching into your heart and asking you to walk with Him. If you stand firm in your new life, you'll discover a supernatural comfort. *Focus on a prayer of clarity*, seeing the old for what it is. Keep asking God for encouragement. Find a mentor!

Blessed are the meek, for they will inherit the earth

As a Christ-follower, you will experience supernatural changes in your

---

[463] "Shalom," https://www.gotquestions.org/Shalom-meaning.html.

heart and mind. The Holy Spirit is working on you from the inside out. You discover an inner strength, resulting in a new confidence in Him. Now you recognize what is happening to the lost. From within you, the Holy Spirit is building a sense of patience and kindness toward the lost. Your family and old friends recognize the change in you. You also see a change in the way you view the world. Focus on the inward/outward journey of your faith. See the Holy Spirit's work within you. *Trust His sovereignty.*

Blessed are those who hunger and thirst for righteousness, for they will be filled

As a maturing Christ-follower, you understand the truth of God's Word. You begin to recognize that righteous behavior is having positive outcomes as well as unexpected blessings. As a result, this life of love, joy, peace, patience, and kindness is creating a supernatural hunger for a deeper relationship with God. Your study, prayer life, and right living grow deeper. You recognize what it means to be Christlike. Focus on learning and asking God for wisdom. Learn to use digital tools for study. Pray unceasingly.

Blessed are the merciful, for they will be shown mercy

You begin to understand what a God-serving leader King David was. You also begin to recognize how deep the evil is in humanity and culture. Your mercy grows for the lost; they have no idea what they are doing to themselves. You are either a slave to sin or a slave to Christ. Your old friends have grown tired of your joy, as well as your concern for them. They ignore your testimony. Within you a deep mercy grows—a goodness and gentleness for the lost. Focus on opportunities to lead and teach. Ask spiritual mentors to include you in their prayer and study.

Blessed are the pure in heart, for they will see God

A new attitude is growing within you. You discover a contentment in God's call to your divine purpose. As a God-serving leader, you are experiencing a call from God to lead. All of your lived experiences and jobs are directed to support God's purposes. Your material wants have lessened. Your conversations with God increase dramatically. With your faith grown, the focus of your heart and mind is God's will only. Ask God for vision of where He is taking you. Pursue His will.

Blessed are the peacemakers, for they will be called children of God

The supernatural wisdom grows within you as a God-serving leader. You see past the hubris of humanity and toward the only answer for the calamities of mankind: peace with God. You understand the sovereignty of God over all the universe. As a God-serving leader, you recognize His intervention daily. A holy self-discipline knifes through the wickedness and corruption you see to reveal God's presence and answers. Focus on where God is leading you. Follow Him when He calls. Pursue His will only.

God wants each of us to be profoundly aware of peacemakers because they live in a fearless reality, serving God alone. In the wilderness, Jesus told Satan, following his third attempt to lure Jesus away from the Father, "You must worship the Lord your God and serve only him."[464]

Peacemakers are fearless because they know that God *is* with them.

> When you go through deep waters, I will be with you. When you go through rivers of difficulty, you will not drown. When you walk through the fire of oppression, you will not be burned up; the flames will not consume you.[465]

To close this chapter, I will share my favorite verse with you. The idea that Jesus could have stepped out on His own to do the work of His Father is an amazing thought. God did everything He could in Eden to raise Adam and Eve with wholesome hearts and minds. But they didn't get it and were lured by Lucifer away from God.

Hallelujah, Jesus became our role model instead. In your relationships with one another, have the same mindset as Christ Jesus. God is the Designer; Jesus is the Builder and the Restorer.

> Who, being in very nature God, did not consider equality with God something to be used to his own advantage; rather, he made himself nothing by taking the very nature of a servant, being made in human likeness. And being found in appearance as a man, he humbled himself by becoming obedient to death—even death on a cross! Therefore God

---

[464] Matthew 4:10. Jesus quotes Deuteronomy 6:13.
[465] Isaiah 43:2 NLT.

exalted him to the highest place and gave him the name that is above every name, that at the name of Jesus every knee should bow, in heaven and on earth and under the earth, and every tongue acknowledge that Jesus Christ is Lord, to the glory of God the Father.[466]

[466] Philippians 2:5–11.

21

SPIRITUAL MATURITY:
A FULL MEASURE OF JOY

ACCORDING TO SCRIPTURES, THERE ARE SEVERAL PIECES OR STEPS TO spiritual maturity, beginning with spiritual formation as described in the Sermon on the Mount. As your soul is being transformed by the Holy Spirit, the fruit of the Spirit—joy—grows you to a Christlike attitude. Spiritual giftings are given by the Holy Spirit to accomplish God's purposes. John records what Jesus said about a full measure of joy:

> I am coming to you now, but I say these things while I am
> still in the world, so that they may have the full measure of
> my joy within them.[467]

All these enhance one's capacity in whatever one's work or vocational talent might be. However, they are all aligned under faith in God's Word, trust in His sovereignty, and pursuit of His purpose for one's life. Everything follows from these critical pieces of the spiritual fruit.

As you study, take no shortcuts. Talk to Him. Ask Him to reveal the whys. Look for the doors He is opening or closing. We have an orderly God: first things first. It all follows from a commitment to make Him the Lord of your life.

PRE-CREATION PLANNING

I can only imagine the discussion regarding the depth of submission and humbling oneself to God. For rational humanity, identifying with the idea

---

[467] John 17:13.

of submitting to God in order to return to relationship with Him is foreign. To those not so immersed in worldly wisdom—the seekers—removing all distractions and trusting God are not so difficult.

I can only imagine that making a way for seekers to discern between humility and pride growth was the challenge. Submission creates an equality, a oneness that does not judge or confer a position of superiority. The responsibility of the peacemaker is to teach discernment through a word planted deep within the hearts of believers. Love is the most significant factor of all.

Believers must desire the fruit of His Spirit. Some will desire the fruit, but too many will focus on the spiritual gifting. Prematurely, Christ-followers believe spiritual gifts will give them significance to God or value among others. The truth is the spiritual gifts *belong* to the Holy Spirit and are imparted as necessary by God. Believers should seek the full measure of spiritual maturity found through the fruit of the Spirit. The beautiful bride will discern and teach love, joy, and peace. Humility and submission will find the fruit of the Spirit.

NT BIBLICAL ACCOUNT

There is a biblical method for discerning, not judging, the spiritual growth of Christians. This method includes Jesus's first major teaching, the Sermon on the Mount. Of the talents and gifts given, we'll look at which is most important. We'll begin with the parable that first addressed the Word of God and how it is planted in the hearts of believers.

This parable is very interesting because Jesus not only presents it, He also explains it. You'll find in His explanation a secret that He reveals about the difference between true believers and nonbelievers.

SEED AND SOIL

This parable is like a cipher that unlocks the mystery of our faith-journey. It is like an assessment tool of spiritual growth. I include this passage in its entirety because it is so important to our understanding. In it, Jesus is asked to explain His use of parables.

That same day Jesus went out of the house and sat by the lake. Such large crowds gathered around him that he got into a boat and sat in it, while all the people stood on the shore. Then he told them many things in parables, saying: "A farmer went out to sow his seed. As he was scattering the seed, some fell along the path, and the birds came and ate it up. Some fell on rocky places, where it did not have much soil. It sprang up quickly, because the soil was shallow. But when the sun came up, the plants were scorched, and they withered because they had no root. Other seed fell among thorns, which grew up and choked the plants. Still other seed fell on good soil, where it produced a crop—a hundred, sixty or thirty times what was sown. Whoever has ears, let them hear."

The disciples came to him and asked, "Why do you speak to the people in parables?"

He replied, "Because the knowledge of the secrets of the kingdom of heaven has been given to you, but not to them. Whoever has will be given more, and they will have an abundance. Whoever does not have, even what they have will be taken from them. This is why I speak to them in parables: Though seeing, they do not see; though hearing, they do not hear or understand.

"In them is fulfilled the prophecy of Isaiah:

'You will be ever hearing but never understanding; you will be ever seeing but never perceiving. For this people's heart has become calloused; they hardly hear with their ears, and they have closed their eyes. Otherwise they might see with their eyes, hear with their ears, understand with their hearts and turn, and I would heal them.'

But blessed are your eyes because they see, and your ears because they hear. For truly I tell you, many prophets and righteous people longed to see what you see but did not see it, and to hear what you hear but did not hear it.

"Listen then to what the parable of the sower means: When anyone hears the message about the kingdom and does not understand it, the evil one comes and snatches away what was sown in their heart. This is the seed sown along the path. The seed falling on rocky ground refers to someone who hears the word and at once receives it with joy. But since they have no root, they last only a short time. When trouble or persecution comes because of the word, they quickly fall away. The seed falling among the thorns refer to someone who hears the word, but the worries of this life and the deceitfulness of wealth choke the word, making it unfruitful. But the seed falling on good soil refers to someone who hears the word and understands it. This is the one who produces a crop, yielding a hundred, sixty or thirty times what was sown."[468]

There are several critical issues here that I would like to unpack. Jesus understood spiritual formation and taught us how to proceed in caring for the lost. Over the years, I have heard many discussions and stories about spiritual maturity, or lack thereof, affecting a short-lived Christian experience. I have found these conversations disappointing because I believe the loss of a *seeker* is equally the fault of the church. I am convinced we have not embraced what it really means to be brothers and sisters in Christ to other believers. We look in their eyes and might see a project. More likely, we see an inconvenience—unless, of course, we determine that they have something to offer. Like a salesperson, we qualify them at the door. If the new believer is well-off, the sales manager will take them. If not, the sales staff will get them. I understand that is harsh, but we *must* learn how to apply the fruit of the Spirit with everyone.

These anecdotal observations are real. God is just. When you choose to make God the Lord of your life, you choose to depend on Him. This is about a relationship in which you depend on God. You have received forgiveness for your sin, but more importantly, you now have a personal relationship with God. Unfortunately, if you don't humble yourself through submission and surrender to this relationship, you miss the intimacy of it. Jesus used examples of believers in this passage—not nonbelievers, but those called by God.

---

[468] Matthew 13:1–23.

THE BARE PATH

I have witnessed hundreds of shallow Christian individuals in my lifetime, ones who have attended church, a small group, or a revival. Consider Joe. Joe prayed a believer's prayer for the forgiveness of his sins and was baptized. He felt much better about becoming a Christian, but soon things went sideways. In chatting with Joe, I found he was a shallow believer. He had expectations of what Christlike behavior looked like. Unfortunately, he never saw that behavior reflected in the lives of other Christians. If he did see brothers and sisters in Christ walking it out, he would compare himself and feel defeated. He put five dollars in the offering. I could not find Joe after a few months.

ROCKY SOIL

Jean made a greater commitment and was filled with excitement. She volunteered in children's church. Unfortunately, she didn't do the real work of growing in her faith-journey. She put ten dollars in the plate each Sunday. Jean liked how it felt when she served, but she lost that feeling soon. She had not developed a Christian worldview on which to stand firmly. She went along with the culture crowd because she could not stand alone. She overindulged with friends at times.

THORNY SOIL

Then there are those who make a consistent commitment, do the consistent church work, and have a dedication to their local church. One couple attended a small group or, more often, led it. They liked reading the Bible, praying in church, and attending every service and church event. They believed God was pleased with their work.

Yet something was not right, because their son had cancer. The bills were growing, so they asked God for help. None came. They believed in a woman's right to her body because it seemed right. They put twenty dollars a week in the offering. This couple hadn't submitted to the sovereignty of God.

GOOD SOIL

A different couple, middle-aged, loved going to church. He led their devotions together every morning. He had a good job as a postal worker. She remained at home with their two high school-aged children. The wife made sure the kids had what they needed.

They talked openly about the challenges of a secular world. The children were often surprised and hurt by teasing they were targeted with because they stood on Christian principles. Mom discussed the hurt and reminded them what the Word says about persecution, praying for bullies, and God's sovereignty. The kids pursued the direction in which they believed God was leading them after graduation. God blessed the husband with a promotion. The family tithed 10 percent—a hundred and fifty dollars each week. The seed of God's Word grew strong.

Needless to say, I have been blessed by God with everything I need and often with what I want. I talk to God minute by minute, from the time I wake up until I lie down for sleep. God blesses those who make a sacrifice for Him.

God is intimately involved in our lives. The spiritually mature learn that dependence on Him is freedom. Here is a remarkable truth, little discussed: *good soil produces the fruit of the Spirit.*

SPIRITUAL MATURITY

Following Jesus's baptism and receiving of the Holy Spirit, He was led to the wilderness, where He fasted for forty days and nights. Then Satan appeared to lure Him away from His relationship with the Father. This was the same approach used by the serpent in the Garden of Eden. Jesus was victorious by believing God's Word, trusting the sovereignty of God, and pursuing God's will *only*!

In His first significant teaching, a major address, Jesus taught His listeners the steps to building their faith and having success over the evil one. In this Sermon on the Mount, He laid out the general process of spiritual formation: being poor in spirit, mourning, being meek, hungering and thirsting for righteousness, being merciful, being pure in heart, and being a peacemaker.

FRUIT OF THE SPIRIT

I want to begin by saying that it seems to me we have *the cart before the horse.* We have placed too much emphasis on the spiritual gifts and motivational gifts when we should be attending to the *fruit of the Spirit*—specifically, teaching and looking for the new believer to demonstrate the mind of Christ through possessing the fruit of the Spirit. I am sure that's the way God intended it to be.

In Paul's stern instruction to the Galatians, he clearly stated the importance of love. The first fruit he described is critical to our unity in Christ.

> But the fruit of the Spirit is love, joy, peace, forbearance, kindness, goodness, faithfulness, gentleness and self-control. Against such things there is no law. Those who belong to Christ Jesus have crucified the flesh with its passions and desires. Since we live by the Spirit, let us keep in step with the Spirit. Let us not become conceited, provoking and envying each other.[469]

To that end, it is obvious he was aware of internal struggles of making comparisons between the spiritual giftings and the fruit of the Spirit.

> If I speak in the tongues of men or of angels, but do not have love, I am only a resounding gong or a clanging cymbal. If I have the gift of prophecy and can fathom all mysteries and all knowledge, and if I have a faith that can move mountains, but do not have love, I am nothing. If I give all I possess to the poor and give over my body to hardship that I may boast, but do not have love, I gain nothing.[470]

Paul connected standing firm in freedom to the fruit of love. Freedom is the trademark of our faith and leads us to walk in the Spirit, who begins

---

[469] Galatians 5:22–26.
[470] 1 Corinthians 13:1–3.

with love. Paul identified the characteristics of the fruit that we demonstrate through our love:

> It is for freedom that Christ has set us free. Stand firm, then, and do not let yourselves be burdened again by a yoke of slavery ... Mark my words! I, Paul, tell you that if you let yourselves be circumcised, Christ will be of no value to you at all ... For in Christ Jesus neither circumcision nor uncircumcision has any value.

> The only thing that counts is faith expressing itself through love.[471]

Finally, Paul gave definition to love as the main fruit of the Spirit:

> Love is patient, love is kind. It does not envy, it does not boast, it is not proud. It does not dishonor others, it is not self-seeking, it is not easily angered, it keeps no record of wrongs. Love does not delight in evil but rejoices with the truth. It always protects, always trusts, always hopes, always perseveres. Love never fails.[472]

We see this fruit in maturing believers, which signals their intimacy with God. Conceit and arrogance spoil or diminish the fruit. As a believer matures, we see a greater measure to a full measure of this fruit in their lives. I believe nourishing the fruit of the Spirit in believers will create a thriving and prospering church body. Pastors, attending to the spiritual formation progression and the fruit of the Spirit in your congregation is more important than motivational and spiritual giftings. It is through the fruit of the Spirit that people will see our love.

> You, my brothers and sisters, were called to be free. But do not use your freedom to indulge the flesh; rather, serve one another humbly in love. For the entire law is fulfilled

---

[471] Galatians 5:1–6.
[472] 1 Corinthians 13:4–8.

227

in keeping this one command: "Love your neighbor as yourself." If you bite and devour each other, watch out or you will be destroyed by each other. So I say, walk by the Spirit, and you will not gratify the desires of the flesh.[473]

Paul also warns us not to be deceived by the slick talk of nonbelievers or, more importantly, misguided believers.

You were running a good race. Who cut in on you to keep you from obeying the truth? That kind of persuasion does not come from the one who calls you. "A little yeast works through the whole batch of dough." I am confident in the Lord that you will take no other view. The one who is throwing you into confusion, whoever that may be, will have to pay the penalty.[474]

Paul clearly identifies that those behaviors are not a part of Christlike behavior. Use this to check your behaviors. I would tell my students, "God is serious about our righteousness."

The acts of the flesh are obvious: sexual immorality, impurity and debauchery; idolatry and witchcraft; hatred, discord, jealousy, fits of rage, selfish ambition, dissensions, factions and envy; drunkenness, orgies, and the like. I warn you, as I did before, that those who live like this will not inherit the kingdom of God.[475]

Jesus made it clear that the relationship we possess with Him is one of love. Neither Jesus nor Paul elevated the spiritual gifts above the fruit of love or character and hope.

A new command I give you: Love one another. As I have loved you, so you must love one another. By this everyone

---

[473] Galatians 5:13–16.
[474] Galatians 5:7–11.
[475] Galatians 5:19–21.

will know that you are my disciples, if you love one another.[476]

You may recall it was following this statement that Peter got into so much trouble with regard to his denial of knowing Jesus. He was being led by his pride to say he would follow Jesus to his death if necessary. Jesus epitomized love in His ministry. Moreover, His healings were demonstrated through love. Love is the key to possessing effectual spiritual gifts.

Paul, in Romans, acknowledged a process. He ended at the critical place for followers of Christ to follow. Growth is a progressive process that takes place as we grow. That growth is often through suffering or trials through which the Holy Spirit leads us.

> Not only so, but we also glory in our sufferings, because we know that suffering produces perseverance; perseverance, character; and character, hope. And hope does not put us to shame, because God's love has been poured out into our hearts through the Holy Spirit, who has been given to us.[477]

The progressive process of spiritual transformation ends in character and hope! Character and hope will allow us to contend with troubles in this world. A Christlike character and hope will give us oneness with the Lord of our lives.

In the apostle John's prayer, he explains an almost out-of-body spiritual experience of perceiving the world and its affairs in another way:

> My prayer is not that you take them out of the world but that you protect them from the evil one. They are not of the world, even as I am not of it. Sanctify them by the truth; your word is truth. As you sent me into the world, I have sent them into the world. For them I sanctify myself, that they too may be truly sanctified.[478]

---

[476] John 13:34–35.
[477] Romans 5:3–5.
[478] John 17:15–21.

John is clearly making a statement about the world being an ungodly multitude, or the whole mass of humanity that is alienated from God and hostile to the cause of Christ.[479]

Distinctly different from humankind's perception of existential self, the Christ-follower's perceptions are of another reality, a spiritual reality that contrasts with the world order and its reality. The mind, in oneness with Christ, sees the kingdom of God on earth. The progressive growth of a Christ-follower brings perceptions born in a new soul-vision.

SPIRITUAL GIFTS

The Holy Spirit is residing in all who made a confession of faith and were baptized. The Holy Spirit provides the spiritual gifts necessary to carry out the work of God.[480] Paul informed the Corinthian church about the spiritual gifts:

> To one there is given through the Spirit a message of wisdom, to another a message of knowledge by means of the same Spirit, to another faith by the same Spirit, to another gifts of healing by that one Spirit, to another miraculous powers, to another prophecy, to another distinguishing between spirits, to another speaking in different kinds of tongues, and to still another the interpretation of tongues.[481]

These gifts are not to be owned. They belong to the Holy Spirit, to be given for the work of God. If someone heals another, they may only be able to do it one time. Or, if someone can discern evil spirits, they may be able to do so on many occasions. God is in control. There are other giftings that God will give to believers as necessary.

The following are what I refer to as motivational gifts, specifically given by God. Paul revealed these gifts to the Romans, to be used by the body of

---

[479] Blue Letter Bible, September 1, 2023, https://www.blueletterbible.org/lexicon/g2889/niv/mgnt/0-1/.

[480] Crosswalk, accessed August 13, 2023, https://www.crosswalk.com/faith/spiritual-lifehow-to-identify-and-effectively-use-your-spiritual-gifts.html.

[481] 1 Corinthians 12:8–10.

Christ, the church. He gave warning that possessing a gift does not give a believer the right to think more highly of themselves.

> For by the grace given me I say to every one of you: Do not think of yourself more highly than you ought, but rather think of yourself with sober judgment, in accordance with the faith God has distributed to each of you. For just as each of us has one body with many members, and these members do not all have the same function, so in Christ we, though many, form one body, and each member belongs to all the others. We have different gifts, according to the grace given to each of us. If your gift is prophesying, then prophesy in accordance with your faith; if it is serving, then serve; if it is teaching, then teach; if it is to encourage, then give encouragement; if it is giving, then give generously; if it is to lead, do it diligently; if it is to show mercy, do it cheerfully.[482]

There is no doubt that the spiritual and motivational giftings are important. However, they should be addressed after the spiritual transformation and the fruit of the Spirit. Done the other way, it would be the cart before the horse. Teach your church body to grow and love first, to thrive and nourish. God is an orderly God. These giftings are given according to the grace given to each, which is different.

A third group are God's vocational gifts. These apply to church leadership and focus on missionary as well as church-planting work. Paul explained this to the Ephesians:

> So Christ himself gave the apostles, the prophets, the evangelists, the pastors and teachers, to equip his people for works of service, so that the body of Christ may be built up until we all reach unity in the faith and in the knowledge of the Son of God and become mature, attaining to the whole measure of the fullness of Christ.[483]

---

[482] Romans 12:3–8.
[483] Ephesians 4:11–13.

> There is no magic formula or definitive test that can tell us exactly what our spiritual gifts are. The Holy Spirit distributes the gifts as He determines. A common problem for Christians is the temptation to get so caught up in our spiritual gift that we only seek to serve God in the area in which we feel we have been gifted. That is not how the spiritual gifts work. God calls us to obediently serve Him in all things. He will equip us with whatever gift or gifts we need to accomplish the task He has called us to.[484]

As a reminder, Paul made a very important and seemingly stern statement regarding spiritual giftings. They are not to be the critical issue of our relationship with God or in doing His work. The Holy Spirit oversees the work. Your job is readiness through the fruit of the Spirit!

Over the years, I have heard arguments and differing interpretations regarding the spiritual gifts. Be very clear about this:

- These spiritual gifts belong to the Holy Spirit. No one necessarily owns a gift.
- They are given by the Spirit to a believer to complete the will of God.
- Too often spiritually immature believers will lay claim to a gifting. *No bueno*! Their boasting will reveal this.
- Too many believe spiritual giftings are not for today. They are wrong!
- Most importantly, a spiritually mature person can discern misuse of the gifts because that person possesses the fruit of the Spirit, which provides a greater level of discernment.

Having said all that, let us focus on the verses driving this chapter. Like Paul, Peter understood spiritual growth as a process. Peter's letter is the focus of our Christian faith-journey. It includes a more detailed analysis of what every believer should do in order to avoid the blindness that nonbelievers possess. Peter maintained that you will not stumble, but will receive entrance into eternal life. Moreover, those who passionately

---

[484] Accessed August 5, 2023, https://www.gotquestions.org/spiritual-gift.html.

pursue a deepened spiritual relationship with God will participate in the divine nature if their faith-journey follows these steps.

> For this very reason, make every effort to add to your faith goodness; and to goodness, knowledge; and to knowledge, self-control; and to self-control, perseverance; and to perseverance, godliness; and to godliness, mutual affection; and to mutual affection, love.[485]

Peter's maturing process focused on the fruit of the Spirit. He studied for knowledge, perseverance, and godliness. These are the specific qualities of Christlike behavior. There is nothing here about spiritual or motivational giftings.

Peter added why this was so critical for each believer:

> For if you possess these qualities in increasing measure, they will keep you from being ineffective and unproductive in your knowledge of our Lord Jesus Christ. But whoever does not have them is nearsighted and blind, forgetting that they have been cleansed from their past sins. Therefore, my brothers and sisters, make every effort to confirm your calling and election. For if you do these things, you will never stumble, and you will receive a rich welcome into the eternal kingdom of our Lord and Savior Jesus Christ.[486]

Here's the point: *in increasing measure* means we are filled with the presence, power, and fullness of God through the fruit; study for knowledge; Christlike behavior; and perseverance. A profound awareness is humble in the presence, power, and fullness of God.[487] You are aware of your deep dependence on God and humbled in your relationship with Him. You know your relationship is authentic. You see God moving and intervening because of His relationship with you.

---

[485] 2 Peter 1:5–7.

[486] 2 Peter 1:8–11.

[487] Blue Letter Bible, accessed August 16, 2023, https://www.blueletterbible.org/lexicon/g4138/niv/mgnt/0-1/.

Let's add that John said:

> A new command I give you: Love one another. As I have
> loved you, so you must love one another. By this everyone
> will know that you are my disciples, if you love one another.[488]

How many times must it be said? Love is the key that unlocks this intimacy with God, because your love for Him and His very authentic love for you is in full measure.

ARMOR OF GOD

Let's first consider a Christlike mind for the workplace—the relationship we have in the workplace and how we should appear to others.

> Slaves, obey your earthly masters with deep respect and
> fear. Serve them sincerely as you would serve Christ. Try
> to please them all the time, not just when they are watching
> you. As slaves of Christ, do the will of God with all your
> heart. Work with enthusiasm, as though you were working
> for the Lord rather than for people. Remember that the
> Lord will reward each one of us for the good we do, whether
> we are slaves or free. Masters, treat your slaves in the same
> way. Don't threaten them; remember, you both have the
> same Master in heaven, and he has no favorites.[489]

Christians are both loved and hated in the workplace. Employers love their work ethic, while teammates will struggle with a Christian's commitment to the job. Do not slip into the trap of acting like the world in the workplace.

> A final word: Be strong in the Lord and in his mighty
> power. Put on all of God's armor so that you will be able to
> stand firm against all strategies of the devil. For we are not

---

[488] John 13:34–35.
[489] Ephesians 6:5–9 NLT.

fighting against flesh-and-blood enemies, but against evil rulers and authorities of the unseen world, against mighty powers in this dark world, and against evil spirits in the heavenly places.

Therefore, put on every piece of God's armor so you will be able to resist the enemy in the time of evil. Then after the battle you will still be standing firm. Stand your ground, putting on the belt of truth and the body armor of God's righteousness. For shoes, put on the peace that comes from the Good News so that you will be fully prepared. In addition to all of these, hold up the shield of faith to stop the fiery arrows of the devil. Put on salvation as your helmet, and take the sword of the Spirit, which is the word of God.[490]

Let's put the armor in order as given to see its specific motif, oneness in Christ:

- stand firm with the truth of who God is and that you know Him personally
- protect your heart with wholesome living
- be balanced in living your life through peace with God
- be courageous and trust God through all the insults and persecution thrown at you
- protect your mind's hold on the truth of what your salvation means
- keep the Word of God close, because it is your weapon to stand firm

To many, these are just words and verses to be memorized. But for Paul, this analogy was a critical series in our oneness as Christ-followers. He meant these words to capture the essence of our battle with the dark world, which is only possible through the pivotal qualities taught by God through trials and suffering. Simply put, God has prepared each of us to stand firm and be courageous as the end times approach. Ask the Holy Spirit to give you each piece. Stand on the truth, wholesomeness, and peace with Him. Trust His sovereignty. Embrace your first love of salvation. Meditate on His

---

[490] Ephesians 6:10–17 NLT.

Word. This is the only way to advance into the horrific and evil darkness of the spiritual forces that are approaching.[491]

THE DREAM EXPERIENCE

It was a couple years after recommitting my life. My biblical study was going well. I learned how to use a concordance and commentary to help in my understanding. I began meeting with some guys in a little town next to the air force base where I was stationed. We gathered on Saturday mornings to pray. And pray we did.

Curiously, I was hearing more and more from the Holy Spirit through a word of knowledge or word of wisdom as I asked God more questions. I would come across a passage I didn't understand and would ask God what it meant. In a couple of days, I would hear back: "You remember when you asked about this passage? Here's your answer." It was spiritually thrilling to me to be in conversation with the Holy Spirit. It filled me with excitement. It happened often and still happens to this day.

There was one particular statement I made—it wasn't a question, but the response was powerful. I had been reading a book about the Israelites and how stubborn they were. God was constantly bringing them back from their disobedience. As I was getting ready for bed, I asked God, "Help me not to be as hardheaded as the Hebrews. Please give me blinders to stay focused on your faithfulness." I went to sleep.

Suddenly, I found myself in space. I mean above-the-earth space, floating over our planet. There was something very real about this. When I realized where I was, I started gasping for breath because I knew this was supposed to be a vacuum, with no oxygen. It was frightening. After a few gasps, I discovered I could breathe, and I relaxed. How could this be?

Then I settled down to take in the view. It was as if I were looking out of an International Space Station portal. It was incredible and now very peaceful. I heard nothing, but I did feel my pantlegs flapping against my ankles in the space wind.

Then I caught sight, in my peripheral vision, of an object floating toward

---

[491] John McRay, *Paul: His Life and Teaching* (Baker Academic, 2003), 348.

me on my right. It was a man in robe. I didn't look directly at the figure—to this day I don't know why. I was mesmerized by my view of Earth.

Then I realized a hand was moving across my shoulders. It rested on my left shoulder. The other hand was pointing back at Earth. There was no audible voice, just a kind of telepathy saying, "He wants them back." There was nothing more, no other mental notes. I woke up well-rested.

I noticed something different as I sat on the edge of my bed. I was experiencing something new from deep within me. It was a joy that went beyond happiness. The joy carried an indescribable peace with it. I was strengthened to know that the dream was from God.

The joy and peace have remained with me since that night back in 1978. It was an experience I will never forget and remains a permanent fixture in my memory. Again, I've told very few about this encounter.

DEVELOPING A PROFOUND AWARENESS

A profound awareness comes as we desire the fruit of God's Spirit. As the fruit ripens, so does our ability to do more through Him. Too often in Christianity, interest in spiritual gifts takes precedence over the desire for the fruit of the Spirit. It is not surprising that this is the case. Understanding and pursuing spiritual gifts can be a more subjective pursuit, as well as being hampered by the believer's emotional excitement. Pursuit of the fruit is more challenging and requires a deeper relationship with Jesus rather than passion for the discovery of one's spiritual gifting.

Chasing after God and being driven by a longing for an intimate bond seem daunting. On the one hand, I want you to know it is not. The focus is different and requires a commitment to conversation and quiet listening. On the other hand, it is a challenge, because it does require a rigorous discipline beyond knowledge acquisition. Many express concern that spiritual disciplines are not spelled out in the Bible and can become a type of legalism. However, many authors and theologians have gleaned from Scriptures some obvious themes and motifs that can strengthen one's relationship with God.

Richard Foster sorts the most common disciplines into three categories. The *inward disciplines* include meditation, prayer, fasting, and study. The second group, the *outward disciplines*, include simplicity, solitude, submission, and service. The *corporate disciplines*, within the church body, are worship, confession, celebration, and guidance.[492]

Scriptures do not provide hard specificity to most of these disciplines. But we do find an encouragement to practice them in our lives. They can intensify one's spiritual formation and relationship with God.

Over the years, I have discovered a correlation between Christ-followers demonstrating the fruit of the Spirit and a joyful adherence to the spiritual disciplines. These faithful followers are profoundly aware of God's intervention in their lives and others. I say this to reinforce all that we've discussed in this book. Those whose soul-deep vision is anchored in their hearts and guided by the Holy Spirit will be fruitful and multiply in their God work! That thriving relationship embraces the spiritual disciplines.

I find it inspirational to listen to popular Christian music at home. Also, I am sure many would agree that Gregorian chants are not inspirational. I do find them worshipful, and I'm not Catholic. Ultimately, solitude and prayer are key. I am entering a new phase in my life of seeking simplicity, so that I might hear Him better.

The purpose in all of the disciplines is to deepen your dependence on God, to hear from Him, and to pursue His plan for your life—not only the big plan, but His daily guidance. Make a plan, but God will guide you where He wants you to go. "In their hearts humans plan their course, but the Lord establishes their steps."[493]

My personal testimony reveals several profound interventions by God in my life. Those events were significant, but they were small in consideration of the many other times that God interceded in my life or answered prayer. Those instances are countless. I know that I know of His involvement in my life.

My path to understanding what I hear from Him is my listening. I have come to learn several things about hearing from God. Not surprisingly, I found my perspective consistent with the experience of the late Dallas Willard. First, *God will be very clear* about something and enter my mind with authority—not overbearing, but serenely clear. He comes when my

---

[492] Richard Foster, *Celebration of Discipline: The Path of Spiritual Growth* (HarperCollins, 1988).
[493] Proverbs 16:9.

mind is not cluttered with other thoughts. Maybe I am driving and listening to Christian music, or in the shower. Something said will send me off to a topic God wants me to think about.

Second, God is to the point. He doesn't use a lot of words, but I get it. Usually, I need many words from someone in order to wrap my head around what they mean. Not with Him. *God is short, sweet, and to the point.*

Finally, what God says always fits into my life or projects, such as writing this book. I am always receiving a word of knowledge or a word of wisdom. Keep in mind: that word *always* fits within the context of what I am writing, and it *never* contradicts the God's Word.

In his book *Hearing God*, Professor Willard shared that God possesses a tone of heavenly instruction. Dr. Willard said that God's communication "enables us to do specific, concrete things that will help us as we seek to know the will of God."[494]

In addition to the fearless nature of God's people is the adamant belief in the joy of their conviction. A conviction in their hope sustains them. "Hope deferred makes the heart sick, but a longing fulfilled is a tree of life."[495]

---

[494] Dallas Willard, *Hearing God: Developing a Conversational Relationship with God* (IVP Press, 1984), 226.
[495] Proverbs 13:12.

22

CHRISTIAN LEADERSHIP: GOD-SERVING MEN AND WOMEN

WE'LL EXAMINE MORE DEEPLY WHAT IT MEANS FOR A MAN OR WOMAN TO move from their humanistic and secular life, which they have belonged to from birth, to the God-serving leader that He has called them to become in oneness with Christ. I'll begin with a quick review of Deuteronomy. It was the last of the five biblical books written by Moses. It is a historical look at where the Israelites came from in Egypt and an encouragement to enter the Promised Land. Moses reviewed the Ten Commandments and reminded the Israelites of their promise to be covenant keepers. Most poignant is a statement referred to as the Shema prayer, which is repeated in the NT at a critical moment when Jesus is asked which commandment is greatest: "Hear, O Israel: The Lord your God, the Lord is one. Love the Lord your God with all your heart and with all your soul and with all your strength."[496]

The Shema captures all of what is meant by possessing a soul-vision. However, Moses added to this some significant remarks on how to use the commandments:

> These commandments that I give you today are to be on your hearts. Impress them on your children. Talk about them when you sit at home and when you walk along the road, when you lie down and when you get up. Tie them as symbols on your hands and bind them on your foreheads. Write them on the doorframes of your houses and on your gates.[497]

---

[496] Deuteronomy 6:4–5.
[497] Deuteronomy 6:6–9.

The soul needs this kind of training: to talk about the commandments when sitting, when walking, when lying down, when arising. Bind them on your forehead. Write them on your doorframe and gate. This approach will build these tenets within your soul, resulting in a "complete devotion to Him and not just an emotional attraction."[498]

The next time we hear the Shema is in a conversation taking place between Jesus and some others. There's a little change in the prayer.

> One of the teachers of the law came and heard them debating. Noticing that Jesus had given them a good answer, he asked him, "Of all the commandments, which is the most important?"
>
> "The most important one," answered Jesus, "is this: 'Hear, O Israel: The Lord our God, the Lord is one. Love the Lord your God with all your heart and with all your soul and with all your mind and with all your strength.'"

Curiously, Jesus added something to the Shema:

> "The second is this: 'Love your neighbor as yourself.' There is no commandment greater than these."[499]

The expert in the law added further explanation:

> "Well said, teacher," the man replied. "You are right in saying that God is one and there is no other but him. To love him with all your heart, with all your understanding and with all your strength, and to love your neighbor as yourself is more important than all burnt offerings and sacrifices."
>
> When Jesus saw that he had answered wisely, he said to him, "You are not far from the kingdom of God."

---

[498] *The Moody Bible Commentary* (Moody Publishers, 2014), 272.
[499] Mark 12:28–31.

And from then on no one dared ask him any more questions.[500]

It is interesting that Mark provided an inside look at what the experts were thinking. Jesus had taken them as far as they wanted to go with this discussion, fearing that He would teach more than they could handle.

Regarding the soul, *The Moody Bible Commentary* states, "[T]he soul denotes the innermost being or emotions."[501] However, when restating Jesus's response, the law expert did not use the word *soul*. He also replaced *mind* with *understanding*.[502] *Understanding*, to the Hebrew lawyer, meant it was all coming together The mind is not a place, but a function of thoughts flowing together.[503] *Faculty* is defined as an inherent mental or physical power.[504] Jesus's usage leads to a distinction for *soul* that we'll be using in this book.

The soul is the harbor of the innermost being, housing the heart, mind, emotions, and will (strength). The soul encompasses understanding, feeling, and desiring through the total work of the heart, mind, and strength. This leads to your behavior. A soul that hungers and thirsts for righteousness is a soul that will become God-serving.

Let's consider this passage more fully. Jesus is teaching a new *love*. It "is a matter of will and action. But He demands decision and readiness for God and for God alone in an unconditional manner which startles His hearers."[505]

For the word *heart*, its larger definition is the center of the inner life. Within the heart dwell feelings, emotion, desires, and passions. It is the seat of understanding, the source of thought and reflection, the seat of the will, and the source of resolve.[506]

On the other hand, Jesus used a different word for *mind* than the word the expert used. Jesus used *dianoia*, which means the faculty of understanding. As used by John at 1 John 5:20, it means a faculty of perception or gift of

---

[500] Mark 12:28–34.
[501] *Moody*, 276.
[502] Proverbs 20:5 NLT. Understanding is discerned through a profound awareness.
[503] Blue Letter Bible, https://www.blueletterbible.org/lexicon/g4907/niv/mgnt/0-1/.
[504] "Usage of faculty," accessed August 20, 2023, https://search.yahoo.com/search?fr=mcafee&type=E211US1500G0&p=definiton+of+faculty.
[505] TDNT. Vol. 1, pg. 45.
[506] TDNT. Vol. 3, pg. 611–612.

apprehension, which includes an orientation to know God, to receive His revelation, and to share fellowship with Him.[507] This understanding not only perceives the world and its ways, but also perceives the supernatural ways of reality.

The word *strength* has to do a person's ability and capacity to carry out the mission. It is a behavior that acquires force through the effective power of prayer. You must have the strength to withstand and to face the buffeting forces against you.[508] The Shema is the rallying cry for Christians to stand their ground. It is the power that is within the greatest commandment: all human strength must concentrate on the love of God.[509]

We learn the greatest commandment because our enemy is found everywhere in humanistic and secular mankind.

> For our struggle is not against flesh and blood, but against the rulers, against the authorities, against the powers of this dark world and against the spiritual forces of evil in the heavenly realms.[510]

Paul gave instructions for living out loving the Lord your God with all your heart and with all your soul and with all your mind and with all your strength. I believe that was the focus of Paul's work. Let's look at the issues Paul raised, beginning with a prayer that Jesus prayed for all believers:

> My prayer is not for them alone. I pray also for those who will believe in me through their message, that all of them may be one, Father, just as you are in me and I am in you. May they also be in us so that the world may believe that you have sent me. I have given them the glory that you gave me, that they may be one as we are one—I in them and you in me—so that they may be brought to complete unity. Then the world will know that you sent me and have loved them even as you have loved me.

---

[507] TDNT. Vol. 4, pg. 967.
[508] TDNT. Vol. 3, pg. 397.
[509] TDNT. Vol 3, pg. 399.
[510] Ephesians 6:12.

Father, I want those you have given me to be with me where I am, and to see my glory, the glory you have given me because you loved me before the creation of the world.

Righteous Father, though the world does not know you, I know you, and they know that you have sent me. I have made you known to them, and will continue to make you known in order that the love you have for me may be in them and that I myself may be in them.[511]

The plan is moving as God ordained from the very beginning, in the pre-creation planning. Jesus wanted to be with us from the beginning.

Here is a quick look at Paul's background. His birth name was Saul. He was a highly educated Israelite and an adviser to the high priest. He was hated by the Christians because he was guilty of putting hundreds of Christians to death. His heart was changed on a trip to Damascus.

As he neared Damascus on his journey, suddenly a light from heaven flashed around him. He fell to the ground and heard a voice say to him, "Saul, Saul, why do you persecute me?"

"Who are you, Lord?" Saul asked.

"I am Jesus, whom you are persecuting," he replied. "Now get up and go into the city, and you will be told what you must do."

The men traveling with Saul stood there speechless; they heard the sound but did not see anyone. Saul got up from the ground, but when he opened his eyes he could see nothing. So they led him by the hand into Damascus. For three days he was blind, and did not eat or drink anything. In Damascus there was a disciple named Ananias. The Lord called to him in a vision, "Ananias!"

"Yes, Lord," he answered.

The Lord told him, "Go to the house of Judas on Straight Street and ask for a man from Tarsus named Saul, for he is

---

[511] John 17:20–26.

praying. In a vision he has seen a man named Ananias come and place his hands on him to restore his sight."

"Lord," Ananias answered, "I have heard many reports about this man and all the harm he has done to your holy people in Jerusalem. And he has come here with authority from the chief priests to arrest all who call on your name."

But the Lord said to Ananias, "Go! This man is my chosen instrument to proclaim my name to the Gentiles and their kings and to the people of Israel. I will show him how much he must suffer for my name."

Then Ananias went to the house and entered it. Placing his hands on Saul, he said, "Brother Saul, the Lord—Jesus, who appeared to you on the road as you were coming here—has sent me so that you may see again and be filled with the Holy Spirit." Immediately, something like scales fell from Saul's eyes, and he could see again. He got up and was baptized, and after taking some food, he regained his strength.[512]

I can certainly sympathize with Ananias, because Saul was a bad man. It is not surprising that he was on fire for the Lord and began preaching and teaching in Damascus. When he went to Jerusalem, the disciples were very unsure of him. Because he was adept at teaching, plots to kill him grew. The disciples moved him to Tarsus. For seven to fourteen years, Saul studied and prepared to return to preaching.

Until then, the prophets, Jesus, and the disciples had been appealing to the Israelites as the chosen people to accept Jesus, be born again, and follow Him. Unfortunately, the Pharisees and Sadducees did everything in their power to dissuade the Jews from listening. If that didn't work with Paul, they intended get rid of him as they had gotten rid of Jesus.

As a result of this backlash from the Pharisees, Paul announced that the Word would be proclaimed to the Gentiles.

When the Gentiles heard this, they were glad and honored the word of the Lord; and all who were appointed for

---

[512] Acts 9:3–19.

eternal life believed. The word of the Lord spread through the whole region. But the Jewish leaders incited the God-fearing women of high standing and the leading men of the city. They stirred up persecution against Paul and Barnabas, and expelled them from their region. So they shook the dust off their feet as a warning to them and went to Iconium. And the disciples were filled with joy and with the Holy Spirit.[513]

Interestingly, the Jewish leaders "incited" the God-fearing women of high standing as well as the leading men in the city. It is likely these women and men were Gentiles from the area, which gave them great influence over the local leaders.[514] Political influence can be an insidious action for the godless powerful.

DEVELOPING A PROFOUND AWARENESS

What we've discussed in this chapter brings up a significant point about the character of one who possesses a profound awareness. This chapter revealed a person, like Paul, who was unaffected by his former character as well as by the nefarious and godless influences of the world. The person experiencing a profound awareness has grown supernaturally into an existential state of emotional detachment from the world. That person has entered a state of soul-deep relationship with God. As a consequence, they are unaffected by the deceitful acts or favor of man. They stand joyfully in oneness with God. A God-serving leader remains above the offenses and focuses on the oneness of God.[515]

The vulnerable behavior of being offended lies deep within humanity and is referred to by John Bevere in his book *The Bait of Satan*.[516] Bevere identifies Satan's bait as some emotional, psychological, or physical attack

---

[513] Acts 13:48–52.
[514] *Moody*, 1703.
[515] John17:15–16. "In the world, but not of the world," https://www.gotquestions.org/in-but-not-of-world.html.
[516] John Bevere, *The Bait of Satan* (Charisma House Book Group, 1994), 13.

that has been perpetrated upon you by another person or persons. Bevere calls it a massive offense.

What happened to Joseph in the book of Genesis is an example. You'll recall that he had dreams of ruling over his eleven brothers. They were offended that he could say or think such a thing. They sold him into slavery. Years later, Joseph had become a high-ranking official in the Egyptian government. Joseph's brothers went to Egypt in search of food during an intense drought in their own land. They discovered their brother in a position of authority. What could have been a very dramatic scene of vengeance became a scene of a warm and joyful forgiveness. This is the object of the story: forgiveness.

We often find ourselves offended by the acts of another. There have been times in my life when the thoughtless behavior of individuals or, worse, friends has offended me. Maybe we could say they hurt my feelings. I would go away mad. It was always the Holy Spirit (or my mother) who would remind me that Jesus had had plenty of reasons to be mad or complain as He hung on the cross. But he said, "Father, forgive them, for they don't know what they are doing." A profound awareness would hold dearly to such a mind of forgiveness.

In Joseph's case, he became profoundly aware of God's actions:

> But Joseph said to them ... "You intended to harm me, but
> God intended it for good to accomplish what is now being
> done, the saving of many lives."[517]

Joseph, as a significant leader for the Egyptian government, possessed the power to imprison his brothers. Joseph was accorded mercy from God. Joseph responded to his brothers with forgiveness.

Jesus and Joseph could have returned evil with evil, but chose not to take the bait of Satan. Instead, they saw humanity in its lost, broken, and desperate state.

Another shining example of this profound awareness is the forgiving state of mind displayed by King David. He was anointed king of Israel, to follow King Saul upon his death. Unfortunately, King Saul took great offense to the boy-king in waiting. Because David was blessed by God, King Saul

---

[517] Genesis 50:19–20.

was envious and jealous and attempted to kill David. Eventually, King Saul's offense tormented his mind and led to his suicide. David's response to this persecution was to treat King Saul as God's anointed.[518]

The disciples experienced both sides of the Resurrection and Pentecost. Prior to the Crucifixion, the disciples seriously lacked understanding. Yes, they knew the Torah. What's more, they knew the Torah well enough to recognize the Messiah. When the Holy Spirit came upon them, the supernatural power gave birth to their testimonies and ministries. They were in the *know*!

---

[518] 1 Samuel 24:1–22.

23

A CHOICE FOR REALITY: KINGDOM OF MAN OR KINGDOM OF GOD

EVERY HUMAN BEING MUST DECIDE FOR THEMSELVES WHAT *REALITY* they will choose to follow. I've discovered in reading the NT that the writers drew a clear distinction between the two realities. One is presented by Jesus as the kingdom of God, the reality the created were taught in Eden. It is a reality of our innocence and relationship with God. The other is the kingdom of man. In man's kingdom, we are born into a reality of science and objectivity. The modern person is raised into a natural approach of viewing and existing in a world as it is, their *reasoned* kingdom.

Every young adult, whether college- or career-focused, must independently make choices as to how they should live. One view is that each person is autonomous and must determine a course of action that leads to self-sufficiency and control over their destiny. On the other hand, those living in the kingdom of God and in dependence on Him will seek His guidance. They are profoundly aware of His intervention in their lives.

HUMANITY: EXISTENTIAL DREAD

Living a life in a kingdom focused on secular humanity is living in the world. Jean-Paul Sarte said this about humanity's choices: "Man is nothing else but what he purposes, he exists only in so far as he realizes himself, he is therefore nothing else but the sum of his actions, nothing else but what his life is."[519] Clearly, for the humanist, your person exists in your personally ascribed purpose. The value you place on yourself is aligned with

---

[519] Jean-Paul Sartre, "Existentialism is a Humanism."

responsible actions, your work. Any inherent value in living does not exist. Accordingly, life itself has no value for humanity. Value comes only from the value a person ascribes to life. Existential dread is the bottom line, and you work your way up from there. The existential dread is without pure vision.

The existentialist assumes there is nothing else beyond this existence, which they qualify as their reality. Humanity is a tiny species on a planet floating around in a humongous universe. In a hundred years, only your children will know you existed. What passes for good news among existentialists is that humanistic psychologists and philosophers have *reasoned* a way for you to understand and accept your existential state.

ABRAHAM MASLOW

Let me be clear: this is a central theme of human existence according to the prevailing winds of existentialism—learning to live in a world without vision and accepting it. So the question becomes, for modern man, "How should we move through our lived experiences?"

From our earliest moments in life, we begin to learn about our dependence on the family. Learning theorists say humans learn the most in the first five years of life. A humanistic psychologist, Abraham Maslow, provided a developmental theory called a *hierarchy of needs*, or choices that will lead to an ultimate goal of human satisfaction, which is happiness.[520] It all makes sense, right?

Not only does Maslow's hierarchy reflect human needs, it also reflects the source of the motivations of our behavior. While we can debate some of his descriptions of our developmental growth, the eerie truth is striking. Every day, whether we realize it or not, the human needs for food, water, sleep, and elimination control our behaviors. Moving up Maslow's pyramid takes us to another realm of critical needs: safety and security. Physiological and safety needs are absolutely critical to all human beings.

Unfortunately, we can experience moments in our lives when these basic needs are in question. These are very frightening moments. A wife and mother in the throes of domestic violence may have to leave her home

---

[520] Accessed October 14, 2023, https://sites.psu.edu/rclerin/2015/04/10/hierarchy-of-needs/.

with her children to seek food, shelter, and safety. I've discovered a high school student sleeping in their car because they were kicked out of their home. An unexpected layoff, for a family living from paycheck to paycheck, may create deep fear of eviction. These are only a few examples of our basic needs coming under threat.

While basic needs are critical, our psychological needs are just as important. Belonging, acceptance, intimacy, and relationship are very important to all of us. To love and be loved is critical to happiness. It is also important to be proud of your accomplishments. This not only means one's work or vocation, but also the academic accomplishment of a fourth grader on their math test. Reaching goals provides a significant level of self-satisfaction. A student who completes high school with honors despite a tumultuous divorce between their parents is proud of their success.

Most human beings exist within their psychosocial and physiological needs. At the top of Maslow's pyramid are self-actualization needs. Not everyone reaches this pinnacle, because their lives are focused on one of the previous stages. The attitude and motivations at the self-actualization level are very different. These individuals want their lives to have meaning. They want their accomplishments to be enduring. They want to achieve something great for humankind. Personal accomplishment and financial gain are not their motivators. They are independent, self-motivated, confident, and magnanimous. They see life from a forty-thousand-foot view and are in it to make a difference beyond themselves. Some will find passion in a blue-collar vocation, a white-collar profession, a military career, or even a nefarious way of life. Most will find a level of satisfaction in marriage. With their partner, they will establish and pursue their goals as well as prepare for retirement Their lives are in search of purpose, and they are often compensated for their selfless pursuits.

The acceptance of Maslow's work is widespread. His work assumes a humanistic and secular reality. His challenge is to accept your plight, be good little human beings, and make the best of life through good choices. You'll find a great explanation of Maslow's theory at simplypsychology.org.[521]

---

[521] https://www.simplypsychology.org/maslow.html.

ERIK ERIKSON

Maslow wasn't the only developmentalist who saw the passage of human beings through stages of life. Erik Erikson developed a different view of human psychosocial development.[522] Maslow focused on how human needs motivate behavior. Erikson believed there is a specific set of internal dynamics within each human being that influences the way we navigate through adulthood. If the passage through a specific stage is stormy or turbulent, this can result in dysfunctional or debilitating behavior in a later stage. Any stage can yield a positive or negative result.

In each stage, there arises a potential conflict in the developmental process. The basic conflict for the infant is mistrust or trust, which is entirely dependent on parenting style. If the parents provide an environment in which the child experiences trust, then in all likelihood, the child will have a good start in the world. However, if life experiences leave the child wounded and harboring a mistrust for others, then this will likely transfer to adult relationships. You'll find a great explanation by Kendra Cherry of the psychosocial developmental stages at verywellmind.com.[523]

Erikson's humanistic approach comes from the existential philosophy we've discussed. He surely recognized the theological underpinnings in American culture, as well as the spiritual influences of "the church" in the home. His daughter wrote in her book, *In the Shadow of Fame: A Memoir by the Daughter of Erik H. Erikson*, about her passage through the developmental stages outlined in her father's work and the personal trauma she experienced.

LAWRENCE KOHLBERG

Another developmentalist produced a similar progressive-stage theory regarding moral development. Lawrence Kohlberg theorized that humanity, in the developmental process, also develops a more informed moral perspective as humans mature, are educated, and experience life.[524]

---

[522] Erik Erikson, "Psychosocial Stages," accessed October 14, 2023, https://studylib.net/doc/8131732/erikson-s-psychosocial-stages-summary-chart.

[523] https://www.verywellmind.com/erik-eriksons-stages-of-psychosocial-development-2795740.

[524] www.psychologynoteshq.com.

His theory starts with the obedient response to parental or other adult authority. It is usually found in yes-no commands. This is followed by the emergence of self-determination—the child decides whether to comply. Unfortunately, the deliberation is superficial and self-interested. A child may love running, but may not recognize the inherent danger of street traffic. As the child continues to mature and gain experience, danger and "bad" consequences are more readily evaluated. Most rules are understood as order over chaos, civility over disharmony.

As a teenager experiences more adult situations, they also begin to understand vague and abstract concepts like freedom, liberty, civil harmony, and love. The ongoing human evaluation of life's circumstances is based upon what is good for the individual and its positive equity for the greater good. Ultimately, morality must transcend selfish interests and be, as Immanuel Kant would posit, a clearly understood moral imperative. There is an outstanding explanation of Kohlberg's theory on the internet at simplypsychology.org.[525]

JEAN PIAGET

Piaget's cognitive development theory is widely used in education, medicine, psychology, and social work as the starting point for understanding perception, learning, and maturation.[526] In fact, all theoretical fields use developmental and motivational theories as the foundation for understanding humanity's behavior. His work is found in many disciplines but most importantly in education and learning psychology.[527]

You'll often hear individuals or parents discussing "age-appropriate" material. That term refers to the work of both Piaget and Kohlberg. Age appropriateness is assessed according to whether the material is considered within the cognitive and moral development of the child. Piaget's followers have elaborated on his work.

---

[525] https://www.simplypsychology.org/kohlberg.html.

[526] "The Psychology Notes HQ," accessed September 20, 2023, http://www.psychologynotesHQ.com.

[527] Accessed September 14, 2023, https://www.pinterest.com/search/pins/?q=Jean%20Piaget%20-%20GGCWiki&rs=typed.

It is uncanny how we can compare our own lived experiences and see each of these developmental stages in our own lives—or, if you're a parent, in the lives of your children. You may notice in Piaget's theory that he identifies formal operational thinking as beginning at twelve years of age. I laughed. As a former school administrator, I'm sure some students didn't reach that stage until much later in their lives.

Piaget's work is still foundational in understanding normal cognitive development. I say "normal" to the extent that dysfunctional mental environments or physiological disruption can lead to abnormal behaviors. Pinpointing the origins of these atypical behaviors is a difficult task, to say the least. However, continued brain research has made incredible advances in identifying the origins of neurophysiological challenges. Moreover, therapies have improved dramatically. Medical advances have saved lives, especially in traumatic home and battlefield environments. Therapeutic work is necessary for resuming a comfortable quality of life. *Simply Psychology* has published an outstanding explanation of Piaget's theory of cognitive development on the internet.[528]

I want to note a concept from Piaget's work, the *schema*.[529] From birth, we are bombarded with perceptions of the world around us. For the rest of our lives, we continue to build categories and mental files for all that we learn. When a person experiences a new set of perceptions through the mind, they will *assimilate* that data into already existing categories. It is critical that new sense data fits properly, even if it is not understood.

If the sense data is new or very different, the person will *accommodate* it in a current mental category or build an entirely new compartment. This is how your worldview is created. Verywellmind.org has a great explanation of our schemas and how we compartmentalize perceptions.[530]

SIGMUND FREUD

Sigmund Freud's psychosexual developmental theory is no longer as widely accepted as the other theories discussed above. However, it did gain attention

---

[528] Accessed April 4, 2024, https://www.simplypsychology.org/piaget.html.

[529] Emily Roberts, "Schema," Verywell Mind, accessed October 10, 2023, https://www.verywellmind.com/what-is-a-schema-2795873.

[530] https://www.verywellmind.com/what-is-a-schema-2795873.

because human sexuality was emerging from the Victorian bedroom, a history we will not discuss here. Additionally, Freud's work on ego defense mechanisms provided insight into the ways we protect the ego, or our self-image.[531] *Simply Psychology* provides a solid understanding of his theory.[532]

Freud's work was heralded as a breakthrough in understanding the interplay between a person's psychosexual and ego development. Freud got his clients to open up and share their thoughts, which was a step forward in developing therapeutic approaches. Specifically, his *talking therapy* encouraged clients to share early-in-life traumatic events, many of which were sexual.

Study the chart referenced in *Simply Psychology*.[533] See how many defense mechanisms you can connect to biblical events. Here are a couple of hints: Peter's denial, Saul's taking on the role of priest to hurry off to battle, Moses's reaction to his newly discovered heritage in the murder of an Egyptian slave master, and Herod's reaction to the wise men.

There have been other developmental theorists, like James Fowler. Fowler applied the same developmental-stages approach to create a developmental model of faith formation. His work never gained any significant traction in scientific circles. For that matter, acceptance of his work was not found in any theological discipline. The challenge for Fowler was applying scientific analysis to a transcendent, all-knowing, ever-present, and all-powerful Being. It smacks of a foolish endeavor. Yet his effort to establish a theory for emerging faith cannot go unnoticed.

I believe the real work in faith formation or spiritual development is anchored in the work of the Holy Spirit. Growing up, I heard nothing about spiritual formation. The discussion was all about salvation. Now there are hundreds of books about spiritual formation.

---

[531] Accessed August 1, 2023, https://www.studocu.com/en-us/document/nova-southeastern-university/concepts-of-psychiatric-mental-health-nursing/defense-mechanisms/4776215.

[532] Accessed March 3, 2024, https://www.simplypsychology.org/psyche.html.

[533] https://www.simplypsychology.org/defense-mechanisms.html Accessed April 4, 2024,

CARL ROGERS

Psychologists believe our schemas are at the base of our happiness because there is *equilibrium*. The famous humanistic psychologist Carl Rogers referred to this mental stability as *congruence*.[534] It is critical that the schemas created be mentally well-defined. If they are not congruent—if a person cannot figure out how to accommodate new schema information—Rogers says *incongruence* occurs. Incongruence leads to mental stress until it is resolved. It can be very disconcerting. A friend who is good at listening or a trained therapist is necessary to assist in accommodating the new information and alleviating the discomfort. Examples of incongruence include someone making fun of your appearance, rejection by a person of the opposite sex, or loss of a big business deal.

Social psychology grows out of a theory called *behaviorism*. Simply stated, social psychology examines the behaviors of people in different environments. In a room full of atheists, a Christian might not initiate a theological discussion. If a person discovers that a party of liberals is present, they might not want to talk about a poor economy. The famous behaviorist J. B. Watson looked at the unconscious roots of behavior. Said another way, behaviorism attempts to observe the behavior but not explain the motivation for that behavior. The focus is on the behavior and what learning leads to the behavior. According to psychologist Saul Mcleod:

> Behaviorism, also known as behavioral learning theory, is a theoretical perspective in psychology that emphasizes the role of learning and observable behaviors in understanding human and animal actions. Behaviorism is a theory of learning that states all behaviors are learned through conditioned interaction with the environment. Thus, behavior is simply a response to environmental stimuli. The behaviorist theory is only concerned with observable

---

[534] "Congruence," accessed October 10, 2023, https://www.thoughtco.com/carl-rogers-4588296.

stimulus-response behaviors, as they can be studied in a systematic and observable manner.[535]

Behaviorism builds on the connections between motivation and observable behavior, with very little regard for the thought process that motivates human action. The key term here is *conditioning*. According to britannica.com, conditioning is "a behavioral process whereby a response becomes more frequent or more predictable in a given *environment* as a result of reinforcement, with reinforcement typically being a stimulus or reward for a desired response." Behaviorists maintain that there are no authentic, thoughtful choices in behavior, only conditioning that provides a favorable outcome.

Marketing works on this associative principle. An advertisement may connect a new automobile with an improved sense of social status or a credit card with financial freedom. Media agencies use the same approach. Present enough negative stories about a candidate, and readers will vote for the other person. Marketing can be less about truth and more about persuasion.

Behaviorists maintain that our actions can be more about the unconscious associations we make than about thoughtful choices. More specifically, all behavior is a form of conditioning from some type of stimulus to a reward. A person will get married because they believe life will be perfect happiness with another, despite the presence of red flags indicating the contrary. Social psychologists often make the claim that they know more about you than you know about you. *Simply Psychology* has a solid explanation about the concepts associated with social psychology.[536]

HOPE VERSUS DREAD

The work of these scientists is outstanding, as is the work by others who followed. Unfortunately, it does not answer the bigger questions of the final or terminal concern(s): What happens next? Most of humanity recognizes that in order to eat, you must work. Maslow is right; each of us pursues a motivational hierarchy. Each day billions of people go to work to feed,

---

[535] Saul Mcleod, *Simple Psychology*, accessed September 30, 2023, https://www.simplypsychology.org/behaviorism.html.

[536] https://www.verywellmind.com/social-psychology-4157177.

shelter, and protect themselves or their families. Once we've attained those material ends or reached those goals, what next? Empty nesters struggle with how to live when their kids are grown and gone, because their motivation was family. Now what? Or, as the years pass and ultimate death looms, "What really mattered?" or "Where to from here?" are profound questions for existentialists. They have no answer and choose to make the state their greatest pursuit.

In comparison, Christ-followers don't share the same dread for their final destination. They believe in an eternal life. They will move on to another dimension of existence with God as Ruler. The Christian has pursued God and His purpose for their life. The motivation is pursuit of a reunion with Him. The joy we experience in the here and now is a precursor to a greater joy!

You must realize by now that these are the ways the world perceives humankind and how the world's wise explain humanity's psychosocial predicament. All that mankind does is a response to dread. All the theories just presented became humanity's explanation for what is. They became the law. You are supposed to follow normative behavior without any crutch of faith. In short, you will serve humanity's expectations, or you will serve right living.

> Don't you know that when you offer yourselves to someone as obedient slaves, you are slaves of the one you obey— whether you are slaves to sin, which leads to death, or to obedience, which leads to righteousness?[537]

Undoubtedly, the world has its way of seeing things, which is very different from God's perspective. Social scientists look at trends in society and make predictions based on the direction of the trend. They refer to this as *social research*. That research is built on science-developed paradigms or algorithms.

Yet there are thousands who see research another way, based on biblical precepts, and give warning regarding the analysis. Humanity will follow the way of their thinking, and those called by God will give warning to the citizens.

---

[537] Romans 6:16.

He said to the crowd: "When you see a cloud rising in the west, immediately you say, 'It's going to rain,' and it does. And when the south wind blows, you say, 'It's going to be hot,' and it is. Hypocrites! You know how to interpret the appearance of the earth and the sky. How is it that you don't know how to interpret this present time?"[538]

In the same way that God placed watchmen on the walls of Jerusalem, so will He set His fearless men and women on the walls to announce the coming evil, as a warning to believers to remain set apart and stand firm.

I have set watchmen on your walls, O Jerusalem; They shall never hold their peace day or night. You who make mention of the Lord, do not keep silent.[539]

In closing this review of human thought, it has become obvious that modern man lives according to what he thinks is right. Despite how the world heralds man's thinking and exploits, it is only a snapshot of how humanity has built its wisdom and reality. Those who have been financially successful, the richest men and women in the world, are fooled by their success (given by God) into thinking they are wise. The same is true of the learned: academic experts also believe their own press.

I love the simple life of farming, the hard work and love for God. A farmer only sees life in its simplest terms: God, family, country, and work. Ultimately, those who choose the scientific, modern-man perspective will struggle mightily with existential dread, even to the point of severe mental stress or suicide. There are signs everywhere that humanity is struggling. This verse comes to mind:

For the wisdom of this world is foolishness to God. As the Scriptures say, "He traps the wise in the snare of their own cleverness."[540]

---

[538] Luke 12:54–56.

[539] Isaiah 62:6.

[540] 1 Corinthians 3:19 NLT.

DEVELOPING A PROFOUND AWARENESS

I give some credit to all these theories. They are viable explanations regarding humankind's growth and development. Scientific man lives by these theories. When I first learned of these theories in college, I was in agreement. I still am to some degree.

However, lived experiences are markedly different between secular man and spiritual man. Secular man is on his own to make life choices. He is alone and possesses an autonomy to determine his own destiny. I've said all along that God gives man the gift of choice.

Spiritual man is in pursuit of God for his life choices. In the prayer for salvation, the Christ-follower has made God the Lord of his life. Spiritual man will be in conversation with God and trust God for guidance.

> I have hidden Your word in my heart that I might not sin against You. Praise be to You, Lord; teach me Your decrees. With my lips I recount all the laws that come from Your mouth.[541]

Following the death of Moses, God said this to Joshua, who would replace Moses:

> Be strong and very courageous. Be careful to obey all the law my servant Moses gave you; do not turn from it to the right or to the left, that you may be successful wherever you go. Keep this Book of the Law always on your lips; meditate on it day and night, so that you may be careful to do everything written in it. Then you will be prosperous and successful.[542]

God instructs His leadership to keep His words on their lips and to follow the plan of wholesome and righteous living. The best news is that if His Word is followed, then we will be a successful people.

The words of Scripture are branded in believers' hearts. It is a soul-deep

---

[541] Psalm 119:11–13.
[542] Joshua 1:7–8.

vision! This is at the very core of why God's words transcend the foolishness of human wisdom. Humanistic man has no ability to dwell in God's thoughts and control. Humanistic man loves to believe he has the capacity to do so, but he does not.

> "For my thoughts are not your thoughts, neither are your
> ways my ways," declares the Lord. "As the heavens are
> higher than the earth, so are my ways higher than your
> ways and my thoughts than your thoughts."[543]

Since the Eden tragedy, humanity has used its knowledge to attempt to build back better than God, ignoring His guidance. Scientific man has made every effort to conquer and to elevate himself above what he refers to as "outdated" and "superstitious" religion. Keep in mind that this is your critical decision. God will not force it on you.

A Christian returns control of their life back to dependence on God, as it was in the garden. The relationship with God is built on believing His Word, trusting His control, and pursuing His plan for our lives. This is dependence. To overcome the shackles of modern man, armed with an educational system that heralds knowledge above all else, the Christian must choose a righteous approach to life that runs after a simple and sweet intimacy with God.

As we have discussed, secular man and spiritual man possess worldviews that are not mutually exclusive. Modern man can attend religious or sacred services, possess a view of supernaturalism not consistent with God's Word, and be happy. This choice is grounded in a reality based on ascribed values determined through human wisdom. What is valued and makes life worth living is a pursuit of happiness in the things of the world, driven by pride. The apostle John stated:

> For everything in the world—the lust of the flesh, the
> lust of the eyes, and the pride of life—comes not from the
> Father but from the world. The world and its desires pass
> away, but whoever does the will of God lives forever.[544]

---

[543] Isaiah 55:8–9.
[544] 1 John 2:16.

Personal ambition can include work, education, music, art, writing, fashion, art, theater, hobbies, and so on. Secular man's pursuit is what he values. Even the seemingly magnanimous work of volunteerism or philanthropy carries an intrinsic feeling of being good. Writers in this secular society identify secular man's self-serving work as a triumph of humanity. All the while, society is seducing its members into believing there is no need for God.

On the other hand, a Christ-follower will participate and exist in the world, but not be of the world. It is not a philosophical decision; it is a theological choice. The choice does not find the value of humanity in its actions. Value is ascribed by God, not man.

The following verses reveal John's keen perspective regarding the traps of the world and Christ-followers' countering eternity mindset:

> See what great love the Father has lavished on us, that we
> should be called children of God! And that is what we are!
> The reason the world does not know us is that it did not
> know him.[545]

> If you belonged to the world, it would love you as its own.
> As it is, you do not belong to the world, but I have chosen
> you out of the world. That is why the world hates you.[546]

Paul solved the confusion for your awareness. You can see it, but you embrace it.

> Do not conform to the pattern of this world, but be
> transformed by the renewing of your mind. Then you will
> be able to test and approve what God's will is—his good,
> pleasing and perfect will.[547]

A profound awareness understands and holds dearly to Paul's statement. Only through a profound awareness will the Christ-follower live by these

---

[545] 1 John 3:1.
[546] John 15:19.
[547] Romans 12:2.

words. First, you truly understand the way in which the world lives because your mind meditates on His Word. Through the renewed mind, you see the world and its trappings. Moreover, you teach others about its snare. Second, and very important, you accept God's control of the world and all that's in it. You never question God's perfect plan. You simply look for His return.

In light of this, Paul could also say:

> And we know that in all things God works for the good of those who love him, who have been called according to his purpose.[548]

Profound awareness is anchored in love for God and will do anything God leads that awareness to do, even if others don't understand it. A hallmark of profound awareness is recognizing and accepting our weakness. Paul referred to weakness of the soul that is "incomprehensible to man."[549] It is an admonition that humanity is deceived by the belief that they are secure in their existential aloneness, when in fact, they are not. Paul admitted to understanding this as a member of humanity, but finds an authentic strength in God's power, protection, and will.

> In the same way, the Spirit helps us in our weakness. We do not know what we ought to pray for, but the Spirit himself intercedes for us through wordless groans. And he who searches our hearts knows the mind of the Spirit, because the Spirit intercedes for God's people in accordance with the will of God.[550]

Paul knew in his heart and mind that our salvation through Christ means we can return to our roots in our garden relationship with God. Paul found confidence that this new covenant placed him on an existential foundation that provides eternal security for the Jew and the Gentile who make God the Lord of their lives. "In their hearts humans plan their course,

---

[548] Romans 8:28.

[549] TDNT. Vol. 1, p.83.

[550] Romans 8:26–27.

but the Lord establishes their steps."[551] Those steps are often guided by the Holy Spirit. Initially, a believer won't respond to the Spirit's leading, but in time, if they learn to reduce the distractions, they will move on the Spirit's leading. Jesus said it like this:

> Jesus answered, "Very truly I tell you, no one can enter the kingdom of God unless they are born of water and the Spirit. Flesh gives birth to flesh, but the Spirit gives birth to spirit. You should not be surprised at my saying, 'You must be born again.' The wind blows wherever it pleases. You hear its sound, but you cannot tell where it comes from or where it is going. So it is with everyone born of the Spirit."[552]

Said differently, Matthew revealed the reality revealed to believers:

> Everyone then who hears these words of mine and does them will be like a wise man who built his house on the rock. And the rain fell, and the floods came, and the winds blew and beat on that house, but it did not fall, because it had been founded on the rock. And everyone who hears these words of mine and does not do them will be like a foolish man who built his house on the sand. And the rain fell, and the floods came, and the winds blew and beat against that house, and it fell, and great was the fall of it.[553]

The Scriptures hold an indomitable truth for Christ-followers to live by. As believers pursue God, His Word becomes the *way* and the *truth*—His Word gives them *life*! Standing on this truth is the basis of our faith as believers. And it is the Spirit who reveals the truth.

The writer of the letter to the Hebrews was succinct. The world is attempting to erase God, His Word, and His actions from our culture:

---

[551] Proverbs 16:9.
[552] John 3:5–8.
[553] Matthew 7:24–27.

> And without faith it is impossible to please him, for whoever
> would draw near to God must believe that he exists and that
> he rewards those who seek him.[554]

An eternity soul-vision is a reality anchored in biblical revelation. Confusion over what dependence on God means is a significant challenge for secular humanism. In all likelihood, secular man truly doesn't know or understand the reality he lives within. Our existential standing rests on these two planks: either it is an attachment to a reality in which each individual decides on their commitment to independence, or it is an attachment to dependence on God. Said another way, you are a servant of the world or a servant of Christ.

Please read through Proverbs chapters 3 and 4. You'll discover an obvious theme about discovering and understanding distinct realities and making life choices. The wise man follows God, and the fool follows the ways of humanity.

> Do not be wise in your own eyes; fear the Lord and shun
> evil. This will bring health to your body and nourishment
> to your bones.[555]

We'll close with this:

> Above all else, guard your heart, for everything you do
> flows from it.[556]

> And the peace of God, which transcends all understanding,
> will guard your hearts and your minds in Christ Jesus.[557]

---

[554] Hebrews 11:6.
[555] Proverbs 3:7–8.
[556] Proverbs 4:23.
[557] Philippians 4:7.

24

THE WHOLE TRUTH: NOTHING BUT THE TRUTH

PAUL WENT TO ROME TO PRESENT THE GOSPEL TO A VERY INTELLIGENT audience. The Romans were the example of a modern people of their time. Paul's presentation made clear the distinction between the two realities: the kingdom of man and the kingdom of God. Paul reviewed what God had done through Jesus Christ. The gospel is about right living and being a righteous people. Humanity cannot live according to their self-assessment that they are a good people. Paul made it clear that the principles of a wholesome morality come through the transcendent power of God, which stands above human wisdom. Eternal life comes through living a righteous life on earth of faith in God, His Son's work on the cross, and the leading of the Holy Spirit.

Paul clearly stated that the people of Rome were living immoral lives—lives that were not pleasing to the Creator God. He told them they were living this way not because they didn't know about the truth of right living, but because they chose to ignore it.

> The wrath of God is being revealed from heaven against all the godlessness and wickedness of people, who suppress the truth.[558]

> For although they knew God, they neither glorified him as God nor gave thanks to him, but their thinking became futile and their foolish hearts were darkened. Although they claimed to be wise, they became fools and exchanged the glory of the immortal God for images made to look like a mortal human being and birds and animals and reptiles.

---

[558] Romans 1:18.

> Therefore God gave them over in the sinful desires of their
> hearts to sexual impurity for the degrading of their bodies
> with one another. They exchanged the truth about God for
> a lie, and worshiped and served created things rather than
> the Creator—who is forever praised. Amen.[559]

Paul recognized that corrupt immorality is a serious step toward a
society's downfall—not only for itself, but for thousands of lost souls for
eternity. Humanity has been given the *choice* and has chosen to ignore God's
truth. Once a society arrives at this point, its downfall is imminent. Paul
did not let the Romans off the hook, because he knew that God had given
warning:

> [W]hat may be known about God is plain to them, because
> God has made it plain to them. For since the creation of
> the world God's invisible qualities—his eternal power and
> divine nature—have been seen, being understood from
> what has been made, so that people are without excuse.
> For although they knew God, they neither glorified
> him as God nor gave thanks to him, but their thinking
> became futile and their foolish hearts were darkened.
> Although they claimed to be wise, they became fools and
> exchanged the glory of the immortal God for images made
> to look like a mortal human being and birds and animals
> and reptiles.[560]

Paul got to the point quickly. The Romans knew the truth. God's power
and what they saw in nature were obvious. Paul repeated his deep concern
for their behaviors. However, through their own choices, the Romans
continued to slip deeper into their unprincipled behaviors.

> Because of this, God gave them over to shameful lusts.
> Even their women exchanged natural sexual relations for
> unnatural ones. In the same way the men also abandoned

---

[559] Romans 1:21–25.
[560] Romans 1:19–23.

natural relations with women and were inflamed with lust for one another. Men committed shameful acts with other men, and received in themselves the due penalty for their error.

Furthermore, just as they did not think it worthwhile to retain the knowledge of God, so God gave them over to a depraved mind, so that they do what ought not to be done. They have become filled with every kind of wickedness, evil, greed and depravity. They are full of envy, murder, strife, deceit and malice. They are gossips, slanderers, God-haters, insolent, arrogant and boastful; they invent ways of doing evil; they disobey their parents; they have no understanding, no fidelity, no love, no mercy. Although they know God's righteous decree that those who do such things deserve death, they not only continue to do these very things but also approve of those who practice them.[561]

Despite the fact that these are the choices of an existential humanity, they are not the wholesome and thriving behaviors that God calls His people to live within.

Paul said that humanity has no excuses: they know what right living is but prefer to give themselves over to debauchery. The humanists do this because they want pleasure, belongingness, or to be loved, albeit superficially. In addition, their hope is that these behaviors will give their lives some sense of meaning or significance. Sadly, that only leads to an eternity in the lake of fire.

God "will repay each person according to what they have done." To those who by persistence in doing good seek glory, honor and immortality, he will give eternal life. But for those who are self-seeking and who reject the truth and follow evil, there will be wrath and anger. There will be trouble and distress for every human being who does evil.[562]

---

[561] Romans 1:26–32.
[562] Romans 2:6–9.

For everyone has sinned; we all fall short of God's glorious standard. Yet God, in his grace, freely makes us right in his sight. He did this through Christ Jesus when he freed us from the penalty for our sins. For God presented Jesus as the sacrifice for sin. People are made right with God when they believe that Jesus sacrificed his life, shedding his blood. This sacrifice shows that God was being fair when he held back and did not punish those who sinned in times past, for he was looking ahead and including them in what he would do in this present time. God did this to demonstrate his righteousness, for he himself is fair and just, and he makes sinners right in his sight when they believe in Jesus.[563]

Paul made clear to the Romans that the blood shed by Jesus had the power to save humanity. However, that truth must be believed—not in word but in an earnest surrender and repentance. As you've read, this began with Abrahamic covenant and ends with the new covenant in Jesus Christ. Humanity faced death via Adam's disobedience and rebellion, but now we have life through the obedience and surrender of Jesus.

Your choice is to be a slave to the culture of humanity or a slave to the goodness of God through His Son. It would seem to me a simple choice to make. Humanity has built and used philosophical wisdom, Eastern religions, and psychological mindfulness as bases for humankind to live by. Whether for ancient Romans or for scientific man today, the challenge remains exactly the same. We will be slaves to the wisdom of modern man or slaves to the everlasting love of God. He created us; He knows what we need to thrive and flourish. He has provided those guardrails for our success.

This seems like a harsh message from Paul, especially for those who feel we live in an enlightened age. We are autonomous human beings given to self-determination. Accordingly, we believe that our reasoned choices, when not affecting others, are our choices to make.

This is true. God has offered you the freedom to choose. However, He has also made it clear that there is a right way and a wrong way to live our lives. As an example, you may think a woman's choice to have an abortion is

---

[563] Romans 3:23–26 NLT.

acceptable. In your wisdom, it may be. However, from God's perspective, it isn't an acceptable alternative for birth control. To God, the egg becomes a fetus, a living human being, a child at conception. When you don't honor the sanctity of human life, you set in motion a range of perverted moral issues. Real choice occurs prior to conception—through prophylactics, withdrawal, the rhythm method, or abstinence until ready. That's responsible human behavior.

Heterosexual behavior, according to the gospel, is a godly choice for humanity. Paul clearly refers to homosexual behavior as being unnatural and shameful.

I am not going to judge either abortion or a gay lifestyle. I will not judge or determine what is worst on Paul's list, which also includes envy, murder, strife, deceit, malice, gossip, slander, insolence, arrogance, and boastfulness, among many other things. Judgment is left to God, on a day in the future only known to Him.

Paul did conclude that passage with this:

> Although they know God's righteous decree that those who do such things deserve death, they not only continue to do these very things but also approve of those who practice them.[564]

Death here is used in the eternal sense, meaning death as eternal separation from God. Hell is a place of torment. Some want to call it a "party" to be in the company of other evildoers. Let me assure you, it will *not* be a party. Consequently, I am culpable for your evil behavior if I don't bring the words of the gospel to your attention.

The good news is that God loves *you*! God does not condemn you. He condemns your behavior and wants you to change. The gospel uses the word *repent*. *Repent* means to "turn away" from your unrighteous behavior to the righteous behavior of God. If you turn your heart to Jesus, you will live a life that is thriving and flourishing. Best of all, you will be able to talk with God at any point in your waking day.

Paul went on to explain in more detail this connection between the nonbelieving individual and God:

---

[564] Romans 1:32.

Those who are dominated by the sinful nature think about sinful things, but those who are controlled by the Holy Spirit think about things that please the Spirit. So letting your sinful nature control your mind leads to death. But letting the Spirit control your mind leads to life and peace. For the sinful nature is always hostile to God. It never did obey God's laws, and it never will. That's why those who are still under the control of their sinful nature can never please God.[565]

Paul points us back to the desires of the self's sinful nature, often referred to as the "flesh," as the controlling party. But he was more specific: the sinful nature overpowers the mind as well. Again, in God's realm is a joy-filled life and peace.

When you come to the place in your life that you want to live in relationship with the God of the universe, you make a prayer of confession. Some refer to it as the sinner's prayer; some more positively refer to it as the believer's prayer. The point is you need to make a statement of confession and repentance. The prayer will sound something like this:

Dear Lord, Your love is everlasting, and I thank You for that. I have come to realize that I have rebelled and been disobedient. Please forgive me. Your Word has revealed to me that my desire to be the master of my universe is wrong. I have tried to replace my relationship with You and my fear with other worldly things, so I hid. Please forgive me. I *will believe* the truth of Your Word. I want to follow Your ways. Thank You for sending Jesus to die the death I deserved. Father, I want You to be the Lord of my life. I *accept Your authority* in all areas of my life. I will turn to You in all circumstances to seek Your will. I will *pursue Your will* for my future and go where You have called me to go, no matter what. I desire the power of Your Holy Spirit to seal this covenant between You and I. Amen.

---

[565] Romans 8:5–8 NLT.

This prayer will connect you with the triune God of the universe. This will be the answer to your life search and the questions you've asked.

This prayer connects with God the Father; Jesus, His Son, who saved you; and the Holy Spirit, who will guide you for eternity. Study the Word, trust God's authority over your life, and pursue His purpose for your life.

Paul discussed the challenging relationship between your sinful nature, its habits, and the direction the Spirit will take you:

> But you are not controlled by your sinful nature. You are controlled by the Spirit if you have the Spirit of God living in you. (And remember that those who do not have the Spirit of Christ living in them do not belong to him at all.) And Christ lives within you, so even though your body will die because of sin, the Spirit gives you life because you have been made right with God. The Spirit of God, who raised Jesus from the dead, lives in you. And just as God raised Christ Jesus from the dead, he will give life to your mortal bodies by this same Spirit living within you.
>
> Therefore, dear brothers and sisters, you have no obligation to do what your sinful nature urges you to do. For if you live by its dictates, you will die. But if through the power of the Spirit you put to death the deeds of your sinful nature, you will live. For all who are led by the Spirit of God are children of God.
>
> So you have not received a spirit that makes you fearful slaves. Instead, you received God's Spirit when he adopted you as his own children. Now we call him, "Abba, Father." For his Spirit joins with our spirit to affirm that we are God's children. And since we are his children, we are his heirs. In fact, together with Christ we are heirs of God's glory. But if we are to share his glory, we must also share his suffering.[566]

This next passage is very revealing. There is a comparison of our present world with that of creation. You are now a child of God. You carry a special

---

[566] Romans 8:9–17 NLT.

place in the universe among His children returning to the new Eden. This world will have suffering because we don't belong here. We will rejoice in a world filled with the fruit of the spirit and innocence.

> Yet what we suffer now is nothing compared to the glory he will reveal to us later. For all creation is waiting eagerly for that future day when God will reveal who his children really are. Against its will, all creation was subjected to God's curse. But with eager hope, the creation looks forward to the day when it will join God's children in glorious freedom from death and decay. For we know that all creation has been groaning as in the pains of childbirth right up to the present time. And we believers also groan, even though we have the Holy Spirit within us as a foretaste of future glory, for we long for our bodies to be released from sin and suffering. We, too, wait with eager hope for the day when God will give us our full rights as his adopted children, including the new bodies he has promised us. We were given this hope when we were saved. (If we already have something, we don't need to hope for it. But if we look forward to something we don't yet have, we must wait patiently and confidently.)[567]

We live in the hope that our place of rejoicing will be a new heaven, new earth, and new Jerusalem, with our Father reigning and His Son at the right hand. For us now is the Holy Spirit.

> And the Holy Spirit helps us in our weakness. For example, we don't know what God wants us to pray for. But the Holy Spirit prays for us with groanings that cannot be expressed in words. And the Father who knows all hearts knows what the Spirit is saying, for the Spirit pleads for us believers in harmony with God's own will. And we know that God causes everything to work together for the good of those who love God and are called according to his purpose for

[567] Romans 8:18–25 NLT.

them. For God knew his people in advance, and he chose them to become like his Son, so that his Son would be the firstborn among many brothers and sisters. And having chosen them, he called them to come to him. And having called them, he gave them right standing with himself. And having given them right standing, he gave them his glory.[568]

This passage makes great sense. You are called according to His purpose. Because of your commitment, you have been made holy and can approach God.

By this point in Paul's letter, I am sure that the Romans were listening carefully. Paul was moving toward closure:

Therefore, I urge you, brothers and sisters, in view of God's mercy, to offer your bodies as a living sacrifice, holy and pleasing to God—this is your true and proper worship. Do not conform to the pattern of this world, but be transformed by the renewing of your mind. Then you will be able to test and approve what God's will is—his good, pleasing and perfect will. For by the grace given me I say to every one of you: Do not think of yourself more highly than you ought, but rather think of yourself with sober judgment, in accordance with the faith God has distributed to each of you.[569]

This is important: be very careful not to compare yourselves with other Christians! It is easy to do but can be very painful. Too often you will witness behaviors that, in your heart, you'll know are not Christlike. Give them grace! You are to listen to the Holy Spirit! Do not be discouraged by others, but be a light and encouragement to them. Listen to what Paul said about the appearance of Christlike behavior:

Love must be sincere. Hate what is evil; cling to what is good. Be devoted to one another in love. Honor one another

---

[568] Romans 8:26–29 NLT.
[569] Romans 12:1–3.

above yourselves. Never be lacking in zeal, but keep your spiritual fervor, serving the Lord. Be joyful in hope, patient in affliction, faithful in prayer. Share with the Lord's people who are in need. Practice hospitality.

Bless those who persecute you; bless and do not curse. Rejoice with those who rejoice; mourn with those who mourn. Live in harmony with one another. Do not be proud, but be willing to associate with people of low position. Do not be conceited.

Do not repay anyone evil for evil. Be careful to do what is right in the eyes of everyone. If it is possible, as far as it depends on you, live at peace with everyone. Do not take revenge, my dear friends, but leave room for God's wrath, for it is written: "It is mine to avenge; I will repay," says the Lord. On the contrary:

"If your enemy is hungry, feed him; if he is thirsty, give him something to drink.

In doing this, you will heap burning coals on his head."

Do not be overcome by evil, but overcome evil with good.[570]

This is different from any moral code. I am sure that those hearing Paul's words were leaning in. Love abounds through the words of Paul.

Jesus had every right to express a righteous anger, but He didn't. There is a passage in Philippians in which Paul described the character of Jesus. Paul communicated to all that if you are of the Spirit, then this is what you'll see:

Therefore if you have any encouragement from being united with Christ, if any comfort from his love, if any common sharing in the Spirit, if any tenderness and compassion, then make my joy complete by being like-minded, having the same love, being one in spirit and of one mind. Do nothing out of selfish ambition or vain conceit. Rather, in humility value others above yourselves, not looking to your own interests but each of you to the interests of the

---

[570] Romans 12:9–21 NLT.

others. In your relationships with one another, have the same mindset as Christ Jesus:

Who, being in very nature God, did not consider equality with God something to be used to his own advantage; rather, he made himself nothing by taking the very nature of a servant, being made in human likeness. And being found in appearance as a man, he humbled himself by becoming obedient to death—even death on a cross!

Therefore God exalted him to the highest place and gave him the name that is above every name, that at the name of Jesus every knee should bow, in heaven and on earth and under the earth, and every tongue acknowledge that Jesus Christ is Lord, to the glory of God the Father.[571]

DEVELOPING A PROFOUND AWARENESS

I have communicated throughout this book my great disappointment in not observing Christlike behavior in Christians and, more importantly, in myself. We should be Spirit-filled and in the mind of Christ. The fruit of the Spirit within is the testimony to whom we belong.

There is one final story I want to leave you with. It isn't about me; it's about the disciple Peter. Peter must have confessed to John what happened, because John recorded the event. You'll recall that Peter ardently supported Jesus. He told Jesus that he would never abandon Him. Peter boastfully said he would die for the One he recognized as "the messiah, son of the living God."[572] Jesus responded that Peter would deny Him three times before the rooster crowed.

Here's the story, beginning with a statement from Jesus and Peter's brash response. He believed he was a strong, spiritual man ready to defend his Savior:

---

[571] Philippians 2:1–11.
[572] Matthew 16:16.

"My children, I will be with you only a little longer. You will look for me, and just as I told the Jews, so I tell you now: Where I am going, you cannot come.

"A new command I give you: Love one another. As I have loved you, so you must love one another. By this everyone will know that you are my disciples, if you love one another."

Simon Peter asked him, "Lord, where are you going?"

Jesus replied, "Where I am going, you cannot follow now, but you will follow later."

Peter asked, "Lord, why can't I follow you now? I will lay down my life for you."

Then Jesus answered, "Will you really lay down your life for me? Very truly I tell you, before the rooster crows, you will disown me three times!"[573]

The next passage describes a scene hours later. Jesus had been arrested. Jerusalem was filled with mayhem and turmoil. A people who days earlier had been dancing in the streets at the arrival of Jesus were now rabid with emotion, believing He wasn't who He said He was. Peter was fully aware of what was happening. He was frightened and hiding under the cover of night, but someone recognized him:

Simon Peter and another disciple were following Jesus. Because this disciple was known to the high priest, he went with Jesus into the high priest's courtyard, but Peter had to wait outside at the door. The other disciple, who was known to the high priest, came back, spoke to the servant girl on duty there and brought Peter in.

"You aren't one of this man's disciples too, are you?" she asked Peter. He replied, "I am not."

It was cold, and the servants and officials stood around a fire they had made to keep warm. Peter also was standing with them, warming himself.[574]

---

[573] John 13:33–38.
[574] John 18:15–18. NIV

> Meanwhile, Simon Peter was still standing there warming himself. So they asked him, "You aren't one of his disciples too, are you?" He denied it, saying, "I am not."
>
> One of the high priest's servants, a relative of the man whose ear Peter had cut off, challenged him, "Didn't I see you with him in the garden?" Again Peter denied it, and at that moment a rooster began to crow.[575]

We can only imagine the gut-wrenching agony Peter must have experienced at the moment the rooster's call was heard. John didn't include this moment of great emotional pain in his account; however, Mark did. Mark had heard the story about his dear friend.

> Immediately the rooster crowed the second time. Then Peter remembered the word Jesus had spoken to him:
>
> "Before the rooster crows twice you will disown me three times." And he broke down and wept.[576]

This is the only time I have quoted from the *Jewish New Testament Commentary*, because I believe it captures Peter's reaction the best. This commentary describes the breaking down and weeping as "beating his chest" and weeping.[577] I personally translate the Greek as "wept bitterly." Without a doubt, Peter was a broken man.

Regrettably, in the same way, I have experienced the ordeals of brokenness, separation from God, and bitter weeping at the realization of my own sin. Having experienced the joy of my salvation, only to encounter my most atrocious behavior as a self-proclaimed Christian, has left me deeply discouraged.

The situation wasn't over. Peter had to face the Christ who had just died for his sins. John was likely present to hear this conversation. It would have

---

[575] John 18:25–27.
[576] Mark 14:72 NIV.
[577] David H. Stern, *Jewish New Testament Commentary* (Jewish New Testament Publications, 1992), 101.

been an unnerving moment for Peter, but it is a reminder for us as Christ-followers: denying Jesus in our lives requires His forgiveness.

> When they had finished eating, Jesus said to Simon Peter, "Simon son of John, do you love me more than these?"
> "Yes, Lord," he said, "you know that I love you."
> Jesus said, "Feed my lambs."
> Again Jesus said, "Simon son of John, do you love me?"
> He answered, "Yes, Lord, you know that I love you."
> Jesus said, "Take care of my sheep."
> The third time he said to him, "Simon son of John, do you love me?"
> Peter was hurt because Jesus asked him the third time, "Do you love me?" He said, "Lord, you know all things; you know that I love you." Jesus said, "Feed my sheep."[578]

Jesus required that Peter repent of his denial.

There was one more moment that revealed Jesus's love for Peter. All of heaven knew of Peter's suffering. We know this because a very specific message was conveyed by the angel at the tomb to make sure the disciples *and* Peter knew where to find his risen Savior:

> But go, tell his disciples and Peter, "He is going ahead of you into Galilee. There you will see him, just as he told you."[579]

My question to the Holy Spirit about that instruction is "Is Peter not considered a disciple because of his denial? Or is that turn of phrase meant as an encouragement for us to understand that Jesus still loved Peter and knew that Peter was hurting?" Since Jesus asked Peter about love three times, does that mean Peter's salvation had been momentarily lost? Or was this a moment of required confession that Jesus wanted to hear from Peter?

There has been no enlightenment from above for me on this. I recognize that Paul understands "grace abound."[580] That means Jesus only asks us

---

[578] John 21:15–17.
[579] Mark 16:7.
[580] 2 Corinthians 9:8.

to make confession and seek forgiveness. Jesus never trifles with issues of salvation and forgiveness. Salvation is more than *belief relief*! Because we believe in salvation, we assure ourselves of eternity. However, our lives must go beyond a doctrinal statement to demonstrate that we are one with Him.

25

ETERNITY: A NEW HEAVEN, A NEW EARTH, A NEW JERUSALEM

WE HAVE LOOKED AT PRE-CREATION PLANNING, CREATION, OT leadership, the Messiah, a new heaven, a new earth, a new Jerusalem, and an eternity unfolding with God dwelling among His people. The new Jerusalem is the bride of the Lamb![581] To explain the meaning of today's church, John wrote, "I did not see a temple in the city, because the Lord God Almighty and the Lamb are its temple."[582] This is our reality check: do we *know* that in church we dwell and worship in the midst of the Almighty God and Christ?

Keep in mind that the One seated on the throne said, "'I am making everything new!' Then he said, 'Write this down, for these words are trustworthy and true.'"[583]

Before going on, let's be very clear about the truth you choose to believe. This decision has eternal consequences. Your choice will be one of either utter joy or a gut-wrenching fear for eternity. As a student once blurted in my class, "God don't play!"

In short, your firm foundation is set on the truth of God, as well as your response to Him in the way you live your life. You use your relationship with God to determine life choices based on the Word, His sovereignty, and the pursuit of His plan for your life. If you have followed what has happened in this book, then you have a renewed vision of the world and who you are in it. This is your truth.

---

[581] Revelation 21:1–9.
[582] Revelation 21:22.
[583] Revelation 21:5.

> Know that the Lord is God. It is he who made us, and we are his; we are his people, the sheep of his pasture.[584]

To review, I'll begin with a summary of spiritual formation. Then I'll consider issues in applying your soul-vision to your daily activities. I'll finish with comments regarding development of profound awareness and spiritual disciplines.

SUMMARY OF THE GOD STORY

The God Story begins in a pre-creation planning meeting. The planning is for our spiritual journey, prepared by the Creator God, His Son, and the Holy Spirit. The universe is the culmination of their work, with Earth being the focal point. It is on this planet that They create a magnificent location called the Garden of Eden. It is in Eden that God creates His crowning work, Adam and Eve. There He communes with the created and gives them *dominion over the planet*. Lucifer's pride then takes advantage of their innocence.

Deceived by Lucifer, the father of evil, Adam and Eve are lured to believe that they can have something better. They become discontented as they contemplate what is possible. Three issues are critical here and continue to be central themes in humanity's demise. First, Adam and Eve did not believe God's warning to stay away from that tree. Second, they did not trust God's sovereignty—that He is the Creator God and they will die. Third, they no longer wanted to pursue God's plan for their lives. They want to pursue their own destiny, choosing to be like God.

God discovers their disobedience because they *hide* from Him. Fear and hiding are insidious qualities that both hinder and drive humankind through its prideful self-determination to its end.

As a result of their *disobedience* and *rebellion*, Adam and Eve are exiled from Eden. They die through a death of *separation from God*. Their separation results in an *unholy fear* and *distrust*.

However, before God sends them out, He covers their *guilt* and *shame* with clothing made from the skins of animals. Blood is shed to cover them. The shedding of blood becomes a crucial theme in Jewish and Christian

---

[584] Psalm 100:3.

cultures. Blood is a dominant aspect to understanding our relationship with the Messiah. The animal skins cover their shame and guilt. Jesus will heal the disobedience and rebellion that is coursing through our veins. Most importantly, through belief in the Story and faith in the work of Jesus, we are cleansed, made holy, and restored to an Edenlike relationship with our Creator.

There is another act of love displayed by God for His created. Keep in mind that there are two trees mentioned in Eden:

> The Lord God made all kinds of trees grow out of the ground—trees that were pleasing to the eye and good for food. In the middle of the garden were the tree of life and the tree of the knowledge of good and evil.[585]

As we know, Adam and Eve were not to eat the fruit from the tree of the knowledge of good and evil. They could eat the fruit from the tree of life. Evidently, this fruit was like a fountain of youth and allowed them to live forever. God reveals this because He prohibits their reentry to Eden:

> And the Lord God said, "The man has now become like one of us, knowing good and evil. He must not be allowed to reach out his hand and take also from the tree of life and eat, and live forever."[586]

God does not want His created living in a state of perpetual rebellion forever, so He places two flaming swords at the entrance to Eden to keep them from returning. He also provides a plan for restoration.

This Story must be told. Adam and Eve tell the story to their children, their grandchildren, and their progeny until their deaths. The patriarchs living under the leadership of Adam and Eve believe and are successful. Unfortunately, Adam and his progeny die, and once again evil abounds. This sets the stage for the Deluge, because the unbelief and sin are great.

Noah, having heard the Story, leads his family to begin anew. Once again, evil runs rampant among nonbelievers. Consequently, God calls on

---

[585] Genesis 2:9.
[586] Genesis 3:22.

Abraham to reveal to his family the Story he has heard. Abraham, in the line from Adam, reveals that God has made a covenant with him, and they will be led to the Promised Land.

In the covenant dream are two figures, God and Jesus. *The covenant is anchored in relationship.* In the cutting of this covenant, Jesus stands in for humanity.

The covenant is passed on to Jacob, Isaac, and Joseph. Due to a famine, the Israelites go to Egypt and seek its plenty. Eventually, the Israelites grow in number and are enslaved by the Egyptians. God sends Moses to bring them out of their captivity and take them to the land promised to Abraham. The covenant is renewed with Moses through the Ten Commandments. God's house of worship is established with His people. Their trek through the wilderness to the banks of the Jordan River is challenging, and the Hebrews behave badly. They send spies into the land to determine a strategy of conquest. In fear of what they find, they disagree with Moses and do not want to enter. Because they lack faith in God, they are returned to the wilderness for forty years. God reassigns Joshua to the role of leadership. Joshua leads the Israelites in the conquest of the Promised Land. The land is divided among the twelve tribes.

In time, the people no longer want God's judges and prophets to lead them. They desire to be like the rest of the world and have a king. God renews His covenant with King David, who brings the ark of the covenant to Jerusalem. David's son, Solomon, builds the tabernacle in which the ark is placed.

Unfortunately, due to developing political turmoil between the tribes, division occurs and splits the kingdom. The upheaval damages the strength of Israel, and the divided kingdoms are plundered. Israel is carried off to Babylon. Four hundred years before the birth of Christ, God goes silent.

Then a star adorns the night sky, leading to the place where Jesus has been born. The prophecies are fulfilled. The Messiah is born to save the world. Because of His obedience, He will make it possible for believers to be restored to a personal relationship with God.

Jesus sheds His blood for the stain of our rebellion and sin, which are removed as far as the east is from the west. Jesus walked with God in Abraham's covenant-cutting dream. This is the foundation of the Christian faith. Jesus represents humanity and takes responsibility for the broken relationship through His death on the cross. Those who believe will be cleansed of their rebellious sin and be set apart for an eternal life in heaven.

Jesus's ministry begins with baptism. He is led into the wilderness to be challenged by Lucifer. The deceiver uses the same approach he used with Adam and Eve, but Jesus is victorious. Jesus calls His disciples and begins His ministry. He brings the kingdom of God and calls believers to become like little children, as it was in Eden.[587] In a significant event, Jesus calls Lazarus, dead for four days and lying in a tomb, to come out of the tomb. After three years of training the disciples to lead, teach, and heal, Jesus's ministry comes to an end.

Jesus is betrayed, crucified, and buried. The disciples are scattered. They are ecstatic to learn of His Resurrection and meet with Him. He tells them to go tell the world what has happened. They are also instructed to await the Holy Spirit.

FROM PRE-CREATION PLANNING

The Story of God began with a pre-creation planning meeting. With His Son, Creation was underway. God knew every step of the way what His design would be and what it would take to draw us back to Him. We bear His image. He gave each of us a soul filled with heart, mind, will, and emotions. He also gave us the freedom to choose or reject His plan. In this love, freedom abounds.

Despite our missteps, He provided a Son who would accept the results of our rebellion and disobedience as a demonstration of His love for us. He provided a way, through surrender and obedience, back to relationship with Him, salvation, and eternal life.

Be sure the divine plan took into account everything that would happen. No human action or response is a surprise to God. However, on occasion, there are situations that result in His feeling remorse for creating humankind and being "deeply troubled."[588] The plan He designed was carried out by His Son and supported by the Holy Spirit. Moreover, the plan for our

---

[587] Matthew 18:3.
[588] Genesis 6:5–6.

relationship with Him includes a renovation of the heart and a renewal of the mind. Heart and mind will be guided by His Holy Spirit and *not* the ambitions of a striving self.

Humanity is bombarded by distractions to the heart and mind that seem good to our eyes, pleasing for our personal gain, and satisfying for our insatiable needs. Sound familiar? Of course it is. The work of the deceiver awaits your attention. The influence of a secular culture defies the value of human life. Abhorrent alternative lifestyles are marketed. We are asked to submit to anti-God physical defiling of children.

Those who possess a profound awareness carry the purposes of God in their hearts. This profound awareness has connected the theological dots from pre-creation planning to the new Jerusalem. Your deep soul-vision is set to teach the God Story and lead the lost. A reminder of what happened in Eden continues to plague humanity.

The following are descriptors of our self-centered focus on the world. These are how humanity glorifies the self through the characteristics of pride:

- independence from God
- self-determination
- self-gratification
- self-actualization
- self-righteousness
- self-worship
- self-reliance
- control of one's own destiny

You must slow your life down to remain present in your relationship with God. God placed the created in a garden and taught them to thrive and flourish with wholesome, life-giving values. Then came the deceiver, who used *pride* to lure humanity. The created:

- failed to recognize evil
- doubted God's truth
- doubted God's sovereignty
- pursued their own destiny

- were filled with discontent
- disobeyed and rebelled
- broke covenant
- feared consequences
- hid from God
- evaded responsibility

As a result of *pride*, secular man pursues idols to gain control over existential dread. Idols are the things of this world that people pursue rather than pursuing God's plan for their lives. Pride is the opposite of humility! Pursuing worldly goals will provide a momentary sense of control over one's own destiny. These goals are also heralded by the culture. It is disappointing to witness an American culture pursuing these goals rather than seeking a deeper relationship with God.

Because of humanity's separation from God, a malaise covers them, causing them to experience discomforting experiential dread in the following ways:

- distorted view of God
- distorted view of humanity
- fear of aloneness
- failure
- lack of belonging
- guilt
- shame
- rejection by others
- self-comparison to others
- poor self-evaluation
- bitterness
- rage
- scarring by trauma
- worry
- insecurity
- impure thoughts
- lust
- addictions

The trek from secular man, who is separated from God, to spiritual man, who is in oneness with God, begins with a prayer of salvation and the earnest desire to submit your self-directed life to pursue a God-directed life. Spiritual formation is our movement back to God and possessing the mind of Christ. Our assigned task on earth is to lead others back to God through the work of Christ on the cross. As *God-serving leaders*, we grow in the character of Christ, which is revealed in our lives by exhibiting the fruit of the Spirit. Through our renewed hearts and minds, we live our lives in the mind of Christ.

The most important theme in the Story of God is Christ's work on the cross. And it was the most significant part of the planning from the beginning. Clearly, the reason for His obedience on the cross was to offer the gift of a restored relationship with the Creator God.[589] Yes, your sins are forgiven, and you are a new creation. But most of all, there is a renewed, intimate relationship you are able to share with God!

It is a tumultuous journey because our prideful nature is revealed to us. We are *all* born in the same state of sin. Paul and the other NT writers have explained what is necessary if we are going to share in the oneness found in the mind of Christ.

THE MIND OF CHRIST OR THE MIND OF MODERN MAN

The following spheres are representations of internal belief structures, categories, or schema.[590] The self responds to the discussions, activities, and lived experiences that create a mindful vision or worldview of the many aspects of life. A secular person with the guiding principles of mindfulness will approach these areas of life based on creating a perceived reality for each person. For the mindful naturalist, the value given in self-determination is important. Everything from judging reality to determining one's own

---

[589] Romans 5:19: "For as through the one man's disobedience the many were made sinners, even so through the obedience of the One the many will be made righteous."
[590] Eric Palmu, "Developing Spiritual Maturity in Ministry Leaders through Whole-Bible Thematic Instruction" (DM.D diss, Southeastern University, 2019), archived in Fire Scholars.

destiny results from their autonomous decisions. The famous Greek Protagoras said, "Man is the measure of all things."[591]

For the God-follower, all reality is determined by Him if the believer submits to and pursues His purposes for their life. The God-vision is one of wholeness or wholesomeness that is sweetly flourishing and thriving with Him, as He intended for a joy-filled creation. The covenants provide a protective barrier for believers that leads to eternity. This is a very different approach to life and living as a spiritual person profoundly aware of the supernatural. For the

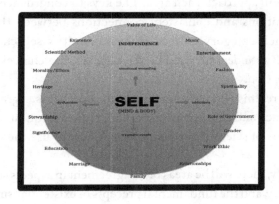

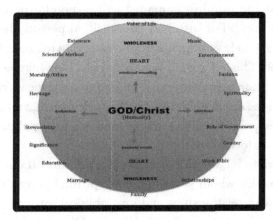

believer, God is in control of all things. And because of that belief, the fruit of the Spirit is anchored deep within the believer.

---

[591] Protagoras, a fourth-century BCE philosopher, determined that humanity would be responsible for its own well-being and all decisions on existential matters, https://en.wikipedia.org/wiki/Protagoras.

The two lives face each category differently. One lives in a perspective of self-satisfaction that their life choices have meaning and value. The other knows their life choices have meaning and value because they are led by the Holy Spirit. Their life choices remain faithful to the biblical precepts found in the Story of God.

Both mindsets will contend with each area. The mindful humanists will seek their own answers, with the idea of creating some form of harmony and unified worldview. Much debate will ensue among humanist intellectuals as to how they will approach each area. The keys to congruence or happiness are the definitions and consistent connections between them. Keep in mind that each category is lived from humanity's self-choices derived from humanity's *independence*. For the believer, life choices are found in *dependence on God*.

The two realms will have agreement in some areas. Agreement can be found in science and the scientific method. However, questions arise from interpretations of scientific evaluations and how to use the results of that research.

Obviously, there will be areas of disagreement in aspects such as valuing life, spirituality, and the fundamental precepts of existentialism. It is obvious the self-guided and mindful humanist will respond differently than the Christ-guided mind. For instance, the spiritual person identifying with Christ will more likely protect life from conception to grave, because life is divinely created. The self-guided person may place qualitative conditions on life from conception to grave because humanity is the measure of all things. The Christ-guided mind, observing fashion, will state that modest is hottest. The self-guided person will say that fashion is a personal decision—wear what you are comfortable with.

With regard to relationships, the secular person will state that you can love and sleep with whom you want. The spiritual person will look for a wholesomeness in relationships and save physical intimacy for marriage. In issues of morality, the secularist will state, "Your truth is not my truth. There are no absolutes. Do your own thing! Do what makes you happy." The person in Christ will say, "There are absolute moral answers in God's Word. Christ-followers should reflect biblical principles in all the facets of their lives. There is no perfection for believers, but there is freedom in forgiveness and grace."

DEVELOPING A PROFOUND AWARENESS

Responding to humanity's existential dread can *only* be accomplished through *pride*. According to Dictionary.com, *pride* is a high or inordinate opinion of one's own dignity, importance, merit, or superiority, whether as cherished in the mind or as displayed in bearing or conduct. Pride, despite all other evidence, maintains that the explanation of reality is the product of humanity's wisdom.

The philosophers developed their version of reality, and the psychologists nursed humanity through the revelation of their dread. Unfortunately, the discovery of this universal aloneness and subsequent real absence of meaningfulness is absolutely startling for the human being when they discover the truth of their significance. The Bible refers to the *wisdom of humanity to be foolish*.

Humility is the opposite of pride. Merriam-Webster defines *humility* as "freedom from pride or arrogance: the quality or state of being humble." The wise will follow the reality God set in motion before the beginning of time. King David said, "The way of fools seems right to them, but the wise listen to advice."[592]

My favorite verse comes from Philippians:

> In your relationships with one another, have the same mindset as Christ Jesus: Who, being in very nature God, did not consider equality with God something to be used to his own advantage; rather, he made himself nothing by taking the very nature of a servant, being made in human likeness. And being found in appearance as a man, he humbled himself by becoming obedient to death—even death on a cross![593]

Humility is paramount in understanding your role as a God-serving leader. Jesus humbled Himself to teach and die so that we could be restored to a right relationship with the Father. To humble oneself means putting everything in one's life under the control of God's Holy Spirit. God is the Designer, Jesus is the Builder, and the Holy Spirit is our Comforter and Encourager.

---

[592] Proverbs 12:15.
[593] Philippians 2:5–8.

26

PROFOUND AWARENESS: IN THE PUBLIC SQUARE

APPLIED CHRISTIANITY

APPLIED CHRISTIANITY CONSIDERS THE INFLUENCE OF BIBLICAL principles and tenets within our soul-vision identity that impact our natural, earthly lives. This includes our influence in the social, political, economic, and cultural worlds as Christ-followers. In the other words, we bring the kingdom of God to earth. There is a term from German philosophy called zeitgeist (zīt gīst) that characterizes an invisible force or guiding spirit that can strongly influence a time in history. Applying Christian beliefs to our culture will create a sort of Christian zeitgeist as opposed to a new age, humanistic, existential, or one-world zeitgeist. (https://www.merriam-webster.com/dictionary/zeitgeist).

Increasingly, I hear church members asking or urging their pastors to become activists in local, state, and federal lawmaking. Apparently, for many members, since many churches have publicly stood against abortion, then churches should engage in other political discourse. I am not sure that is the organizational structure the church was built for. Christ-followers are to lead and teach. The pastors have done what they are called to do. The hearers are to become the doers. The responsibility falls upon believers to be led by the Holy Spirit to influence the nefarious world!

Jesus was very clear about the purposes of the gospel as well as the purposes of humanity and its government. His ministry focused on the salvation of the lost. The instruction to go and teach is clear. Pastoral focus must be on God's Word and caring for His people. However, that doesn't preclude Christ-followers from engaging the public square, armed with a biblical message. Christ-followers are to be beacons in their homes first, and then in the public square.

Please be clear: humanity's goal for government is shared power. Unfortunately, that doesn't always happen. Power does not corrupt; corrupt humanity abuses power. Too often, governmental growth reveals a leadership headed toward control of the people.

In the kingdom of God, government can be built with wholesome and thriving principles that reward effort and minimize sloth. The Constitution was built on biblical principles. I have presented several of the common areas of concern for Christ-followers and their message in the public square.

VALUING HUMAN LIFE

A successful humanity and its government must begin with valuing our relational life as humans. Everything begins with valuing life. Both human and ecological success begins here. Everything we do in life begins with honoring humanity and the earth in all stages, from conception to death. God knows you in the womb, and your relationship with Him begins there.

> For you created my inmost being; you knit me together in my mother's womb.[594]

> From birth I was cast on you; from my mother's womb you have been my God.[595]

Describing a fetus as anything but an embryo from the Creator God violates the sanctity of human life. If we don't honor the fetus from the moment of conception as a living, breathing member of society, then we run the danger of establishing a slippery slope to dehumanization at all levels. Abortions devalue human beings. Euthanasia has been a practice widely discussed as abhorrent to our senses. Assisted suicide continues to be a discussion for ending one's life on the grounds of pain, suffering, and poor quality of life conditions. Clearly, they are bad ideas.

Scripture holds that God knew us as fetuses in the womb, and that we

---

[594] Psalm 139:13.
[595] Psalm 22:10.

are called to pursue His purpose for our lives. From His perspective, this clearly indicates our value at birth through a return to eternity.

Our XX and XY chromosomes are determined by God. Today, we find that many experience a discontent with their sexual selves. As a result, there is movement in medical science to alter the discontented soul's outward appearance and/or internal, hormonal, bodily function. Proponents are allowing and coaching children to alter their sexuality via drugs and/or surgical mutilation without parental or moral guidance. This is the result when humanity devalues life and desires to live on human terms because people are discontented with the way they are.[596] Reminder: human pelvic structures differ between male and female.

Teach family members that they are the valuable people God created them to be. He knew them in the womb. Ladies, you do have a choice: it is a pro-life decision. Honor what God has created. The choices for young marrieds are prophylactics, preconception birth control, withdrawal, or the rhythm method. For pre-marrieds, the choice is abstinence. Abortion is NOT a choice. Abortion is a way to evade responsibility. The real choice is BEFORE conception! It is YOUR body, take responsibility for your behavior prior to conception. This is the **true pro-choice stance:** prophylactics, coitus interruptus (withdrawal), the rhythm method (post-menstrual cycle), pre-conception birth control, mutual stimulation (non-penetrating), or abstinence.

HUMAN SEXUALITY

Ordained by God, human sexuality is a gift from Him. You are born with the XX (male) or the XY (female) chromosomes, and gender is determined accordingly. God created it so. He also established a capacity for physical oneness between the male and female only. Despite modern man's attempt to reframe human sexuality in culture and in medicine, the biological processes of procreation were created by God and to this day remain. Let us not forget that heterosexuality is the driving force for a society and species to continue. All other alternative lifestyles are a slippery slope to self-destruction.

---

[596] Dr. Miriam Grossman is a board-certified child psychologist. She works with a legal and medical association referred to as Do No Harm. She appeared before Congress in August 2023 to debunk the political purposes of gender ideology. See https://www.youtube.com/watch?v=abTMFKoytMo.

The sexuality of human beings is most importantly to be experienced between married partners. It is a precious and divine experience for marriage. It is a detriment to a thriving and wholesome life and not meant to be a self-gratifying experience. And there is plenty of evidence to support that the rampant growth of STDs is an indicator. Sexual humanity was *not* designed for multiple partners.

Place a greater value on yourself than the world gives you. Those called by God recognize they are round pegs in a square world. Your sexual passions are to be focused on one partner of the opposite sex. That partner will be sent to you from God. Read the story of Abraham, Isaac, and Rebekah in Genesis 24. Treat your sexuality as a sacred and pure gift from God.

WORK

God placed Adam and Eve in the garden to care for it. Work was and is a critical theme in God's work. Laziness is not good for humanity. If you do not work, you bear the consequences. It is critical for each man and woman to pursue the work that God has called them to do. The kind of job does not matter. What matters is that you are doing what God has called you to do.

For young persons, your family can help you to see what divine purpose God has called you to fulfill. I did not like going to school. I graduated in the bottom decile of my high school class. God then called me to teach high school social studies.

MARRIAGE

Marriage is a divine ordinance from God, to be enjoyed for a lifetime and not to be broken. Marriage is a divine covenant, a bond of three: God, the man, and the woman. It is the most critical step enabling a society to continue. Heterosexuality gives humanity a future!

The reason God hates divorce is primarily due to the broken relationship caused by the rebellion of Adam and Eve. His heart was in turmoil because of the broken covenant.[597] As it was and still is, marriage is the cornerstone of a society and its culture. Family is a critical outcome of marriage and should

---

[597] Genesis 6:6.

295

be protected at all costs. Some will find a level of satisfaction in marriage. With their partner, they will establish and pursue their goals as well as prepare for retirement.

> God, not you, made marriage. His Spirit inhabits even the
> smallest details of marriage. And what does he want from
> marriage? Children of God, that's what. So guard the spirit
> of marriage within you.[598]

Most will find a passion in a blue-collar trade, white-collar profession, entrepreneurship, military career, or criminal activity. Ultimately, if a believer follows God's guidance into marriage and work, they are likely to be more satisfied and fulfilled.

Ask God to lead you to the person He has prepared for you. Be patient! This will be your person for life. He will bless you in incredible ways.

PARENTING

Parenting is a combination of love and reasonable rules. Parents have specific roles as they raise their children. Parents must create balance in their authority because they are the child's critical role models in the same way Christ is the role model for the parents. The family must thrive and flourish as a unit because the unit is the foundation for raising children. If we are to build fully functioning children for a healthy society, then children must be raised in wholesome and nourishing environments.

> Fathers, do not exasperate your children; instead, bring
> them up in the training and instruction of the Lord.[599]

Get into a young family small group to learn about ways to parent your children. Most churches have great parenting programs for young families. Many great Christian writers have addressed family topics. Christian radio also has awesome parenting programs on the air.

---

[598] Malachi 2:15 MSG.
[599] Ephesians 6:4.

EDUCATION IN THE PUBLIC SQUARE

Educating your children is a critical issue for every parent. It always centers on a single issue: the decision to send your child to a public school, private school, or homeschool.

A public school is a viable way to educate your children. The issue you need to examine in that decision is the community and local school board. A school governed by a school board that possesses your values is the critical piece to this puzzle. Additionally, whether it is a county-run district or a community-run school board plays a role.

If the county in which you live holds a conservative approach to teaching social studies, then it is a good fit. By conservative social studies education, I am referring to a culture that values a belief in God, traditional American history, a belief that we are creations of God, and the view that the XX or XY decision is made at conception. Every conception is a valued human being. The values a school board possesses are seen in its approach to teaching social studies education. It is that simple. This approach allows your faith system to be honored.

If the school board possesses a liberal, humanistic approach to its social studies education, then it will herald humanity as the determiner of all things. There will be no place for God. They will teach your children to accept alternative lifestyles. More importantly, your faith system will not be honored.

If you consider a private education, again it must be determined if it is liberal or religious setting for your child. Does the school administration possess your values?

Obviously, if you choose to homeschool, your values will be preserved and passed along. As of late, parents are becoming more aware of their local school districts and the boards that either honor or deny their values. Protect your children from the reign of evil: no drag queens in any school!

Pray! Get involved in your local school board elections. Look for candidates who possess the mind of Christ. This is critical. Pray for and encourage Christians to run for the board.

ECONOMICS IN THE PUBLIC SQUARE

Given their distinctive views on human nature, secular man and spiritual man propose economic theories differently. As an example, a humanistic thinker sees humankind as basically good and believes everyone will participate equally in the work; therefore workloads will willingly be shared equally. On the other hand, a conservative thinker sees humankind as basically selfish. Not everyone will participate equally. Ultimately, conservative people will work as hard as they need to get what they need and want.

At the base of these two approaches is whether one believes one has control over one's life. Psychologists refer to this as the *locus of control*. Verywell Mind provides a great explanation of this internal human dynamic.[600] Locus of control will influence every aspect of your life, including your economic decisions. Put simply, some people believe in their internal abilities to overcome obstacles. Others believe that external circumstances control their success. The former prefer less government; the latter prefer greater government to help them have success.

Humanistic thinking holds that the selfishness of the wealthy class abuses the working class. Consequently, liberal politicians (Democrats, Progressives, Socialists) don't trust the wealthy (those who own the means to produce goods and services). They build a large governmental structure to control the wealthy. Their goal is to persuade a citizenry that the wealthy are the bad guys. Consequently, a liberal government offers *all* citizens the same level of material well-being, as determined by the government. This is a socialist economic system. A socialist government will determine how the rewards for your work will be equally shared, despite a person's work ethic.

Sweden tried this structure in the 1970s and 1980s. They almost entirely abandoned it for two reasons. First, the citizens wanted more than the government was providing. Second, the structure could not control costs of the production of good and services.[601] Truth is the ruling government becomes the wealthy, like Venezuela.

The conservative thinker understands human nature's selfish desire for a better life. Since people are unique, they want different things. The only way to provide those differing goods and services is to let the market, also

---

[600] https://www.verywellmind.com/what-is-locus-of-control-2795434.

[601] https://www.wsj.com/articles/how-sweden-overcame-socialism-11547078767.

known as consumer demand, produce it. If there is a want, then someone will figure out a way to provide it and, as a producer, get paid for it. Conservatives prefer a capitalist system. The marketplace determines the reward earned based on what each person has contributed to the product. You will receive what you put in. The only role of government is determining a level ground of accessibility, equity, and safety.

The most important issue regarding financial stability for the Christ-follower is working to support the local church and its mission through tithing. Tithing is a response of gratitude for all that God has done for you and your family. Your life-focus must be the work of God. Please don't get this wrong!

Most conservatives rely on God and His blessings.[602] The work you do and the reward you gain is given back to God through tithing and, by choice, offering above and beyond the tithe. Since becoming a tither, I have wanted for nothing and never been without work. You see, it all belongs to God! This is a mystery of supernatural proportion. Get your priorities straight: God first (10 percent), savings next (10 percent), and daily living on the rest (80 percent).

Get excited about tithing. When you're making that deposit in the church, tell God you will continue this practice of gratitude for the rest of your life, no matter what. Our life-focus is not about you or me; it is about Him!

The following biblical passage is synonymous with a capitalist system. The employer gives a reward to those who earned it.

> Again, it will be like a man going on a journey, who called his servants and entrusted his wealth to them. To one he gave five bags of gold, to another two bags, and to another one bag, each according to his ability. Then he went on his journey. The man who had received five bags of gold went at once and put his money to work and gained five bags more. So also, the one with two bags of gold gained two

---

[602] Conservatives are made up of both believers and nonbelievers. What they have in common is a great dependence on their own efforts to provide for themselves and their families, *not* government.

more. But the man who had received one bag went off, dug a hole in the ground and hid his master's money.

After a long time the master of those servants returned and settled accounts with them. The man who had received five bags of gold brought the other five. "Master," he said, "you entrusted me with five bags of gold. See, I have gained five more."

His master replied, "Well done, good and faithful servant! You have been faithful with a few things; I will put you in charge of many things. Come and share your master's happiness!"

The man with two bags of gold also came. "Master," he said, "you entrusted me with two bags of gold; see, I have gained two more."

His master replied, "Well done, good and faithful servant! You have been faithful with a few things; I will put you in charge of many things. Come and share your master's happiness!"

Then the man who had received one bag of gold came. "Master," he said, "I knew that you are a hard man, harvesting where you have not sown and gathering where you have not scattered seed. So I was afraid and went out and hid your gold in the ground. See, here is what belongs to you."

His master replied, "You wicked, lazy servant! So you knew that I harvest where I have not sown and gather where I have not scattered seed? Well then, you should have put my money on deposit with the bankers, so that when I returned I would have received it back with interest.

"So take the bag of gold from him and give it to the one who has ten bags. For whoever has will be given more, and they will have an abundance. Whoever does not have, even what they have will be taken from them."[603]

Capitalism provides any person with the drive to do so to present any product to the free marketplace and secure the gains from it. Private owners

---

[603] Matthew 25:14–30.

control their businesses. From the liberals' perspective, this is the biblical passage they would use to support equality:

> All the believers were one in heart and mind. No one claimed that any of their possessions was their own, but they shared everything they had.[604]

In socialism and communism, the government owns all the business products and shares the rewards for making them equally among the workers. Most importantly, God blesses those whom He blesses. What He calls you to do will be blessed.

POLITICS IN THE PUBLIC SQUARE

Our country was built on a belief that man should have the right to pursue life and own property. His freedom and liberty would be protected through our Constitution. It is the job of government to ensure that people have access and capacity to possess property through liberty.

A person's locus of control plays a role here. You choose the political approach that will give you access to your needs and wants. Progressive socialists believe external forces like the wealthy control their destiny. Conservatives believe they are capable of overcoming external forces, so they are more likely to be independent or libertarian. Each person can make their own decision. Less government is the best government.

After much study and research, the founding fathers built a unique form of democracy that gave everyone a say in the operation of government and represented the people's wishes. It was called a representative republic with three branches of government. Many of the authors were theists and believed God was in control.

> Everyone must submit to governing authorities. For all authority comes from God, and those in positions of authority have been placed there by God. So anyone who rebels against authority is rebelling against what God has instituted, and they will be punished. For the

---

[604] Acts 4:32.

authorities do not strike fear in people who are doing
right, but in those who are doing wrong. Would you like to
live without fear of the authorities? Do what is right, and
they will honor you. The authorities are God's servants,
sent for your good. But if you are doing wrong, of course
you should be afraid, for they have the power to punish
you. They are God's servants, sent for the very purpose
of punishing those who do what is wrong. So you must
submit to them, not only to avoid punishment, but also
to keep a clear conscience.

Pay your taxes, too, for these same reasons. For
government workers need to be paid. They are serving God
in what they do.[605]

In all likelihood, submitting to governmental authority came from
this passage. The primary requirement of all citizens was to pray, vote, and
then accept the outcome as directed by God. Paul's letter to Timothy gave
additional instructions regarding submitting to authority:

I urge, then, first of all, that petitions, prayers, intercession
and thanksgiving be made for all people—for kings and all
those in authority, that we may live peaceful and quiet lives
in all godliness and holiness. This is good, and pleases God
our Savior, who wants all people to be saved and to come to
a knowledge of the truth.[606]

We can agree that *honoring those in authority is expected in applied
Christianity.* The citizens must decide the level of control given to politicians
through voting. Some elected officials believe it is their responsibility to
make decisions for you. Others will listen to the voters and work in their
interests. The role of government will directly impact its size and the taxes
assessed to support it.

---

[605] Romans 13:1–6 NLT.
[606] 1 Timothy 2:1–4.

THE ROLE OF GOVERNMENT

How one sees the role of government will determine their political affiliation. As a government takes on more responsibility the cost of government operation (taxes) increases.

More Governmental Control <—> Less Governmental Control

Liberal   Moderate   Conservative

**THIS PERSPECTIVE RESULTS IN THE
FOLLOWING POLITICAL GROUPS**
Socialists Progressives Independents Libertarians Anarchists

Democrats ------------------ Republicans

Some political groups will increase the size and level of intervention to permit government to operate. Others will desire smaller government, much less intervention, and lower taxes. Many people desire the government to have less involvement in their lives. In short, they believe they are capable of handling their life choices without governmental intervention. Others prefer governmental authority in most areas of their lives because they can't get where they want to be, so they prefer government to secure their goals.

We are really not in need of a government, because we live by a soul-vision given by God. So government is not critical for our lives. His purpose for my life is critical. Therefore, our government, if necessary, should be built on the Word of God.

KINGDOM ON EARTH

I am not taking an anarchist position of "down with the government." I am suggesting that we should take our Christian vision into the marketplace. Get involved in those events that support your belief. Go to the rallies protesting at abortion clinics. Consider boycotting the following for:

- corporations or its ownership that support abortions. This is public information that can be found on the internet.
- companies or its ownership that support a woke ideology. This is public information that can be found on the internet.
- companies or its ownership that discriminate against conservative employees. This is public information that can be found on the internet.
- hospitals or its ownership that support the mutilation of young people under age of twenty-one through gender-affirming surgeries. This is public information that can be found on the internet.

Attend local school board meetings to ensure that your local school board is teaching wholesome values to your children. Elect politicians who are committed Christ-followers!

Keep in mind that the government and companies will *not* bring salvation to the world! Judas thought in those terms; that didn't work out so well for him. The church is not responsible for getting us into heaven. God placed the responsibility of choice solely on the individual to surrender to Jesus. Remember this:

> Be on your guard; stand firm in the faith; be courageous; be strong.[607]

> Therefore, put on every piece of God's armor so you will be able to resist the enemy in the time of evil. Then after the battle you will still be standing firm.[608]

The discussion of the kingdom of heaven coming to earth is a discussion about our culture, not the laws or politicians. The discussion revolves around what we believe and how it should influence our culture. We have the Spirit of God within us. It should make a difference in our response to our family and our community. We as the people of God can reclaim this land in one federal election cycle.

Get involved in your local politics. Find out what your politicians stand

---

[607] 1 Corinthians 16:13 NIV.
[608] Ephesians 6:13 NLT.

for. Check their records. Let your local politicians know what you believe. Elect believers to local, state, and federal positions.

It is *not* the job of the church to speak from the pulpit regarding these matters. The pastor can lead or support a midweek group to discuss local issues and provide a Christian worldview. Start with prayer. Ask God where you should enter the political process. Most importantly, *pray* and *vote*!

RELIGION IN THE PUBLIC SQUARE

Existentialism, commonly referred to as *secular humanism*, is regarded by natural man as the approach we should own in response to life. In short, if we can't feel, touch, taste, see, or hear a phenomenon, then it doesn't exist. Therefore, man should live by scientific proof that requires evidence and measurement. That includes resisting any inclination toward God because He is beyond the natural. Existentialists accept their place in the universe: existential dread. Humanists choose to ascribe value to what they choose to do. Moreover, secular humanity seeks to erase any references to belief in anything beyond our existence, as well as celebrate humanity's independence. As humanity attempts to escape its dependence on God, it finds itself searching for other bigger-than-life pseudo-faith alternatives, such as Eastern thought, Hinduism, Buddhism, and New Age beliefs. All of them are empty of significance.

Faith systems are an integral part of any culture. A significant issue in the public square is the many denominations of Christianity. Most denominations use the same revealed Word, the Holy Bible, but they interpret it or focus on theological points differently. As a result, their doctrines are often different. However, the tenets of the faith are the same.

Political parties may align themselves with a denomination. Others don't believe. Both groups exist within government and develop policies that are consistent with their beliefs. Consequently, it is incumbent upon Christians to know their faith and vote accordingly. Churches may not discuss these issues from the pulpit, and rightly so. Christian citizens should vote the principles and tenets of their faith.

Again, let's be clear: *not* all faith systems are the same. Spirituality is not the same from one system to the next. Some faith systems claim spirituality but will focus on what seems right, looking for love and peace.[609] You'll hear such terms as *mindfulness*, defined as a conscious awareness of self, well-being, and others in my space.[610] All of which celebrate humanism.

Islam is a faith system created by Muhammad. He was dissatisfied with the ancient Hebrew writings and decided to copy what he liked and omit what he disagreed with. His Muslim followers pray to Allah. Please understand, Allah is not Yahweh or the Christian God. The attributes and behavior of Allah and God are completely different. The Christian God does not require you to kill nonbelievers. Islam expects you to do violence to nonbelievers.[611] Muhammad did not understand the grace and mercy offered by Yahweh.

Islam understands Jesus to be a prophet but not the Son of God. Islam maintains you are born with a clean slate; you are sinless. To enter eternity requires good behavior, but there is no assurance that good behavior will be good enough. You don't need your sins forgiven through the work of Christ. Most importantly, they do not believe that Christ died to redeem believers back to God.[612]

Much of the Koran is not a sacred text as claimed. Islamic holy writings use many of the stories from the Hebrew Torah, so the Koran looks familiar. Muslims' reward of getting into heaven is based on their good works, not on belief in Jesus as the Son of God. Islam is a man-created faith that utilized the Hebrew Torah for legitimacy, making Muhammad the first to plagiarize the God Story. Muslims are duped into believing the Koran was revealed by God. Muhammad completed his copied work circa AD 632. Keep in mind

---

[609] Proverbs 14:12.

[610] Surah 2:191, "And kill them [non-Muslims] wherever you find them ... kill them. Such is the recompense of the disbelievers [non-Muslims]," https://www.healthline.com/health/mind-body/what-is-mindfulness.

[611] https://www.jacksonville.com/story/opinion/columns/mike-clark/2015/02/03/islam-quran-itself-preaches-violence-against-nonbelievers/985431007/.

[612] Huda. In the Quran, there are many stories about the life and teachings of Jesus Christ (called 'Isa in Arabic). The Quran recalls his miraculous birth, his teachings, the miracles he performed by God's permission, and his life as a respected prophet of God. The Quran also repeatedly reminds us that Jesus was a human prophet sent by God, not part of God Himself. See https://www.learnreligions.com/what-does-the-quran-say-about-jesus-2003787.

that anyone who alters or changes Christian sacred writings will pay a heavy toll. Islam's battle is Allah's battle with the King of the universe.

Clearly our focus must be heavenward. We are to be eternity-minded for this reason:

> But God shows his anger from heaven against all sinful, wicked people who suppress the truth by their wickedness. They know the truth about God because he has made it obvious to them. For ever since the world was created, people have seen the earth and sky. Through everything God made, they can clearly see his invisible qualities—his eternal power and divine nature. So they have no excuse for not knowing God.
>
> Yes, they knew God, but they wouldn't worship him as God or even give him thanks. And they began to think up foolish ideas of what God was like. As a result, their minds became dark and confused. Claiming to be wise, they instead became utter fools. And instead of worshiping the glorious, ever-living God, they worshiped idols made to look like mere people and birds and animals and reptiles.
>
> So God abandoned them to do whatever shameful things their hearts desired. As a result, they did vile and degrading things with each other's bodies. They traded the truth about God for a lie. So they worshiped and served the things God created instead of the Creator himself, who is worthy of eternal praise! Amen. That is why God abandoned them to their shameful desires. Even the women turned against the natural way to have sex and instead indulged in sex with each other. And the men, instead of having normal sexual relations with women, burned with lust for each other. Men did shameful things with other men, and as a result of this sin, they suffered within themselves the penalty they deserved.
>
> Since they thought it foolish to acknowledge God, he abandoned them to their foolish thinking and let them do things that should never be done. Their lives became full

of every kind of wickedness, sin, greed, hate, envy, murder, quarreling, deception, malicious behavior, and gossip. They are backstabbers, haters of God, insolent, proud, and boastful. They invent new ways of sinning, and they disobey their parents. They refuse to understand, break their promises, are heartless, and have no mercy. They know God's justice requires that those who do these things deserve to die, yet they do them anyway. Worse yet, they encourage others to do them, too.[613]

The wrath of God targets *anything* that violates a wholesome, thriving, and nourishing theology regarding the kingdom of heaven. Idolatry—the worship of anything that distracts you from trusting God's right living—is no joke with God. Evil and wicked behaviors of humanity can include drugs, homosexuality, sexual immorality, New Age philosophy, Eastern religion, mindfulness, dark arts, transgenderism, and abortion. Idolatry means you love these dehumanizing activities more than God.

Do you inquire of the Lord in all things? Remember, your relationship with God is between you and the Holy Spirit. Your spiritual formation is proportional to your depth of surrender and submission to God. How deep is your love for the work of Jesus and His Crucifixion? He made holiness possible. He enabled you to approach God in intimacy. Is He Lord of your life? Are all facets of your soul driven by your covenant relationship with God?

This is what we've discovered together:

- Your body is a *living sacrifice*. Treat it well.
- Your mind perceives the world around you, which produces your *thoughts* and *feelings*. Be sure to fill it with Word of God.
- Your heart is home to the Holy Spirit, who is the Interpreter of your experiences that direct your *will* and *behavior*. Make sure you fill it with conversation and guidance from the Holy Spirit.[614]

Pray for God's guidance and presence in all matters, and vote!

---

[613] Romans 1:18–32 NLT.

[614] Dallas Willard, *Living in Christ's Presence* (IVP Books, 2014), 135–145.

MEDIA AND HOLLYWOOD

• There is an effort by media to control how we see ourselves and the world around us. This is the battle of worldviews between existential humanity and the soul-vision God has called us to walk in our journey with Him. The media is setting its claim to redefine social context for all humanity. This humanistic perspective is heard in news reporting and has even seeped into marketing. Watch closely for their subtle messages that your life choices are yours alone. For believers, our choices are driven by our relationship with God. Our decisions will carry us into eternity with God.

Hollywood is considered by many to be the voice of this new age. Too many writers and actors use their positions to further the goals of immigration, sexuality, government control, and defiance of traditional marriage. These folks live in our world of fantasy and make-believe. In those fantasies, they attempt to rewrite the reality God has given us. Pedophiles are creating new scenarios for their own gain. Please watch carefully for the mixed messages found in a popular television series. Don't be driven by your emotions; be driven by the truth of heaven on earth.

PERSONAL DECISIONS ABOUT MAKING A LIVING

The question for each person to answer is how they will provide a living for themselves and maybe a family. These are the marketplace employment options:

- *Business ownership*—this could be a service business, like a medical practice, daycare center, or tailor shop; or a product business, like a factory or a grocery store
- *Employee of a business*—sell your labor to the highest bidder
- *Military service*—there are four branches to choose from
- *Nefarious or criminal activity*—take from others or sell an illegal product

Every one of us has seen the truth of human nature from our very first employment experience. Not everyone pulls on the oars equally. Some work harder than others. This isn't just to make the boss happy, though that may factor in for some. People work hard to get a bigger reward.

Growing up just south of the Flint, Michigan, auto plants, I heard the stories of the workers. The biggest complaint was about carrying the load of another person who was lazy. What made the complainer angrier was that they all got paid the same. And this did not only happen in the factories—it was the same in my work experience, even in the military.

This is an ages-old human characteristic: jealousy because someone made more money and worked less. A number of issues affect differing pay scales. Most often, pay is determined by what the marketplace will accept. Generally, plumbers make more money than teachers, but teachers only work for nine months. Doctors make more than auto plant workers, but the workers don't make life-and-death decisions. The coffee shop manager's base pay is more than the car salesman's base, but the car salesman earns a commission for every car sold. On and on it goes. There is great envy of those who are paid large incomes. If you don't like the income you have, then seek a better job. Under socialism or communism, you may change jobs, but the pay will be similar.

Capitalism is not a government-ordained theory. It is an economic system that allows every human being to prosper to the degree of their work ethic. Socialism is a government-ordained economic system designed to control the means of production and individual earnings.

Please understand that capitalism frees consumers to pursue their own vocational choices. Socialism, an economic and political philosophy developed by Marx and Engels, is anything but freedom.[615] Learn to recognize a government's increasing control of the economy. Socialism's goal is to empower government to control everything from employment to the marketplace. Inform your local, state, and national politicians that you expect them to keep a free-market system in which your family will prosper.

DEVELOPING A PROFOUND AWARENESS

Let me review the most critical aspects of our spiritual formation. I have shared my thoughts regarding the fruit of the Spirit. We should exhibit the characteristics of the fruit.

---

[615] https://en.wikipedia.org/wiki/Socialism.

Paul shared a revelation in his letter to the church in Galatia. Pay close attention to his introduction:

> So I say, let the Holy Spirit guide your lives. Then you won't be doing what your sinful nature craves. The sinful nature wants to do evil, which is just the opposite of what the Spirit wants. And the Spirit gives us desires that are the opposite of what the sinful nature desires. These two forces are constantly fighting each other, so you are not free to carry out your good intentions. But when you are directed by the Spirit, you are not under obligation to the law of Moses.
>
> When you follow the desires of your sinful nature, the results are very clear: sexual immorality, impurity, lustful pleasures, idolatry, sorcery, hostility, quarreling, jealousy, outbursts of anger, selfish ambition, dissension, division, envy, drunkenness, wild parties, and other sins like these. Let me tell you again, as I have before, that anyone living that sort of life will not inherit the Kingdom of God.
>
> But the Holy Spirit produces this kind of fruit in our lives: love, joy, peace, patience, kindness, goodness, faithfulness, gentleness, and self-control. There is no law against these things!
>
> Those who belong to Christ Jesus have nailed the passions and desires of their sinful nature to his cross and crucified them there. Since we are living by the Spirit, let us follow the Spirit's leading in every part of our lives. Let us not become conceited, or provoke one another, or be jealous of one another.

There are two things of note. First, the fruit of the Spirit is central to our behavior. The fruit produces wholesome and thriving behaviors in the believer. In addition, the fruit allows you to hear from Him.

Second, the order in which Paul places the fruit of the Spirit is pivotal, because I believe it reveals the maturational order of our spiritual formation. Moreover, the fruit is necessary for discernment and leadership.

In each step of your spiritual transformation, an increasing measure of fruit is required. When you submit your life to God, you'll initially experience supernatural love, joy, and peace. As a peacemaker, you will experience a self-control filled with all aspects of the fruit: "love, joy, peace, patience, kindness, goodness, gentleness, faithfulness, and self-control."

Human attachment to the world, its wisdom, and all it offers is an insidious and deceptive lure away from dependence on God. Humanity places stock in what the world offers for happiness, but God offers more than a superficial or momentary happiness.

Movement away from our sinful nature and toward the kingdom of God reflects a deeper relationship with God. He offers joy when we return to the original relationship He desires, which is our dependence on Him as experienced in Eden. Possessing the fruit of the Spirit is not individual stages, but what I describe as the nine layers of an onion or facets of a diamond. *Fruit* is singular but plural in its aspects.

I've observed extraordinary and supernatural spiritual growth revealed in some Christians over and over again for sixty years. The lived experience of bonding with God will initially result in an overwhelming love that gets the spiritual-formation ball rolling. This supernatural experience of love for your relationship with God will be both intense and sincere. I've witnessed this in each person touched by God. Nothing ever produced in human emotions can compare.

However, it is obvious there is a clear separation from the psychological grasp of the world's enticements to a supernatural freedom! I refer to this as the *joy measurement*. When I've made these observations of a person filled with a love for the divine, what I see is freedom from the world and its entrapments. If this seed is watered by a passionate pursuit of God, the love transitions quickly to joy and peace.

The remaining aspects of the fruit are patience, kindness, goodness, faithfulness, gentleness, and self-control. They are not necessarily in chronological order. However, the apparent pinnacle of one's growth in the fruit is self-control. While it could be argued that the anecdotal evidence of observation is not objectively reliable, interviews with those adorned with self-control will reveal a maturational process.

A deepening faith begins with believing the Word, trusting God's sovereignty, and placing dependence on His control over your lived experiences. It will manifest in the fruit of the Spirit. Separating yourself from humanity's hubris is the mysterious secret to your growth, which will ultimately come to a peaceful acceptance and trust of His control, displayed as self-control. I often refer to this process as the *joystick*, the measure of the fruit in your soul-vision. There is a biblical expectation for accountability.

> As iron sharpens iron, so one person sharpens another.[616]

> Therefore confess your sins to each other and pray for each other so that you may be healed. The prayer of a righteous person is powerful and effective.[617]

> Therefore encourage one another and build each other up, just as in fact you are doing.[618]

We should be providing guidance to one another through discernment of each other's spiritual growth.

Paul's letter to the Ephesians is succinct in his instructions:

> With the Lord's authority I say this: Live no longer as the Gentiles [nonbelievers] do, for they are hopelessly confused. Their minds are full of darkness; they wander far from the life God gives because they have closed their minds and hardened their hearts against him. They have no sense of shame. They live for lustful pleasure and eagerly practice every kind of impurity.

> But that isn't what you learned about Christ. Since you have heard about Jesus and have learned the truth that comes from him, throw off your old sinful nature and your former way of life, which is corrupted by lust and deception. Instead, let the Spirit renew your thoughts and attitudes. Put on your new nature, created to be like God—truly righteous & holy.

---

[616] Proverbs 27:17.

[617] James 5:16.

[618] 1 Thessalonians 5:11.

So stop telling lies. Let us tell our neighbors the truth, for we are all parts of the same body. And "don't sin by letting anger control you. Don't let the sun go down while you are still angry, for anger gives a foothold to the devil.

If you are a thief, quit stealing. Instead, use your hands for good hard work, and then give generously to others in need. Don't use foul or abusive language. Let everything you say be good and helpful, so that your words will be an encouragement to those who hear them.

And do not bring sorrow to God's Holy Spirit by the way you live. Remember, he has identified you as his own, guaranteeing that you will be saved on the day of redemption. Get rid of all bitterness, rage, anger, harsh words, and slander, as well as all types of evil behavior. Instead, be kind to each other, tenderhearted, forgiving one another, just as God through Christ has forgiven you.[619]

This letter hits to the heart of our soul-vision: to be a wholesome and thriving people who encourage one another. Profound awareness requires truth in love spoken through the gentleness of the fruit of the Spirit. This thriving and nourishing soul-vision is necessary to the way in which we respond to the challenges in our lives, because we are called to be peacemakers!

Review the discussion regarding spiritual disciplines. Remember to talk with God unceasingly. That is our prayer life. Study His Word. Meditate on the Word. Listen for the Holy Spirit's enlightenment. Holy is the directing of the Holy Spirit; practice it. Keep your life simple. Avoid distractions of the world. Find solitude to dream your dreams. Most important, delight in the Lord.

Then will appear the sign of the Son of Man in heaven. And then all the peoples of the earth will mourn when they see the Son of Man coming on the clouds of heaven, with power and great glory.[620]

---

[619] Ephesians 4:17–32 NLT.

[620] Matthew 24:30.

For he stands at the right hand of the needy, to save their lives from those who would condemn them.[621]

A dear friend once told me that we must not look for the spectacular like the world does. In God's realm, the Christ-follower looks for the supernatural. A profound awareness will distinguish between the two.

A FINAL REMINDER

Ultimately, life has two options. One is to live it with an individual choice to strive for my own purposes as I face the existential dread. The second is to believe God's Word, trust His intervention in my lived experiences, and pursue God's purpose for my life.

---

[621] Psalm 109:31.

APPENDIX 1

SPIRITUAL FORMATION

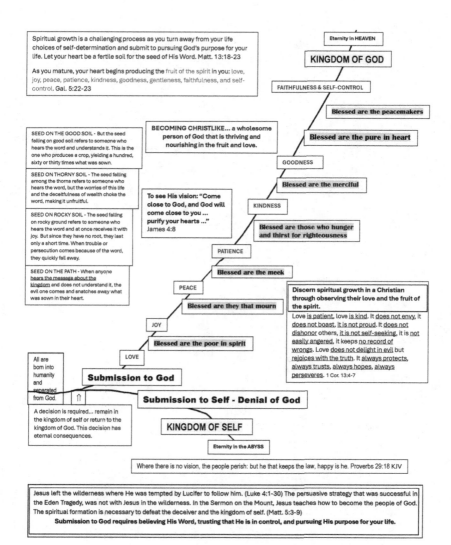

Spiritual growth is a challenging process as you turn away from your life choices of self-determination and submit to pursuing God's purpose for your life. Let your heart be a fertile soil for the seed of His Word. Matt. 13:18-23

As you mature, your heart begins producing the fruit of the spirit in you: love, joy, peace, patience, kindness, goodness, gentleness, faithfulness, and self-control. Gal. 5:22-23

Eternity in HEAVEN

KINGDOM OF GOD

FAITHFULNESS & SELF-CONTROL

Blessed are the peacemakers

SEED ON THE GOOD SOIL - But the seed falling on good soil refers to someone who hears the word and understands it. This is the one who produces a crop, yielding a hundred, sixty or thirty times what was sown.

BECOMING CHRISTLIKE... a wholesome person of God that is thriving and nourishing in the fruit and love.

Blessed are the pure in heart

GOODNESS

SEED ON THORNY SOIL - The seed falling among the thorns refers to someone who hears the word, but the worries of this life and the deceitfulness of wealth choke the word, making it unfruitful.

Blessed are the merciful

To see His vision: "Come close to God, and God will come close to you ... purify your hearts ..." James 4:8

KINDNESS

SEED ON ROCKY SOIL - The seed falling on rocky ground refers to someone who hears the word and at once receives it with joy. But since they have no root, they last only a short time. When trouble or persecution comes because of the word, they quickly fall away.

Blessed are those who hunger and thirst for righteousness

PATIENCE

SEED ON THE PATH - When anyone hears the message about the kingdom and does not understand it, the evil one comes and snatches away what was sown in their heart.

Blessed are the meek

PEACE

Discern spiritual growth in a Christian through observing their love and the fruit of the spirit.

Blessed are they that mourn

Love is patient, love is kind. It does not envy, it does not boast, it is not proud. It does not dishonor others, it is not self-seeking, it is not easily angered, it keeps no record of wrongs. Love does not delight in evil but rejoices with the truth. It always protects, always trusts, always hopes, always perseveres. 1 Cor. 13:4-7

JOY

Blessed are the poor in spirit

LOVE

All are born into humanity and separated from God.

Submission to God

A decision is required... remain in the kingdom of self or return to the kingdom of God. This decision has eternal consequences.

Submission to Self - Denial of God

KINGDOM OF SELF

Eternity in the ABYSS

Where there is no vision, the people perish: but he that keeps the law, happy is he. Proverbs 29:18 KJV

Jesus left the wilderness where He was tempted by Lucifer to follow him. (Luke 4:1-30) The persuasive strategy that was successful in the Eden Tragedy, was not with Jesus in the wilderness. In the Sermon on the Mount, Jesus teaches how to become the people of God. The spiritual formation is necessary to defeat the deceiver and the kingdom of self. (Matt. 5:3-9)
   Submission to God requires believing His Word, trusting that He is in control, and pursuing His purpose for your life.

APPENDIX 2

THEMATIC LESSONS TO THE WHOLE COUNSEL OF GOD

Trinitarian conclave for pre-creation planning: God (Designer),
Jesus (Builder), and Holy Spirit (Comforter/Sustainer) *before the
foundations of the world* to plan a universe and its inhabitants.
*Created: Adam and Eve, male and female, *choice, marriage, work.*
Choice: the gift of love. The pivotal theme for humanity to choose.
*Eden: built to commune with the created in holiness
to teach the created about wholeness.
*The angels were given a choice, but *no option for redemption.*
*Evil: an *angel's decision*—
A broken covenant between the created and Creator.
*In an act of love, God refuses man's return to Eden
and the tree of life. A return would have meant living
apart from God forever. *God's everlasting love.*
*The Story of God and the tragedy in Eden were
told to seven generations by Adam and Eve.
*The believer's response to entering this relationship is *to believe
God's Word, trust His sovereignty, and pursue His purpose for your life.*
*God uses the covenantal structure *to lead
humanity to relationship with Jesus.*
*Blood: a theme of sacrifice, restoration, and movement
away from disobedience and rebellion.
Blood is shed *to cover* the stain of their shame
and the guilt of disobedience.
*Flood: cleansing the earth of evil.
*Noah: begins anew.
*Covenant: built to *teach love, linking* believers to
God in the beginning and to eternity.

*Abraham: *drawing together the eternal family of God.*
*A crucial theme: *the smoking oven is God; the flaming torch is Jesus.* Jesus cuts the covenant to represent all mankind.
*Abraham is the earthly leader of a *familial covenantal relationship* with God.
*Led by God, Moses establishes the *Law* (*Commandments*) and *worship* (*tabernacle*). Behavioral boundaries and worship are monumental themes for God's people.
*King David: *a man after God's own heart.*
*David's intimacy with God was authentic. He *inquired of the Lord* with his decisions.
God-serving leadership is a complete dismissal of your rights and wants to serve God's vision and purpose for your life and His will. *All* believers are called to be part of His leadership.
*A *covenant relationship* is about a dynamic and extreme pursuit of intimacy with God—most importantly, on His terms.
*The *soul-vision* connects us to God.
*God is serious regarding you *trusting Him only*!
*Jesus faced the same temptations found in the Eden tragedy. Jesus defeated Lucifer's strategy.
*The soul is *home to the heart, mind, will, and emotions.*
Vision refers to a realm of perfect spiritual understanding, *a supernatural epiphany, or an "aha" moment that permeates the soul.*
God will not allow His holiness to be diminished, even by His called leaders.
*Your faith-walk will be different from mine. No two journeys with God are the same, because the soul is as unique as your fingerprints. *You are known.*
*Accepting His love that *restores you to relationship with Him* is your choice.
*Your decision: to *submit to Him or reject Him.*
*The essential qualities of faith require a submission and surrender to 1) *believe His Word,* 2) *trust His sovereignty,* and 3) *pursue God's purpose for your life.*
*Jesus presents *a progressive nature to our spiritual transformation* in his Sermon on the Mount.
The blood of Jesus, shed at the cross, *removes the stain of sin* for those who will believe.

*Practicing the spiritual disciplines should never be a regimen. As you practice them, you'll meet the Holy Spirit. *Seek the first fruit of love, peace, and joy as you wade into the disciplines.*

The Sinner's (Believer's) Prayer

Father God, I renounce the selfish, rebellious, and disobedient behavior (sin) I was born into. My sin has separated me from You. I confess that you are the King of the universe, and I was lost and heading to an eternity with Satan. I believe Jesus is your Son and died a horrible death so that I can be restored to relationship with You. He accepted on the cross my sin. I accept His sacrifice for me. He is the way to You, the truth of who You are as Creator, and the life eternal of living in joy, peace, and love with you. I now choose to make you Lord of my life! I will believe your Word, trust your intervention in my actions and decisions, and pursue your purpose for my life. Amen

Make this your definition of love (1 Cor. 13:1-13)

If I speak in the tongues of men or of angels, but do not have love, I am only a resounding gong or a clanging cymbal. If I have the gift of prophecy and can fathom all mysteries and all knowledge, and if I have a faith that can move mountains, but do not have love, I am nothing. If I give all I possess to the poor and give over my body to hardship that I may boast, but do not have love, I gain nothing.

Love is patient, love is kind. It does not envy, it does not boast, it is not proud. It does not dishonor others, it is not self-seeking, it is not easily angered, it keeps no record of wrongs. Love does not delight in evil but rejoices with the truth. It always protects, always trusts, always hopes, always perseveres.

Love never fails. But where there are prophecies, they will cease; where there are tongues, they will be stilled; where there is knowledge, it will pass away. For we know in part and we prophesy in part, but when completeness comes, what is in part disappears. When I was a child, I

321

talked like a child, I thought like a child, I reasoned like a child. When I became a man, I put the ways of childhood behind me. For now we see only a reflection as in a mirror; then we shall see face to face. Now I know in part; then I shall know fully, even as I am fully known. And now these three remain: faith, hope and love. But the greatest of these is love.

APPENDIX 3

GOD'S DESIGN

Trinitarian Design & Covenantal Structure of the God Story

The design's most critical challenge is teaching the Created the freedom and liberty in love of the Creator.

Trinitarian Conclave
Pre-Creation Planning
"before the creation"
w/Father, Son, Holy Spirit
Teach Love, a choice
Covenant w/Jesus (to restore)
The Designer
The Builder
The Encourager
With the end in mind
A Holy God

A Divine Reality
(supernatural & God-serving)

Covenant w/Adam
Gen. 1:1-4:26
Created Imago Dei (m/f)
Dominion over the Earth
Eden (Jesus teaches love)
Work
Marriage (F&M)
Broken covenant
Leaders after banishment
Blood shed to cover sin
Cain & Abel
Seven Generations

R E B E L L I O N

A Humanistic Reality
(naturalistic & Self-serving)

Covenant w/Noah & His Sons
Gen. 5:1-11:32
Build the Ark
Reset the Earth
Teach about God
Tower of Babel

Covenant w/Abraham Issac, Jacob, Joseph
Gen. 12:1-50:26
Covenant Dream
Altar & Honoring God
Gather the nations

Covenant w/Moses Joshua & Judges
Exodus 1:1-Ruth 4:22
Exodus from Egypt
Relational Boundaries (Law)
Establish Worship
Family of God in the Promised Land
Sacrificial system

1) BELIEVING God's Word

Covenant w/David Solomon (Wisdom)
1Sam. 1:1-Songs 8:14
City of God
Ark of the Covenant
Keep & protect Israel

Failure, Prophets, & Prophecy
2Chron. 10:1- Malachi 4:6
Kingdom split (North & South)
Jerusalem destroyed & exile
Isaiah, Jeremiah, Ezekiel
Daniel, Hosea, etc
Intertestamental Period

2) TRUSTING God's Authority

Covenant w/Jesus & Believers
Matt. 1:1-John 21:25
Our Forgiveness (salvation)
Restoration to Creator
Lesson of Love (resurrection)
Submission to the Divine Reality
Grace & Mercy
Blood to remove sin

3) PURSUIT of God's Plan for your life

The Church, End Times, & Christ's Return
Acts 1:1-Revelation 22:21
Church - a people set apart
Spiritual formation
Growing in the fruit of the Spirit
Establishing the Kingdom of God on Earth
One mind with Christ, a oneness
A new reality, living in His presence

Altar Ministries
Dr. Eric J. Palmu 12/2024

Printed in the United States
by Baker & Taylor Publisher Services